Software for Optical Storage

Supplements to
Optical Information Systems

1. Essential Guide to Interactive Videodisc Hardware and Applications
by Charles R. Miller, III
ISBN 0-88736-091-2

2. Authoring Systems: A Guide for Interactive Videodisc Authors
by Peter Crowell
ISBN 0-88736-084-X

3. CD-ROM Applications and Markets
edited by Judith Paris Roth
ISBN 0-88736-332-6

4. The Librarian's CD-ROM Handbook
by Norman Desmarais
ISBN 0-88736-331-8

5. Software for Optical Storage
edited by Brian A. Berg and Judith Paris Roth
ISBN 0-88736-379-2

Software for Optical Storage

edited by
BRIAN A. BERG
and JUDITH PARIS ROTH

Meckler
Westport • London

Library of Congress Cataloging-in-Publication Data

Berg, Brian A.
Software for optical storage/edited by Brian A. Berg and Judith Paris Roth.
p. cm.
Bibliography: p.
Includes index.
ISBN 0-88736-379-2 (alk. paper) : $
1. Optical storage devices. 2. Computer software. I. Roth, Judith Paris
II. Title.
TK 7895. M4R68 1989
004. 5 ' 6--dc19 88-37335
CIP

British Library Cataloguing in Publication Data

Berg, Brian A.
Software for optical storage.
1. Computer systems. Data. Storage.
Software
I. Title II. Roth, Judith Paris
005.73

ISBN 0-88736-379-2

Meckler Corporation, 11 Ferry Lane West, Westport, CT 06880.
Meckler Ltd., Grosvenor Gardens House, Grosvenor Gardens,
London SW1W 0BS, U.K.

Printed on acid free paper.
Printed in the United States of America.

For Joyce, Elizabeth and my parents

B.A.B.

For Bryan, Rachel Annaliese and my father
with love

J.P.R.

Contents

Section III: Jukebox Software

Section IV: Optical Disk Evaluation and Performance Issues

Appendices

List of Trademarks

Company	**Trademark**
Intel Corporation	8088, 80286, 80386
Xerox Corporation	Ethernet
Sun Microsystems	Sun, SunOS, NFS
Novell	Novell, Netware
Oracle Corporation	Oracle
International Business Machines	Micro Channel Architecture (MCA), IBM-PC, IBM PS/2, OS/2, SNA, PC-DOS, PC/AT
Microsoft Corporation	MS-DOS, Xenix, Windows/386
Apple Computer	Apple, Macintosh
Eastman Kodak Company	KIMS
Micro Dynamics, Ltd.	MARS
Perceptics Corporation	LaserStar, LaserWare, WORMS-11
FileNet Corporation	WorkFlo
KOM, Inc.	OptiServer, OPTIFILE
Cygnet Systems, Inc.	JIMS
U. S. Design	JukeVOS, VOS
FileTek, Inc.	HYPERchannel, Storage Machine/1
Digital Equipment Corporation	VAX, Micro VAX II, VMS, Unibus, Qbus,RSX-11M, RSX-11M/PLUS, RT-11, MSCP, Files-11, DEC
AT&T Bell Laboratories	Unix
N. V. Philips	Megadoc
Drexler Technology Corporation	LaserCard
Quarterdeck Office Systems	DESQview
Plexus Computers	XDP (Extended Data Processing)
Banyan Systems, Inc.	Banyan
Informix Software, Inc.	Informix
3Com Corporation	3Com
Sybase, Inc.	Sybase
Britton-Lee, Inc.	Britton-Lee

Foreword

Optical storage is one of the most exciting technologies to emerge within the last two decades. While most of us relate to it by our familiarity with digital audio compact discs and their players, another revolution has begun in the area of computer storage. Optical storage of computer data on small, low-cost removable cartridges promises to have a profound impact on not only the way information is stored, but also on the tasks we ask our computers to perform.

The advent of low-cost removable storage with hundreds of megabytes available for random access will open up a wealth of new applications that need this kind of storage. Applications using multi-color graphics and images are taking advantage of this new medium. Such applications coupled with the improved display technology now starting to appear will change forever the man-machine interface of computers.

Removability is the key feature for many applications for optical storage. If the media can be removed from the drive on which it was written, what guarantee exists that it can be read by another drive? What if we want to move the media to a different drive on a different system? The need for recognized standards for removable optical media is apparent and urgent.

For the past 30 years, the only independent means for true interchange of data between computer systems has been magnetic tape. Originally in 7-track format, then later in 9-track format, a reel of 1/2-inch tape has been the only recognized standard medium for information exchange between computer systems.

Optical storage now offers the potential for a new and more efficient means of information exchange between systems. Both the space needed for a given amount of storage and the time required to access date are radically reduced as compared with magnetic tape. However, with its random access capability, optical storage is not a direct replacement for tape.

The nature of Write-Once, Read-Many (WORM) storage places some constraints on software that are unlike those of either tape or magnetic disk data storage. Since an existing record cannot be rewritten in place, any update to a file means new sectors must be written and linked back to the original file.

Solutions to the problems faced by optical storage users can develop independently, or via a cooperative effort, in order to enable true interchange between drives, systems and operating environments. Such interchange of removable media requires agreement between many companies on several levels of technical specifications. The task is complicated by the fact that much of the specifics regarding the new technology are considered proprietary by the companies that participate in its development. Members of technical standards committees have thankless jobs. They carry more responsibilities than the average engineer within their company. Just finding the time to read the proposals submitted to a technical committee is a challenge. Nevertheless, the work is critical to the development of the information industry.

Levels of agreement include such simple issues as the physical dimensions and tolerances of the removable optical disk cartridge, the optical characteristics of the media, the recording method used to mark the media, and the decoding method used to read it. Beyond the issues of physical interchange lies the challenge of logical interchange.

The standardization efforts taking place within the U.S., Europe and Japan have begun to produce some impressive results. Proposed standards now exist for 130mm (5.25-inch) WORM media within ANSI (American National Standards Institute) and at the ISO (International Standards Organization) level. Work on a proposed standard for 130mm rewritable media is expected to be complete by Spring 1989. These standards deal with the size, shape and tolerances of the optical disk cartridge, the tracking and servo methods, and the recorded format.

A proposed standard on File Structure and Labeling for optical disks (independent of media diameter) is under review at the time of this writing (December 1988). The proposed structure is based on the previously approved standard for File Structures on CD-ROM, ISO 9660 (also known as the "High Sierra Group" standard). [Editors' note: See Schwerin, Julie, Parke Lightbown, Connie Bailey and Howard Kaikow, *CD-ROM Standards: The Book* published by Learned Information and InfoTech, 1986.] Changes to allow for rewritable media and to accommodate multiple volume data sets are among the issues being added.

This book reflects various problems and solutions dealing with the idiosyncrasies of optical storage and specifically WORM optical storage. Many of the designs in this book do not conform to standards under consideration by the technical committees under ANSI or ISO. However, there is merit in examining and understanding some of the current approaches taken by various companies today. Anyone who would like to contribute to the optical storage standardization effort is encouraged to contact the ANSI Secretariat or myself.

Kenneth J. Hallam
Chairman, ASC X3B11
ENDL Associates

Preface

The use of Canon's removable erasable 5.25-inch optical disk drive in Steve Jobs' NeXT Computer has dramatically increased attention on the field of optical storage. Certainly, the NeXT Computer's gamble with magneto-optic (erasable) optical disk technology as the primary computer storage device is a precursor of the advent of optical storage in the next decade and the 21st century.

It is over ten years since the announcement and introduction of the first optical storage devices. By 1980, Magnavox and DiscoVision Associates had introduced the interactive videodisc, Drexler Technology Corporation had licensed the LaserCard™, and Philips' WORM-based Megadoc™ office automation system was being installed in Europe. Optical storage is making inroads in virtually all image processing and document storage segments of the information management industry.

Today, WORM technology is being used in a steadily growing number of areas including legal document storage, on-demand printing, new drug information applications, insurance documentation, credit card receipts, mortgage applications, scientific data distribution, and engineering image and document storage and distribution.

The list of companies and government agencies who have announced their utilization and implementation of these optical disk-based systems is impressive. Many of the Fortune 500 firms are slowly investing in optical storage as a cost-effective technology that offers a competitive business edge. These firms include IBM, American Express, USAA, Citibank, Fairchild Communications and Electronics, Home Savings Bank of America, and Monsanto Laboratories.

Special niche markets are rapidly developing. One example is the pharmaceutical industry. From the list of drug companies such as Upjohn, Marion, Pfizer, Glaxo, and others who are now submitting new drug information applications to the U.S. Food and Drug Administration, it is evident that the pharmaceutical industry has wholeheartedly embraced WORM technology.

Government agencies and organizations who have installed WORM-based systems include the Library of Congress, U. S. Air Force at Wright Patterson, NASA, the National Archives, Fort Belvoir, the U. S. Army Electronics Technology and Devices Laboratory, and the IRS. Local state and municipal governments currently using WORM technology include the States of Florida, Arizona, and California, New York City, and the number of governmental agencies committing to WORM technology is steadily growing.

Wang Laboratories, IBM, AT&T Network Systems, Sony, Toshiba, Scientific Micro Systems, Hitachi, Unisys, Hitachi, Panasonic, Matsushita, FileNet Corporation, Eastman Kodak, FileTek, Pioneer, Fujitsu, Plexus Computers, and DEC are just a few of the companies offering optical disk-based image and document storage and retrieval systems to their customers. Apple Computer and other PC manufacturers are evaluating various erasable and write-once optical storage drives for integration with existing microcomputer-based retrieval systems.

Computer manufacturers and systems integrators are becoming convinced that the integration of optical storage devices—CD-ROM, write-once and erasable—into existing and future micro-, mini-, and mainframe computer systems is inevitable as we enter the next decade. As a result of this ever-increasing activity, today's end-users can choose from a growing array of write-once and erasable optical disk subsystems compatible with popular operating systems such as MS-DOS, OS/2, Unix, Xenix, PICK, Macintosh, and VAX/VMS.

Software for Optical Storage is directed toward current and potential users of WORM and erasable storage drive and jukebox devices. The intent of this book is to inform and educate computer professionals evaluating optical storage software for use in an existing or planned computer system. Topics addressed include different perspectives on software requirements, off-the-shelf versus customized software, data formats and standards, operating system dependence/independence, benchmark testing of WORM drives, evaluating jukebox software, and the use and impact of SCSI.

In order to assist the reader in understanding what is involved in implementing a WORM drive into a particular operating environment, we have included specific chapters on five well-known operating systems: MS-DOS, Unix, VAX/VMS, OS/2, and Macintosh. We have attempted to provide the reader with as much implementation level information as possible given proprietary concerns, and the current state-of-the-art.

Organization of this Book

We have assumed that this book's reader is a computer professional involved with systems integration, software development, and systems design. We have also assumed that the reader has a basic understanding of optical storage technology.

We have organized the book moving from general to increasingly technical and specific topics. However, readers should be able to read individual chapters as standalone documents. Chapters have been written by skilled system designers, programmers, system integrators, and soft-

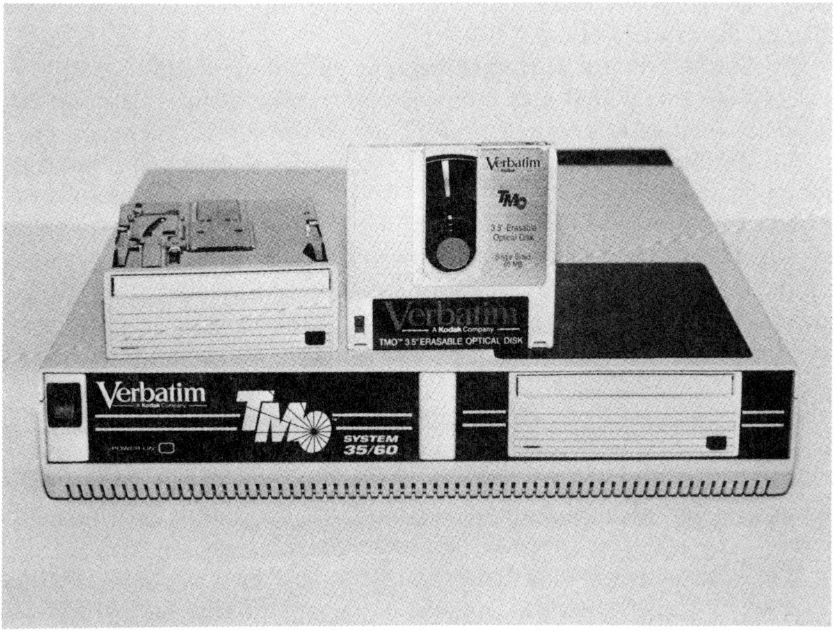

Verbatim Corporation's initial 3.5-inch TMO erasable optical disk system. (Courtesy Verbatim)

ware engineers with hands-on experience with WORM technology. Contributors include authors of operational systems, both currently available and upcoming.

Software for Optical Storage is divided into the following six substantive sections.

I. Optical Storage Market Requirements addresses specific market and functional software requirements for designing an Optical Disk File System (ODFS).

II. Optical File System Implementations includes specific optical disk implementations for MS-DOS, OS/2, the Macintosh, Unix, and VAX/VMS. This section also features an innovative approach to the design for an ODFS specifically for WORM drive.

III. Jukebox Software deals with the selection and evaluation criteria for WORM jukeboxes, and shares a jukebox end-user's experience integrating and implementing jukebox software.

IV. Optical Disk Evaluation and Performance Issues deals with benchmark testing of WORM drives, and offers a technique for sector interleaving across WORM multiple drives (striping) which can moderate drive performance problems.

V. Standardizing Software Interfaces addresses the role and impact of SCSI on WORM and other optical storage devices, and a SCSI-based architecture to streamline this device driver development process.

VI. Optical Standards focuses on optical disk hardware, software and media standards work by the ANSI X3B11 Optical Media Committee.

A set of appendices at the end of the book includes charts comparing the major WORM and erasable drives currently available on the market and a technical glossary. A list of recommended readings and an annotated directory of organizations and individuals mentioned throughout this book is offered to readers who wish to pursue additional information.

We appreciate Ken Hallam's interest in our efforts and willingness to take time out of a busy and demanding schedule to write the forward to our book. This book's glossary was compiled with the generous assistance of Ed Rothchild of Rothchild Consultants, Lou Edwards of Verbatim Corporation, and John Levy of Computer Structures.

We acknowledge with thanks the editorial assistance and guidance provided by Tony Abbott and Doreen Beauregard throughout the electronic preparation of this book. And we are deeply grateful to Alan Meckler for his continuing support and interest in optical storage technology.

This book would not have been possible without the emotional support, intellectual interest and encouragement of our spouses, Bryan and Joyce, and our respective daughters, Rachel Annaliese and Elizabeth, to whom this book is dedicated. Their willingness to spend weekends and evenings without our company reflects their generous and patient spirits.

As optical storage technology continues to mature and gain industry-wide acceptance by both computer manufacturers and end-users, the need for standardized software has become apparent and necessary. We believe that establishing software standards for optical media offers the promise that it will be more widely embraced as a useful and appropriate storage media by computer and communication professionals alike. The creation of the CD-ROM standard, ISO 9660, has helped to enhance the growth and acceptance of CD-ROM as an international publishing medium. It is our hope that the work of the ANSI's X3B11 Optical Media Standards Committee can help to advance the implementation of WORM and erasable optical storage as we prepare for the next decade.

Mention of any company, product or service does not imply endorsement. The errors, inaccuracies, and misstatements contained in this book are ours. We welcome reader comments and critiques. We hope that this book is informative, useful, and challenging for both potential system developers and integrators, drive and jukebox manufacturers, and the emerging optical storage industry at large.

Judith Paris Roth
Brian A. Berg
January 1989

1
Introduction

BRIAN A. BERG

The optical storage industry has been "on the verge of making it big" for most of this decade. All too often the drive and jukebox manufacturers have had a love affair with the hardware and have not themselves addressed the software required to be able to sell these devices to the people who would like to use them.

The primary software elements necessary to make these devices usable are a device driver, and software to command this device driver to perform drive functions. A device driver communicates directly with the optical disk drive. It sends the drive requests, and sends and receives data to and from the drive. Software to command this driver to perform useful functions may already exist, it may be in the form of some special utilities, it may be in the form of a large collection of programs which center around use of the optical drive, or it may be a combination of all of these.

This book raises many issues that are unique to optical devices. It also discusses the Small Computer Systems Interface (SCSI). Although SCSI is the most common interface for communication with optical disk drives, the issues discussed are applicable to computer peripheral devices in general.

Much of the potential of optical storage devices has been slow to gain acceptance due to the lack of standards for both physical and logical formats. The need for a physical format standard is easy to understand — physical incompatibilities immediately prevent the interchange of media. The need for a logical format standard is only necessarily an issue if the device cannot be immediately usable with current popular operating systems such as MS-DOS, Unix, VAX/VMS, and Macintosh.

WORM Software Implementation Methods

There are two basic categories of software that have been developed to support WORM devices. The first includes application- and company-specific products which store data on WORM disks in a proprietary format. The second includes turnkey products which are intended for general-purpose use. These turnkey products often emulate the magnetic file system of the host computer.

In the products which use a proprietary format, typically no attempt is made to emulate any particualr magnetic disk file system. These systems are either created as a subsystem of a commercial product or are purely for a single company's use. Examples of companies with commercial products which take this approach are Plexus Computers, Raytel Systems, FileNet and Wang Laboratories. In none of these systems is the end-user aware of the format being used for storing data on the WORM disk.

An example of a WORM-based system that was created for a single company is one built for American Express by TRW Financial Systems which stores compressed images of customer charge slips on WORM disks in a series of jukeboxes. Another example is the system created for Federal Express by Integrated Automation which uses jukebox-based WORM storage for compressed airbill images. Most American Express cardholders and Federal Express customers have no idea that WORM storage and jukeboxes are an important part of the operation of these companies, but these systems demonstrate just how entrenched optical storage systems have become.

For most turnkey products created for general-purpose use, data is stored in such a way as to be able to create the impression that the host's magnetic file system exists on the WORM media. However, a special logical disk format and algorithm must be used to create this illusion. Some of the vendors who have created such products have contributed to this book.

These turnkey products have not always been received with great success. This is in great part due to the fact that these products have often been "kludgy", e.g., they often required special utilities and large memory buffers. In addition, these products often did not allow existing programs that used magnetic storage devices to use optical storage devices in a similar manner without modifications to the customer's software.

The Future of WORM Software

Until recently, the software which implemented the erasability emulation algorithm used by many of the general-purpose turnkey products discussed in Section II of this book always ran in the host. Hence, it had to co-exist with or be integrated with the host operating system. Such an architecture has proved difficult to implement without some compromises in performance or device usability.

It is such an architecture that has been used by numerous products created for simple single-user operating systems such as MS-DOS. Implementations for complex multi-user operating systems such as Unix have been much slower in appearing on the marketplace. If the software to create the impression of rewritability can be made to be independent of the host operating system, device integration becomes a much simpler task. This approach is being implemented by some vendors by moving this software into the drive itself, i.e., by including it in the drive's firmware. Hence, with WORM-specific software no longer host resident, the WORM drive looks like an erasable disk drive.

WORM Versus Erasable Optical

Although some would say that the market for WORM drives and WORM-based software will disappear now that erasable optical drives are becoming available, this proposition is debatable. Certainly many applications which required the high data density and removability afforded by optical storage were forced to contend with its write-once nature. These applications will eventually evolve to make use of erasable storage. However, WORM devices have created a niche for applications that require its non-volatility.

In addition, integration of an erasable emulation capability in the drive itself as described above can create the best of all worlds: full file system update and access capabilities with standard software, guaranteed data permanence on the WORM media, and the ability to access older versions of files using utilities created for this purpose. These last two characteristics can make WORM technology more appealing than either magnetic or erasable optical devices.

It is not possible to achieve these capabilities without sophisticated software. Such software consists of two elements: the controller firmware embedded in the drive and utilities running on top of the operating system which harness the archive capability. This book is directed toward the goal of proliferating this kind of sophisticated software as well as the creation of flexible device drivers which can access optical and other kinds of devices on a common interface.

Acknowledgments

I would like to thank some of the people who made this book possible. First, I would like to thank my wife Joyce for her patience, for proofing my writing and for creating the figures used to illustrate my chapters. I would also like to thank Dave Engle who gave me my first consulting job involving WORM storage back in 1985. I wish to acknowledge Ernie Rael for his design work on the Arix Unix implementation. I would also like to thank Ron Voss for the use of his modem, his editorial comments and his help with some of the figures.

Finally, I would like to thank my co-editor, Judith Paris Roth, for giving me the opportunity to speak at the annual Optical Information Systems Conference and Exposition and for asking me to co-edit this book with her.

SECTION I
OPTICAL STORAGE MARKET REQUIREMENTS

2
Market Requirements for Optical Disk File Systems

ROY J. SLICKER

WORM technology provides a cost-effective, efficient solution for organizations requiring permanent storage for critical data. It offers the ability to store massive quantities of data in a relatively small amount of space. WORM's mass storage capacity has allowed a growing number of organizations improve their management of all forms of information. During the past ten years, the storage capacity of WORM disks has substantially changed. Originally introduced as a 12-inch device, there are now 14-, 8-, and 5.25-inch WORM drives. Some of today's 12-inch WORM disks have a capacity of 2.5GB per side and these densities are increasing. Yet, while these figures are impressive, the market has been slow to capitalize on the potential of WORM technology.

Generally, the data processing industry has had difficulty understanding and appreciating the role of optical storage, particularly WORM, in information management. The absence of industry standards and a perception that WORM is immature has discouraged would-be implementors and end-users of the technology. Providing an optical software solution to a user's diverse needs requires a balance of both hardware design attributes and the required application functionality. **Thus, the challenge is how to design and bring to market software products that harness WORM's enormous application potential and serve user needs over the long-term.**

Not all applications will be able to use the same approach. For example, an Optical Disk File System (ODFS)[1] solution for a medical records image storage and retrieval application will not necessarily be appropriate for a database application. From both technical and marketing per-

[1]ODFS refers to a generic WORM file system.

spectives, software developers are faced with a number of complex, intertwined issues concerning the level of compatibility that is really needed in an ODFS.

As of late 1988, there are two common approaches to an ODFS. The first approach uses a device driver that emulates the host operating system's magnetic storage file system by writing data to the WORM disk the same way it would be written to a magnetic disk. The second approach uses a unique file system designed specifically to take advantage of WORM's special characteristics. Although there is considerable debate concerning the "right" approach, both approaches have a place depending on the user's needs.

This chapter discusses the major market requirements of an ODFS. It will address such issues as data reliability, transportability, transparency, coexistence with other magnetic and optical formats, and costs associated with ODFS software.

Reliability of Optical Disks

Reliability is an important marketing feature of an ODFS because the end-user must be assured that critical information will always be accessible. Furthermore, the ODFS' error detection and correction (EDC) scheme must be implemented without the involvement of the end-user, who needs to only know that data is stored safety and is free of media errors.

Since WORM disks have an inherently high data error rate, data must be stored in a manner that compensates for media flaws. Disk drive hardware generally includes controllers that identify or flag "bad" spots upon an optical disk and compensate for "bad spots" or "bad sectors" identified during the write process. The optical head assembly is directed by the controller to write data that was first written to the damaged disk area to a replacement sector in some pre-determined location called "the automatic bad sector reallocation area." The controller keeps track of user data within this reallocation area. While this method may be sufficient for reliability, it has drawbacks which should be overcome by the ODFS.

The optimal ODFS uses a scheme that disables the automatic reallocation of bad sectors feature and performs its own error checking and bad sector flagging in real-time. Bad sectors encountered during a write process are mapped "out of availability" and writing takes place on the next good sector. From a marketing perspective, this feature offers the user the advantage of faster access to the data. It is much quicker to access contiguous data than to seek all over the disk to retrieve scattered information.Another advantage of disabling this feature is more efficient disk utilization and the resultant reduction of the number of disks required. Experience has shown that bad spots on a WORM disk are usually found in adjacent tracks, not adjacent sectors. Any scheme that makes entire tracks unavailable greatly reduces the amount of storage available on the WORM disk to the end-user.

There is much discussion about the archival life of a WORM disk. Accelerated aging tests have been conducted and estimates of a 100 year shelf-life has been predicted. However, it is not possible to state with 100 percent certainity that the media is totally reliable. An ODFS should implement a scheme that considers WORM's potentially long shelf-life.

How directory information and data are structured on the disk by the ODFS are extremely important considerations. A certain amount of redundancy is required within the directory to ensure that proper information about files residing on the optical disk exists at all times. By immediately checking a duplicate sector for comparative results, redundancy provides the needed security for directory information and fast access to data without time- consuming reads of a single sector. An ODFS feature that automatically creates another good directory sector and flags the original as outdated should be added to ensure that directory sectors are always in excellent condition.

The ODFS should compensate for potentially bad sectors by ensuring that the sector chosen is over the marginal classification. Experience indicates that WORM media is extremely reliable and the most secure media for storing long-term information.

Writing and Accessing Data on a WORM Disk

Many integrators and end-users have placed unrealistic requirements on WORM file management systems. This is due partly to the inability to grasp the significant differences between magnetic and WORM disks. While a product that uses the MS-DOS file structure on a WORM disk can be more transparent to applications than an ODFS approach, using a WORM disk in a magnetic disk application can have drawbacks. The end-user becomes painfully aware of these drawbacks as data begins to fill the disk and updates are made. To understand these drawbacks, it is important to have an appreciation for how data is written to a WORM disk and later accessed.

Data is written contiguously to a WORM disk but is randomly accessible. When a file is written to the WORM disk, data is physically located in one chunk of disk space rather than scattered about the disk. The ideal WORM ODFS allows users to only write one file at a time. When the ODFS finishes writing one file, it moves to the next. This prevents a user's file from being scattered on the disk. When a user wants to add or change a data file, information can be tagged at the end of the data heap and a directory entry written tagging that portion for later identification. Through an elaborate magnetic disk or memory caching scheme, this directory can be read and maintained on magnetic disk or in memory for rapid access to the data heap on the WORM disk. An ODFS with a built-in caching scheme allows the user to browse through the WORM disk's directory stored on magnetic disk without actually moving the optical head assembly, thus saving access time.

It is possible to change data once it is written to the WORM disk. This is most efficiently accomplished by the ODFS writing versions or pieces of a file to the WORM disk and later linking them together to show the file as a whole. Another method is to rewrite entire file changes or append to a new location on the WORM disk and update the current directory entry with pointers to the new file. However, this latter approach tends to use a lot of disk space, especially if a significant number of changes are made.

Allowing updates and appends to files stored on a WORM disk is an essential feature that should be incorporated into an ODFS. However, the user must understand the ramifications of making changes to data written to a write-once media. When changes are made to data stored on a WORM disk, there is either reduced access time or a loss of available storage capacity since previous versions of data files still exist on the media.

Tranportability

Transportability means that data stored on a WORM disk is hardware and operating system independent. The ODFS must be compatible with most of the major optical disk drives that are available on the market. Additionally, WORM disks written in a single drive or daisy-chained environment can be transportable to a jukebox and be readable without data file conversion.

Transportability also means that WORM disks written on a PC can be transported to a network operating system (such as Novell, 3COM, or Banyan) and read without file conversion. A properly designed ODFS can provide transportability between these and other operating systems (such as Unix or VMS) without conversion.

To understand why transportability is so critical, it is necessary to examine what is currently happening in today's workplace. Organizations have begun to move away from single-user computers to LANs and multi-user systems and are recognizing the need to share data across operating system and hardware boundaries. Many organizations have purchased and are using different types of computers. The costs of replacing all of this equipment and retraining end-users is significant. Consequently, networks are becoming very important in the information exchange and interchange process. Increasingly, organizations are purchasing computer systems that provide the ability to access information created on a variety of different systems.

A growing number of these systems require compatibility with different brands and sizes of WORM disks. An ODFS-based product offers system developers the capability of using many different optical disk drives without having to change application software code. Different drive compatibility is achieved by changing device drivers in the MS-DOS CONFIG.SYS file.

This compatibility is a major selling tool for system integrators because it enables them to offer a low-end, entry level system based on a 5.25-inch WORM drive while allowing an upgrade path to more drives or a jukebox. Various ODFS products on the market today allow integrators and users to access information stored on WORM disks via networks. Using this approach, the integrator can add both 5.25-and 12-inch WORM disks to a network and provide the user with an upgrade path to the higher capacity 12-inch drives.

It is important to appreciate that end-users conceptualize transportability in terms of their particular needs. An ODFS needs to provide flexibility in integration for application independence. When developing an ODFS, the system integrator must understand that developing a WORM product that cannot adapt to future operating systems is a short-term solution for a long-term need.

Machine/Operating System Independence

When data is written to an optical disk, it must be written in a consistent, non-operating system-specific manner. As new host operating systems begin to replace current operating systems, it is likely that data stored on a WORM disk under obsolete operating systems will be accessible only by using special conversion utilities. Since WORM disks have a long shelf-life, it is important to consider the life expectancy of MS-DOS and other currently used operating systems. Will they be available for the next 50 to 75 years?

An ODFS based a generic design and written using a program language such as "C" is more adaptable to new and different operating systems. By providing "hooks" on the top and bottom of the ODFS, the systems integrator can recompile ODFS "C" code under different operating systems, adding system interfaces and device drivers specific to different current and future operating systems.

Transparency

Transparency refers to the ability to access a device through normal operating system calls or utilities. Generally, the ODFS should be as compatible as possible with the host's normal utilities because certain operating system commands written specifically for magnetic disk drives are not relevant to a WORM disk. For example, the MS-DOS CHKDSK program provides the user with magnetic disk space utilization information. Because this utility was written for magnetic disks, it may not function well with WORM disks due to their different logical data formats. Such differences cause problems for the ODFS designer, and raise the following question: **What are the requirements for optical format compatibility, and at what transparency level?**

The real transparency issue centers around whether WORM disks should be used with off-the-shelf MS-DOS application software. MS-DOS was written for small capacity erasable magnetic disks and cannot directly access foreign file systems. Operating systems such as Unix were designed to allow access to other file systems through "hooks" provided within the operating system. Most off-the-shelf MS-DOS-based application software assumes the use of magnetic disks, and was not intended for compatibility with WORM disks. Most MS-DOS application developers have been unaware of end-user interest in using WORM disks with normal application software. As a result of this growing end-user interest, many application software packages make use of temporary work files and other processing techniques inappropriate for write-once storage. Although PC users demand total transparency, limited transparency is needed for vertical market specialists. However, making a WORM disk totally transparent to MS-DOS is difficult. This is because once the basic ODFS has been designed, the systems integrator must interface it with MS-DOS through system calls, many of which are undocumented.

The ODFS should be compatible and transparent with any application software package utilized by the end-user. The end-user should notice only minimal differences between the WORM and magnetic hard disks. The ODFS should not impose any restriction upon the end-user that hinders normal use of any application software package. Support for all documented operating systems programming calls and utilities should be provided as long as they pertain to a storage device and not magnetic disk specifically. Application software packages that "patch" or otherwise modify an operating system's internal BIOS may or may not be supported depending on the type of modification made to the operating system.

Properly designed and implemented, an ODFS can work with both WORM and erasable optical disks. Drive manufacturers have announced their intention to introduce multi-functional optical drives, i.e., optical disk drives that are capable of writing and reading both WORM and erasable optical disks, and possibly reading CD-ROM disks. This is a perfect fit for an ODFS designed for interchangability.

Conclusion

The optical disk industry has failed to live up to its potential and to meet market requirements for a variety of reasons. A lack of hardware and software standards and confusion about the technology and its appropriate application has made the end-user leery of incorporating WORM drives into existing data storage environments. A serious lack of vertical applications has also prevented the expected growth of this market. The emergence of a standardized ODFS is a necessity for achieving the market requirements of optical technology.

If this ODFS provides users with a transparent, reliable, transportable and cost-effective way of storing mass amounts of information, WORM technology can become the preferred media for storing critical information for short and long-term applications.

Hardware manufacturers must also consider standardization to be a priority because media must be interchangeable between drives. The success or failure of the ANSI X3B11 standards committee will play a significant role in WORM technology's ability to meet market requirements.

3
A Manufacturer's View of WORM Software Requirements

DR. AL MCDOWELL

Many WORM disk drive manufacturers and vendors have failed to anticipate the need for a convenient system interface for this new device type. Fortunately, independent system software vendors are now supplying these missing links between existing systems and new WORM devices. More generally, the market for WORM optical storage has been poorly understood and the system software which is now emerging offers the key to resolving this misunderstanding.

Drive and computer system manufacturer alike have always carried a prejudice that computer storage should be erasable. The fact that the first practical writable optical recording systems did not allow physical erasure has been considered an unfortunate compromise to be overcome by the next generation of erasable drives.

Optical media's removability allows a single WORM drive to be able to access many gigabytes of data on multiple media. In addition, the relatively small cost of buying new media, instead of erasing and reusing old media, is quite justified for many applications. Data may be saved for months or years as an archival record. There may be value in having complete a audit trail through the historic development and updating of a database. When taken to court as legal evidence, the jury will more easily believe that the data has not been altered if it is recorded on an unalterable medium.

For data which needs to always be online with a split-second access time, fixed magnetic drives are faster and less expensive than optical drives. If a multi-second access time is acceptable, or if split-second access times are needed only intermittently, then optical disk storage can achieve substantially lower costs by sharing each drive among many pieces of media.

As a result, WORM disk users will tend to have many more disks than drives. Many WORM disks will store very large databases which consume a lot of time and money to develop. Very large databases are likely to be used for a long time and to be updated relatively slowly over time. WORM media is quite appropriate for such applications.

So, why has WORM storage often been viewed as merely an inconvenient step along the way to erasable optical storage? One reason is that all existing application software and operating systems are designed for erasable storage. Moreover, WORM drive manufacturers and vendors have been slow to recognize the need to provide a system level interface which makes these drives look like something that existing applications and operating systems can understand.

Packaging WORM drives with system software that make these disks look erasable solves this problem. In fact, the "functional erasability" which the software provides to WORM storage is all the erasability that many applications really require. As long as this functional erasability makes it easy to interface with WORM without modifying application programs, the physical "unerasability" of the media can be accepted as an advantage for the reasons suggested above.

There is another way to solve the problem which is widely used today. New application programs can be written which do not expect optical storage to be erasable. The customized file management system inherent in each application can be optimized for its particular application. A number of optical disk based-document and image storage systems comprise a large share of the early optical storage implementations.

While system vendors can write or rewrite application software to interface directly with the low-level SCSI commands of optical drives, this solution is generally too difficult for end-users. Moreover, the data recorded by customized file management structures is only transportable to systems running the same or compatible software.

Vendors of customized systems will continue to use the low-level optical device interface. However, the broader market requires that the device interface be masked by system software to make the device as easy to use as magnetic storage. Ideally, the user should be able to use WORM optical storage with the same command and application calls provided by the operating system for using magnetic disk storage.

Three Ways to Emulate Erasable Storage

The current commercially available WORM disk software uses one of the following three approaches to make this disk look like erasable magnetic storage.

1. *Tape emulation.* Many of the earliest products enable optical disks to be written and read with conventional magnetic tape drive commands. In avoiding the complexities of dealing with random access to files through disk directories, the random access capabilities of optical disk storage are sacrificed.

2. *Disk emulation device driver.* The most direct way to emulate a

magnetic disk drive is to install a special device driver for the WORM disk controller. In order to present a magnetic (erasable) drive appearance to the operating system and yet update data on an unalterable disk, such a device driver must translate the logical addresses assumed by the operating system to different sector addresses for use by the optical controller. Moreover, the device driver must maintain a map of these address translations. This map must be updated after each file write, and must be recorded on the WORM disk at some point before its removal from the drive.

When the operating system intends to rewrite a block of data in place, the device driver writes the new data in a new location. When the operating system updates directories and the records of file locations, there is often a lot of redundant data rewriting. For example, an entire directory may be rewritten, even though only one entry in the directory was updated. In order to minimize the waste of WORM disk capacity, many device drivers will cache the frequently updated sectors which contain the file location data and directories.

Caching of directory and file location data, either in memory or on a magnetic disk drive, will increase search performance, but there are several undesirable side effects. One is the possibility that the backward linked list describing previous versions of files could be broken. This could happen if a disk was removed or power was lost before cached data was dumped on the optical disk. More importantly, mounting a disk could be time-consuming if directory structure information must be extracted from the disk and cached. Dismounting could also be time-consuming when this cached data is dumped to the disk.

Perhaps the most severe side effect results from the fact that optical device drivers will necessarily record structural data in a different format for each operating system. This shuns an excellent opportunity to use WORM disks as a means of data transport among dissimilar systems.

3. *An Optical Disk File System (ODFS).*[1] A new file management system, optimized for WORM storage, can replace the operating system's file management code for use with these drives. This is the most recent, and most difficult to develop, approach to making WORM disks look like something that applications already understand. The ODFS responds directly to the same user commands and function calls defined by the operating system for magnetic disk storage. As with disk emulation device drivers, WORM disks appear as transparent extensions of the file structure provided by the operating system.

An efficient ODFS will write only the incremental directory and file location information for each file write or update, minimizing the use of capacity. This structural information is usually recorded in a common area

[1] OFDS refers to this magnetic storage emulation approach within this chapter only.

separate from the files themselves, speeding searches through directory and file location data to locate files. Moreover, an ODFS can record this structural data in the same format for any operating system, providing data interchange among different systems. For example, files written on a PC/ MS-DOS system can be read and updated under Unix, or vice-versa.

Requirements for a WORM ODFS

The objectives of efficient use of disk capacity and file interchange among different operating environments dictates the development of a file system which is optimized for WORM storage. This file system will define a new format for recording directory and file location information. General requirements for a WORM ODFS are outlined below.

1. *Transparent extension of the operating system.* The basic objective of the software is to enable users and existing application programs to use the WORM disk as if it were a conventional magnetic disk drive. The mounted side of the WORM disk should appear as a "transparent" extension to the file structure defined by the host operating system. The optical system software should respond properly to all relevant application function calls and user commands. An error message should be returned for magnetic disk commands that are irrelevant to the WORM disk, such as the format command.

2. *System environments.* Optical system software architecture should allow for implementations with all popular mini- and micro-computer operating systems whose file structure is hierarchical. PC/MS-DOS, Unix, VMS, and Macintosh should be among the first implementations. Thus, the functions provided by the software will be a superset of what is provided by current operating systems with hierarchical file structures.

3. *System file interchange.* The format for recording directory and file location information on the WORM disk should be common for all operating system implementations. This would facilitate the transfer of files between systems of different types. An important side benefit would be the reduction of software development expense.

Differences in functionality required by different operating systems will require interpretation as files move from one environment to another. For example, the file access permission stored with Unix files will be ignored under PC/MS-DOS, and PC/MS-DOS files will be universally accessible under Unix. These translation issues have been resolved in various network protocols which allow client and file server nodes with different operating systems. One way to resolve these translation issues, and to facilitate the integration of the ODFS into many environments, is to port it to some of the popular network file server interfaces such as Novell and the Sun Network File System (NFS).

4. *Standards.*[2] Interchange within a organization can be accomplished by using the same optical system software and compatible WORM drives throughout the organization. Interchange among organizations requires that the software products from different vendors use the same format for recording directory and file location information on the optical disk.

Since software products meeting most of these objectives will be available before a standard is established, an additional objective for the early products would be to provide a compatible transition to the future standard format. This would require the current software products to be designed with format flexibility which would allow a future version to handle both the current format and the yet undefined standard format.

5. *Data integrity.* All directory and file location information should be recorded and updated on the optical disk at the conclusion of each file write or update. In at least one mode of operation, caching of files, directories, and file location information on either magnetic drives or in host memory should not be required. Optional additional modes of operation are preferred in which directory and file location information is cached in user-selectable amounts of host memory to improve system performance.

6. *Volume partitions.* Users should be able to partition each optical disk surface into sub-volumes and use the same logical drive naming convention as that provided by operating systems for magnetic drives. In addition, partitions and files in partitions should be allowed to span more than one WORM disk surface.

Any file size or partition size limits of the operating system should be eliminated for optical disk storage. The PC/MS-DOS 32MB disk partition size limit is an example.

7. *Multiple opens.* In order to support multiple users accessing the WORM drive, the software should support the file and record locking functions provided by the host operating system. Multiple simultaneous opens should be allowed for writing of different files and/or reading of any files. In other words, end-users should be able to open any file anytime for reading and any file for writing which is not already open for writing. Note that simultaneous writing of different files will cause fragmentation and/or interleaving of file data as data is written sequentially to the WORM disk, but this is transparent to the user.

8. *File updates.* When a file is updated by copying the new version to the WORM disk with the same file name, the new version should be compared with the stored previous version, byte-by-byte. Only the changed or added sectors should be recorded. Updated files should con-

[2]The ANSI accredited X3B11 technical committee and ECMA in Europe are developing logical file format standards.

sist of a sequence of segments; each segment consisting of one or more contiguous sectors in various physical locations on the WORM disk.

A user-selectable parameter at installation should define a maximum number of segments per file, beyond which a fragmented file will be automatically rewritten as one contiguous segment.

In addition, files should be updatable by appending or by selective update of bytes or records as enabled by the host operating system for magnetic disk storage. Only the updated sectors should be recorded until the user-specified level of fragmentation occurs.

9. *File and directory version history.* All previous versions of updated files and directories should be recoverable by new user commands to step backward from the current version to earlier versions. This new function is unique to WORM storage.

New commands will be required for this function. Unless the history commands are used, searches should go directly to the latest version of a file, without seeking through data for earlier versions.

10. *Program execution.* Programs should be executable from the WORM disk.

11. *Disk format.* The optical system software should be optimized to operate with WORM drives meeting the ANSI/ISO specification for 5.25-inch media. These standards define fixed block formats of either 512 or 1024 bytes per sector. All directory and file location information will be written in user data areas with the same error correction and recorded format as file data.

Under this standard defect management is handled transparently by the device. To the extent that the spare sector locations are not defined outside of the device controller and marginally written sectors are relocated in spare sectors, the system software will refer to "logical" rather than physical sector addresses.

12. *Performance and efficient use of capacity.* Updates to directory and file location information should involve writing only the incremental new data (e.g., time, date, file size, and location of the updated file). It should also include a minimum of additional pointer, vector or table data to enable directory path searches for a file with a maximum of more than two disk seeks per directory level in the path specification.

This will result in fragmentation of the information for a given directory into several physical disk sectors. In order to expedite searches, it is expected that the directory and file location information will be written sequentially and chronologically from the end of a disk partition inward. Also, files and file updates will be written sequentially and chronologically from the start of the disk partition inward.

Illustration of Architectural Feasibility

Since the feasibility of meeting all these requirements could be widely questioned, the remainder of this chapter outlines an architecture for accomplishing these objectives. The intent is only to describe the basic features of one approach; it is not to specify in detail a complete file system.

The final product is assumed to be packaged in three modules:

1. System interface that intercepts file management requests for WORM disks, and translates function calls and user commands peculiar to a specific operating system to the standard functions of the ODFS.

2. The ODFS, written in a language such as C, can be compiled to run in virtually any micro- or mini-computer system.

3. Device interface that will be customized to the SCSI commands for a particular optical device.

The ODFS will write files and file updates sequentially and chronologically from the start of the disk inward. Since the WORM disk track is a spiral, files of any length can be read without one-track seeks at each track to interrupt the flow of data.

Directory and file location will be written, separately from files, in normal user data sectors, sequentially and chronologically from the end of the disk inward. One or more of these structural data sectors will be written after each file write or update.

Unless multiple files are written simultaneously, a file will be written initially as a continuous sequence of logical sectors. Updates may fragment a file into several segments, each a continuous sequence of sectors. The location of a particular version of a file will be recorded as the logical starting sector number and length in sectors of the first segment. This will be followed by the starting sector and length of each additional segment.

The file location and all of the directory information for a particular file version will be contained in "File Descriptor." The File Descriptor will contain the file name, file version number, the previous version's File Descriptor starting sector number, the file size in bytes, the date and time that the file version was created, the file owner identification, access permission information, and the locations of the segments of this version of the file.

Each directory in the file hierarchy is described by a "Directory Pointer List." This List will include:

- Directory name
- The names of each file and sub-directory in the directory
- Number of the sector which contains the beginning of the previous version of that directory
- Directory ownership and access permission information

- The File Descriptor starting sector number for each file in the directory
- The Directory Pointer List starting sector number for each sub-directory of that directory.

The File Descriptors and Directory Pointer Lists are stored in the structural data sectors which are written from the end of the disk inward. There is no fixed length to either File Descriptors or Directory Pointer Lists. Each is delineated with special starting and ending characters, and either type of record may span sequential sectors. The first entry in a File Descriptor is the file name. The first entry in a Directory Pointer List is the directory name facilitating the location of either record type by way of the sector number containing the beginning of the record.

Immediately after a file is written or updated, one or more structural data sectors are written as required to record the File Descriptor, a new Directory pointer list for the sub-directory containing the file, and new Directory Pointer Lists for each higher level directory up to and including the root directory.

With this architecture, the current version of the file structure is available on the optical disk for file searches using the directory path to any file. Even if the disk is unloaded from the drive and reloaded at a later time, the file structure is easily accessed by first scanning the disk from the end inward to find the last written sector and then reading that sector to find the pointers to every file and sub-directory in the root. These pointers will direct the search to one more seek for each sub-directory in the pathname, leading finally to the File Descriptor which contains the specific logical address of the file.

In this system, there is no need to reserve sectors for file or directory updates. Sectors are used as required for both file and structural data. In contrast, systems which reserve sectors for an unpredictable number of future updates result in wasted capacity. The system suggested here could achieve a virtually 100 percent utilization of disk capacity.

While this system records the same directory and file location information that is recorded on magnetic disks by the operating system, this structural data is reformatted to more efficiently use the capacity of WORM disks. For example, relative to PC/MS-DOS, this system replaces the File Allocation Table (FAT) with the file location data in the File Descriptor. The directory information for files is fragmented into File Descriptors for each of the files in the directory, and directories are tied together by the Directory Pointer Lists. The result is that the amount of redundant rewriting of directory information is greatly reduced from the format which PC/MS-DOS uses to maintain the same information.

Conclusion

With an ODFS as described in this chapter, WORM storage can be immediately and freely used without modifying application software and without learning new file system commands. Users will need to be aware of the additional media costs when using WORM storage for short-lived data. For many applications, however, this blend of functional erasability and physical unerasability will be strongly preferred to conventional erasable storage.

SECTION II
OPTICAL FILE SYSTEM IMPLEMENTATIONS

4
An Operating System-Independent WORM File System

DR. JOHN V. LEVY

The peculiarities resultant from write-once optical media should lead to reconsideration of the structure of file systems. However, few implementers are motivated to redesign an entire file system for the following reasons:

- Write-once media will coexist in systems with read/write media, and it is advantageous to have the same file structure on both media.

- File systems on magnetic read/write media are highly evolved and optimized for the characteristics of Winchester disk technology. Therefore, these systems are not easily adapted to a fundamentally different technology.

- It is quicker to implement interfaces to file systems at lower levels (for example, at the block-retrieval level) because the model of interaction is simpler.

In addition, systems manufacturers are rarely motivated to design or implement a file structure which is explicitly designed for multiple hardware platforms and operating systems.

In this chapter, the design of an Optical Disk File System (ODFS)[1] is presented which goes against all of the above expectations. The file system was designed starting from a clean slate using the characteristics of

[1]As used in this chapter, ODFS refers to this particular WORM design.

WORM media as the basis. It includes features common to the file systems of four operating systems: MS-DOS, Unix, VAX/VMS, and Macintosh. Finally, it is expected (perhaps most ambitiously) that the application program interface of this file system will appear exactly like a read/write file system running under each respective operating system.

A layered implementation keeps all incremental file information on the optical disk volume. The unit of allocation on the disk is a variable-length record, rather than a sector. Control information, including a journal of directory updates, is stored in tagged records which are embedded in the same stream as the file data. The objective is to provide a common on-disk structure for all of these systems while implementing the equivalent of a read/write file system on an erasable medium. Efficiency of storage space usage and file reading and writing time were of equal importance.

Optical Disk File System (ODFS) Development Environment

This ODFS was developed for use with the Ricoh 5.25-inch optical disk drive. The Ricoh drive, a WORM device capable of storing 400MB of information on each side of a double-sided cartridge, contains an internal SCSI controller. This drive is currently marketed in the United States by Maxtor Corporation as the RXT-800S. The Ricoh disk cartridge is constructed of organic methine dye material using a spin-coating method. The expected media life is more than ten years after recording.

A preliminary version of the ODFS has been operating since November, 1988 using MS-DOS on a PC/AT equivalent system. It is in development using SunOS Version 3 on a Sun-3 based system [Sun Microsystems, 1986], and the code is written in C.

Advantages of the ODFS Design

The ODFS makes the WORM disk look like a read/write medium. This makes the medium much easier to use, and immediately makes the optical disk available for use by a wide range of application programs.

Since the file structure created on the optical disk is uniform and independent of operating system, WORM disks may become an interchange medium between systems. There is little learning required by application developers because the file structures and interface are well-defined and the file system functions are similar to those for Unix files.

The ODFS achieves high performance by using the following techniques:

- Minimize the number of times a file or a directory must be copied when it is updated.

- Write the latest file data, directory update and file control information in the same disk area to minimize seek distance.

- Use the minimum space necessary to record the current relevant information.

- All of these techniques serve to compensate for the inherent low speed of data access on the optical medium.

The ODFS design uses much less storage space than other write-once file system designs. It has a very flexible allocation method since it uses as many "Extents" as required to store file information. The ODFS recovers the use of sector space that would ordinarily be wasted, and uses small segments of information to code the contents of directory entries and "Journal" records.The ODFS maintains the integrity of the optical disk data at all times. In case of power failure or program error, all files which have been closed and all data which has been written will be recoverable in subsequent use. No auxiliary files on read/write media are required. In case of media failures, losses are limited to data in sectors which literally cannot be read. In addition, all previous versions of every file can be retrieved if desired because a detailed change history is maintained.

The ODFS is designed to accommodate future expansion to larger disks while maintaining backward compatibility. A file system version number is maintained in system records, and file control information is kept separate from user data. Reference to locations of data on the optical disk is accomplished with an expandable "record handle" which is independent of the sector size.This chapter concentrates on explaining the unusual design characteristics of this file system. The design concepts may be applicable to future file systems even if the particular implementation described here does not gain widespread use. In particular, the design is likely to be applicable to any storage medium where seek time dominates the access time to data, or where data write time is slower than data read time. One of the future digital storage media which may find these methods useful is Digital Audio Tape (DAT) when used as a block-addressable digital storage volume.

Design Alternatives

Most alternatives proposed for optical disk file systems involve keeping the concept of blocks or sectors, and allocating space in groups of blocks. The Unix file system is so oriented to the block concept that is impossible to implement a disk structure under it which does not support fixed-sized units of allocation. Unix also depends on having certain information stored in fixed places on the disk (the superblock and the inodes, in particular). For those who maintain the block-level interface, there is the advantage that Unix does caching and other optimization of buffer management at the block level in a manner transparent to the device driver.

However, **implementors of WORM software with lower-level interfaces to existing block-oriented file systems must deal with the problem of Logical Block Address (LBA) remapping**. This remapping requires a data structure to be created and maintained to enable the translation of a requested LBA into the block's real disk location. This poses the following problems or constraints:

- What is the typical size of this structure? Where will it be kept on the disk?

- How often will this structure be moved to the disk to keep the file system self-contained and recoverable on the single volume?

- How large can this structure become? How many times will a single block be remapped? What is the maximum size of a file in blocks? How many bits should be allocated for the LBA remapped address?

- What information can be kept on disk to allow recovery in case of a failure while the remap structure is in memory?

When a system has file directory management under the control of an operating system's file manager, and block allocation and remapping under the control of a subsidiary device-oriented software module, there is a lot of needless functional duplication. Both software modules are managing data structures pertaining to the creation, updating and deletion of storage space (files or allocation blocks); both are concerned with buffering of data (including caching for performance) and with recovery from errors. Attempts at designing efficient low-level block-remapping modules suffer from the fact that they have no information about the file structure to be created or accessed. Hence, they cannot optimize either allocation or buffering. Large performance advantages could thus result from re-conceptualizing the entire file system structure.

The promise of better performance and the difficulty of the questions above lead to this heresy: **disk allocation can be done in variable-sized chunks, and "control" information (the journal records and the system's file information) can be embedded in the same data stream as the user file information.** Numerous advantages became apparent in the course of the design. Ultimately, the brave course of total file system re-implementation was chosen.

The Concept of a Journal

The concept of a journal comes from several sources. Informally to writers and to laboratory workers, a journal is a permanent record of ideas and activities. In the accounting profession, a journal is a formal record of all transactions. A related concept in accounting is the audit trail which is a record of transactions which is adequate to reconstruct and validate results which are compiled or computed from the transactions.

In databases and transaction processing systems, audit trails and journals are commonly used for transaction management and for roll-back recovery activities. There is also a concept called "differential databases" in which all data related to updates of the main database are maintained in a separate small database. The small database is used like a cache memory. Retrieval attempts search the small ("differential") database first before moving to the large database.

In the ODFS, a journal has been implemented for recording updates to directories. The journal concept fits neatly with the optical medium for two reasons. The first reason is that the natural allocation method is linear from one end of the disk to the other, so that journal entries are written in sequential and chronological order on the medium. The second reason is that by embedding the journal entries in the same write stream as the user file data, the space overhead is very small, especially in view of the potential space wasted if partially-filled sectors were written.

Actual directory updates are not performed until a disk is to be dismounted, or an explicit **sync( )** operation is requested. This process may be time-consuming, as explained later in this chapter.

ODFS Features and Design Requirements

What follows are brief descriptions of the key features of the ODFS.

1. While maintaining a file system that appears to be read/write/erase, it minimizes the data copying that would be necessary to keep files and directories up-to-date.

2. All standard features of a read/write file system are implemented, such as those of Unix.

3. By implementing a "journal" of update notations, the volume (on a removable cartridge) is always self-contained: it can be removed at virtually any time without losing the ability to reconstruct the latest state of the file system.

4. The storage cost of maintaining the journal is very low because the control records implementing the journal are intermixed with data records, often using space that would otherwise be wasted inside the fixed-size sectors.

5. By implementing variable-length records at the lowest level, the ODFS allows file directories to define variable-sized "extents" naturally. This leads to further efficiencies in directory file size.

6. The lowest level (which implements tagged, variable-length records) can reasonably be contained in a disk controller's firmware.

7. The design minimizes operating system specific features, i.e., it implements all common features in a layer so that the operating system-specific portion becomes a thin layer.

8. This file system is designed to be interfaced with minimum difficulty to a wide variety of operating systems. Initial implementations are under way for MS-DOS and SunOS (Unix); the next implementations will be for Macintosh and VAX/VMS.

9. The layered definition of the ODFS allows information hiding so that the implementation of each layer is independent of the others.

Some of the requirements imposed on the file system design were:

1. Volume integrity is to be maintained at all times. Each volume is to be self-contained: all information needed to determine the contents and character of the data stored on the volume is stored on the volume (i.e., not stored on a magnetic disk).

2. Consistency of the data (and directories) is to be maintained or be reconstructible at all times, so that a failure such as power loss will not lose content or structure information for any file. [Note: Writing data to the disk can be delayed at the Level 1 stage. A **flush( )** function (described later in this chapter) is provided so the delay can be overridden in critical applications.]

3. A desirable feature is the ability to recover all previous versions of a file. This is attained with the rewrite of a "file header" each time that a file is closed.

4. The on-disk storage overhead (space taken by data structures not created by the file user) is to be small compared with the files and directories themselves.

5. Overhead time should be small for frequently-used file operations and should be amenable to trade-off for RAM space used.

6. File open is an operation whose time should be minimized. This is primarily dependent on minimizing the number of disk accesses and the seek distance during the operation.

7. In general, control information such as file headers and journal records should be located close to the file contents to which it relates.

8. File sizes, extent sizes and number of extents per file should not be arbitrarily limited. It should therefore be possible to fill an entire volume with one file, to have a single extent that makes up a volume-sized file, and to have a volume-sized file made up of small extents.

Figure 1. ODFS Architecture

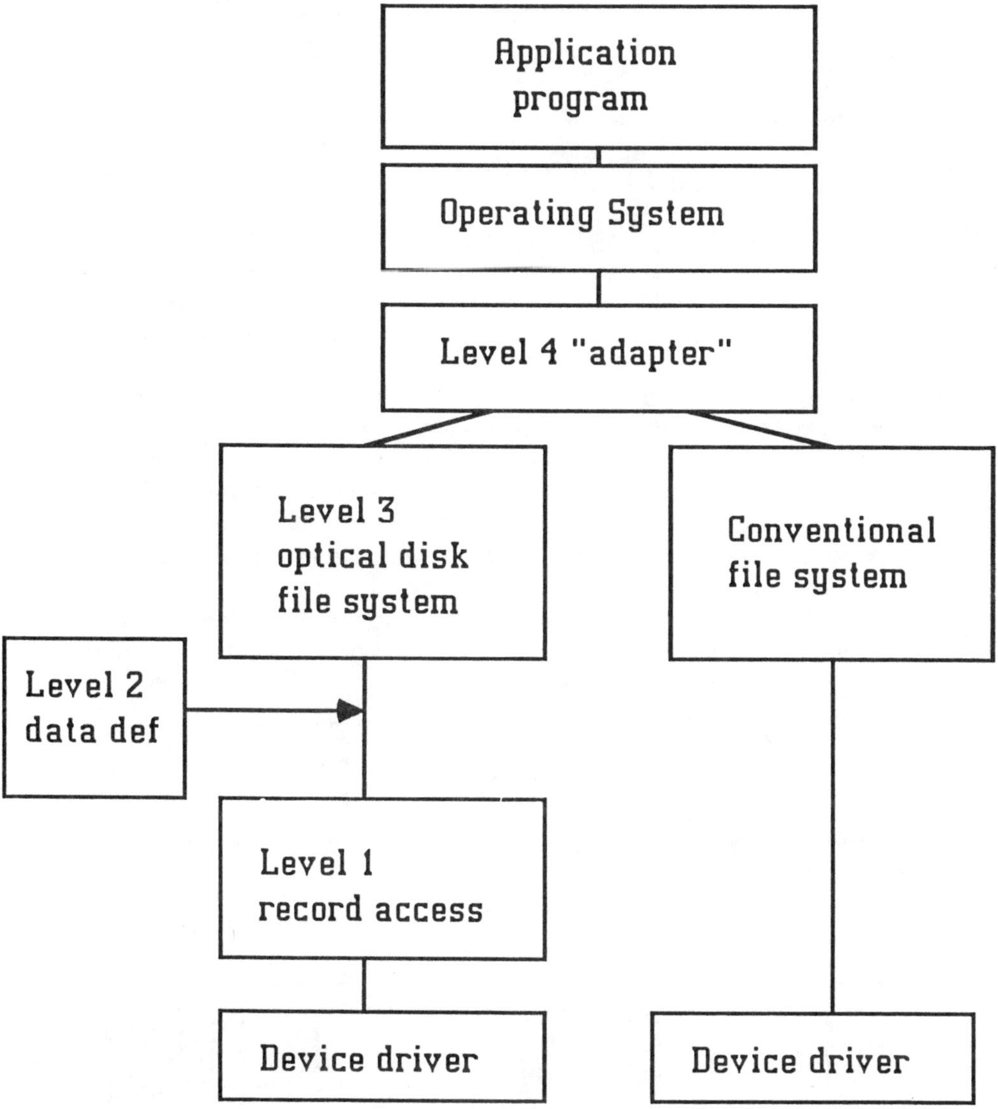

Implementation

The requirements were met in a design which divided functionality into four implementation levels, as show in Figure 1. These levels are described in this section.

Figure 2. An ODFS Record

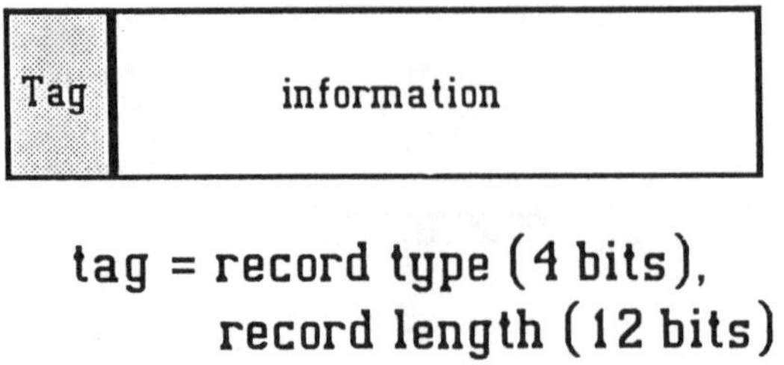

Level 1

Level 1 implements a volume of variable-length records, so that the sectorized structure of the optical disk is no longer visible. Instead, the Level 1 interface provides two streams: a user data stream accessed by the **d_read( )** and **d_write( )** functions, and a control stream accessed by the **read_record( )** and **c_write( )** functions. The former function pair perform multiple-record read and write operations, while the latter perform single-record read and write operations.

Records are tagged variable-length strings. (See Figure 2.) Each record is prefixed by a 16-bit Tag. A Tag is composed of a 4-bit Record Type and a 12-bit Record Length. Record Length is the number of bytes in the string. The type indicates whether the contents of the string are to be regarded as data or as control information.

Although the control information stream does not interfere with user data streams, it makes use of frequently unused portions of the sectors. A

Figure 3. Storage of Records in Sectors

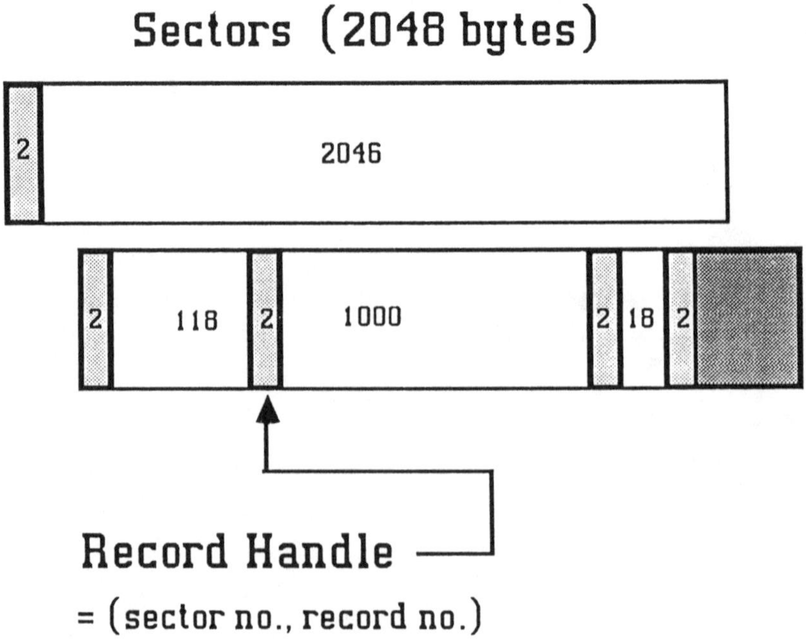

data write length may exceed the distance to a sector boundary. In this case, a new record tag is inserted at the beginning of the next sector and the data stream spans a series of records. Reference to records is by Record Handles. A Record Handle is a number used to locate a particular optical disk record. It is analogous to the Logical Block Address (LBA), but composed of two components: a sector number, and a record number within the sector. (See Figure 3.)

There is a sector buffer in the Level 1 implementation which is used to hold portions of the control and data streams yet to be written to the storage medium. In case a bad sector is detected at the time of a write, the bad sector is skipped and the next sequential sector is used.

Each record in the control stream represents a control object. Some example control records are: a File Header (similar to an inode in Unix), a File Extent Continuation (similar to a block containing additional block numbers), the Unmount Record, and a Journal Record containing update information for a directory entry. Each of these records contains a one-byte Control Type number in its first data byte which identifies the type of the Control Record.

The user data stream is implemented as a series of tagged records, but with no further tagging. Data writes cause variable-length data records to be written beginning at any point in a sector and continuing until the entire data buffer contents is transferred. A series of contiguous data records is defined as an Extent. An Extent Descriptor refers to the first record in the series and the length of the data in the Extent. In this implementation, 32 bits are allowed for the length of an Extent. It appeared unreasonable to restrict the length of a single data write function call to 64KB.

Level 1 Functions Definitions

A tag is composed of two components, **RType** and **RLen**.

RType is the Record Type field, containing 4 bits. Its assigned values are:

0 = Data Record
1 = Control Record
2 through 15 = Reserved

RLen is the Record Length field, containing 12 bits. Its assigned values are:

0 = zero-length record, a null record
1 through 4095 = length of record in bytes

The length of a record is less than or equal to the number of bytes remaining in the sector.

When a Tag is written on the storage medium, the Record Type field (in the high-order half of the byte) and the high-order 4 bits of the Record Length field (in the low-order half of the byte) are written first, followed by the low-order 8 bits of the Record Length Field.

A Record Handle (RH) contains a reference to a Sector Number (SN) and a Record Number (RN) within the sector (independent of record type). The first record in a sector is referenced with RN=0.

The RN field is 8 bits long. Its values (0 through 255) represent the first through 256th record in the sector (independent of **RType**).

The SN field is 24 bits long. Its assigned values are:

000000H[2] to FFFEFFH = sector numbers 0 to 16777199
FFFF00H to FFFFFFH are reserved for special use:
  FFFFFFH = invalid record ("undefined")
  FFFFFEH = reserved
  FFFFFDH = Latest Unmount Record sector

When a 4-byte Record Handle is created, the high-order byte is the 8-bit RN, and the low-order 3 bytes are the SN.

Level 1 Function Descriptions

d_read( )

Reads data records beginning at a designated record and continuing with subsequent data records until the user data buffer has been filled. This is the operation which is normally used to read one extent. An Extent is defined in Level 2 as the contents of a contiguous series of data records.

d_write( )

Writes data beginning at the next available space on the optical disk. Returns the record handle of the first record of the data just written. This Record Handle is used to create an Extent descriptor.

The data is actually moved into a write buffer which is not written to the

[2]The H suffix indicates a hexadecimal value.

optical disk until it is full. The buffer is written starting at the first unwritten sector on the disk, i.e., just after the High Water Mark.[3] This function always uses up the remaining space in the write buffer before going on to another.

flush( )

The contents of the write buffer is written to the current sector of the optical disk. If there is room in the write buffer for a null record, one is inserted before writing.

read_record( )

Reads exactly one record beginning at a designated record handle. Returns the type and the length of the record read. If there is no record at the exact location designated, a warning is returned and the next record on the optical disk is read. This function is also used to read the latest Unmount Record by specifying a special reserved value of the record handle to be read.

c_write( )

Writes a single control record at the next available space on the optical disk. Returns the record handle of the record written. If the record is too long to fit in the remainder of the write buffer, the write buffer is written to the optical disk before the record is inserted in the buffer.

c_write_ur( )

Writes the contents, if any, of the write buffer to the optical disk and then inserts an Unmount Record as the first record in the write buffer. The sector number which is the eventual destination of the contents of the write buffer is set to the successor of the latest Unmount Record sector (one less than the latest Unmount Record sector).

get_remainder( )

Returns length and a record handle of a (not-yet-existing) record which, if written, would exactly fill the write buffer. This function is used to determine how much space remains in the write buffer so that variable-sized control information can be sized to fill it. It can also be used to determine the size of the write buffer.

[3]The High Water Mark is the sector number of the last-written sector on the optical disk, not including Unmount Record sectors at the very end of the disk.

get_rrh( )

Returns the type, record handle, and length of the last previous record actually read.

get_freespace( )

Returns the total number of bytes remaining in the blank sectors of the optical disk, assuming each sector was written with a single record. A fixed number of blank sectors are reserved and are not included in computing the total.

Level 2

The Concept and Use of the Journal

Having arranged for control records to be embedded transparently in the stream of records stored on the medium, the concept of a Journal (a sequence of Control Records) is defined at Level 2. These records contain notes about changes to the file directories. In addition, the File Header records, which are the Control blocks related to files, are written as Control Records any time they are changed. Since control records are skipped over while reading data, they do not interfere with normal data reads and writes.

The purpose of the Journal is to delay as long as possible the rewriting of file directories. In file systems on normal read/write media, the information related to a given file is continually updated. For example, whenever a file is written to or modified, the file header must note the date and time of the last update. The length attribute of the file is modified often while it is being written.

Updating of data (for example, the contents of a directory) is expensive in a WORM environment. In the ODFS, updating of directory entries is delayed until a **sync( )** or **unmount( )** operation is invoked. In the meantime, a list of directory entry updates is kept in a data structure called the Journal. This structure is kept in RAM as well as on the optical disk.

Whenever a directory is to be retrieved from the disk, a search is first made through the Journal to see if the desired directory entry has been updated. If so, the updated value is taken from the Journal entry.

As new directory changes are made, new Journal entries are made in the RAM Journal and are also written to the optical disk as Journal records. The cost of the Journal in space on the disk is minimal because the control records are small, and they typically fit in portions of sectors which would otherwise go unused.

Figure 4. A File Extent List

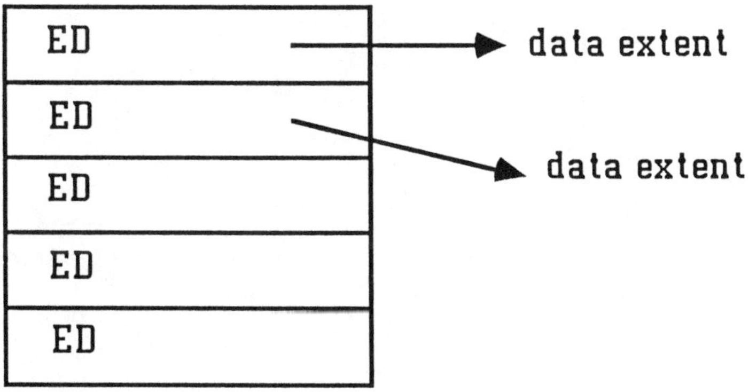

At the time of **unmount( )** or **sync( )**, all directory updates are applied to the old directories in a sequence which makes it necessary to rewrite each modified directory only once.

On **mount( )**, the ODFS expects to find all directories up to date and the latest Unmount Record containing the latest High Water Mark (the highest numbered sector which has been written). If there are any records written beyond the High Water Mark, they were necessarily written after the last previous **unmount( )** call. This situation can occur if power was shut down without doing an **unmount( )** or a **sync( )**. On encountering non-blank sectors beyond the High Water Mark, the Mount process simply reads all Journal records in sequence and rebuilds them into a RAM Journal.

Extents and File Headers

Files are named collections of data stored on the volume. The data consists of variable-length sequences of bytes, known as Extents. Extents are located using Extent Descriptors. The collection of Extent Descriptors related to one file is called its File Extent List (FEL). See Figure 4 for a list of the File Extents.

The File Header (FH) corresponds to an "inode" in the Unix file system [Bach, 1986, 61]. It contains all of the information about a file except for the file's name. Access to a file always begins by retrieving the FH. A short version of the File Extent List is contained in the FH. (See Figure 5.) When the number of Extents in the file exceeds four, the structure of the File Extent List on the optical disk becomes more complex with the addition of File Extent Continuation (FEC) records. (See Figure 6).

Journal records contain information about changes which are to be made to the directory entry for a file. Each record contains a code

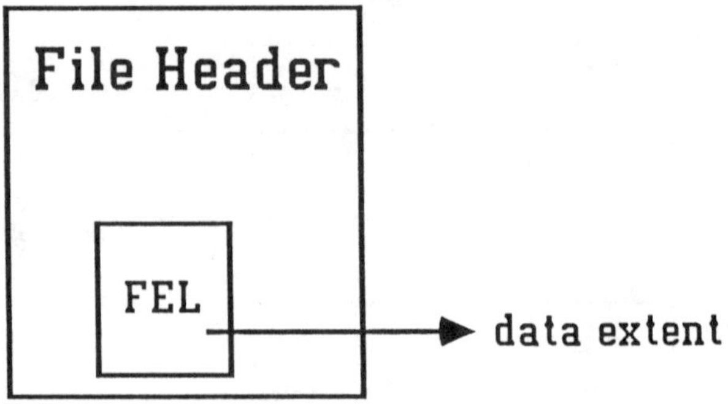

**Figure 5.
A File Header**

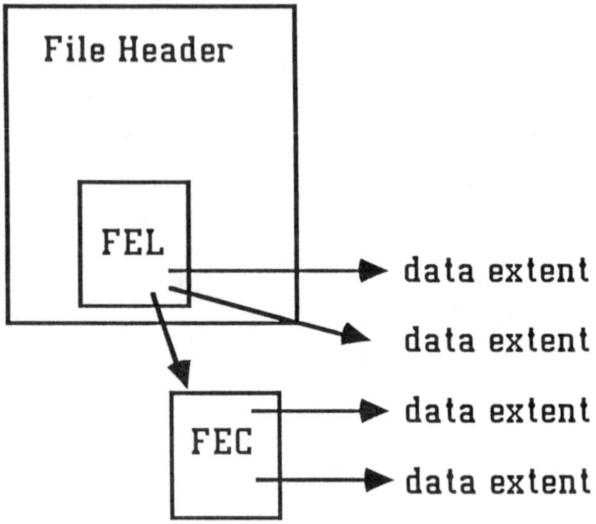

**Figure 6.
File Extent
List Structure**

indicating whether the change is "create", "update" or "delete", along with other information identifying the file and its parent directory.

The Unmount Record is a unique record. Unmount Records are written reverse sequentially, starting at the last sector on the disk. (See Figure 7 for a diagram of the usage of sectors on the optical disk.) Each Unmount Record represents the state of the file system at the time of a **sync( )** or an **unmount( )** call; that is, a time when all directories were up-to-date and consistent. The Unmount Record contains the value of the "High Water Mark" which is the number of the last-written sector in the data and control stream. It also contains the Volume Identifier. An entire sector is allocated each time an Unmount Record is written.

The Root File Header (RFH) is a File Header associated with the Root Directory. The Root Directory is the key to locating all files on the

Figure 7. ODFS Disk Layout

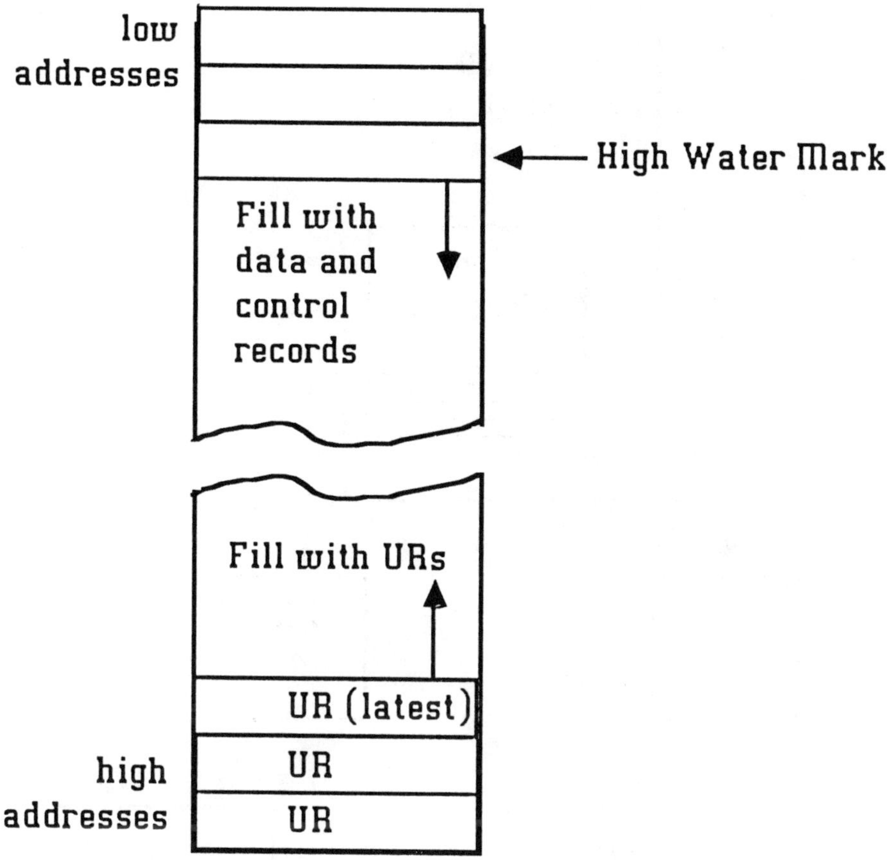

volume. To make access to it easy, the latest RFH is always stored in the same sector as the latest Unmount Record. (See Figure 8.)

The File Extent List and the Maximum Length of Files

The File Extent List (FEL) is a structure containing one Extent Descriptor (ED) for each extent in a file. In the current implementation, this structure is represented in memory as the Long FEL, a linear array of EDs. While it may not be practical in future implementations to keep all EDs in memory, this approach is adequate for a first version.

Figure 8. Access Pathways for Directories and Files

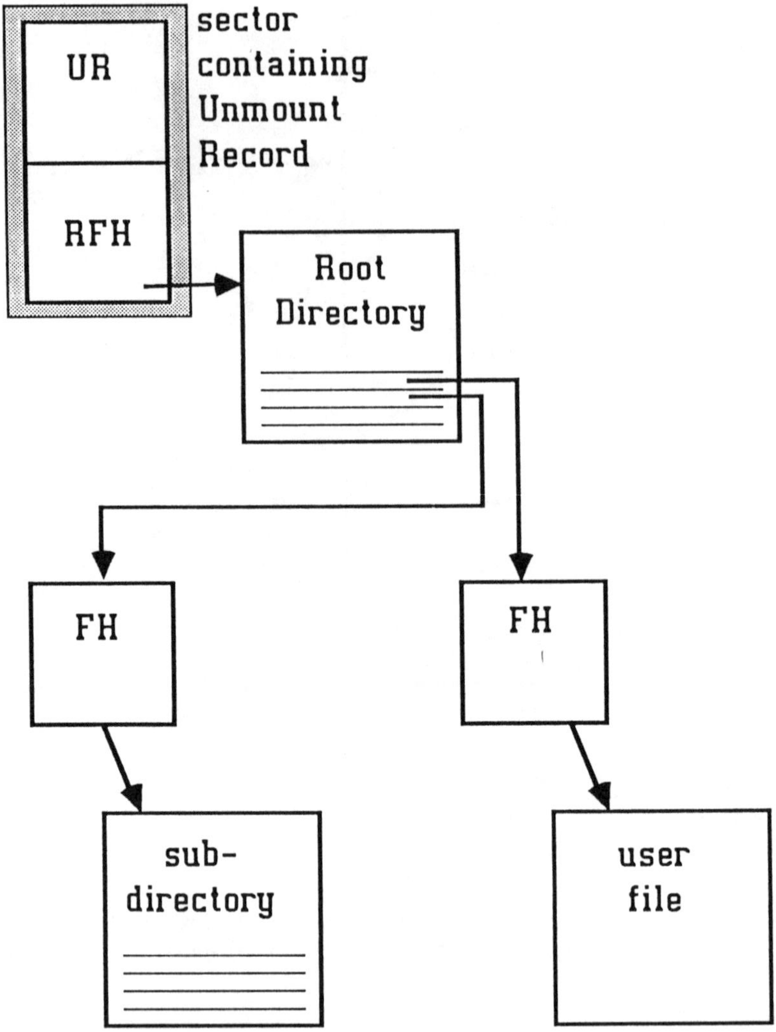

The "Short FEL", a data structure contained within the File Header, consists of seven elements:

ED1 The first extent descriptor
ED2 The second extent descriptor
ED3 The second-to-last extent descriptor
ED4 The last extent descriptor
FECD1 The first "File Extent Continuation" descriptor

FECD2 The last "File Extent Continuation" descriptor
FERCD The "File Extent Root Continuation" descriptor

The first four elements comprise the "first level" of the file extent list (FEL). Each element is an eight-byte descriptor of a file extent, consisting of a 4-byte Record Handle and a 4-byte Extent Length. The Record Handle portion refers to the first record of the extent. The Extent Descriptor contains all the information needed to retrieve the extent using the Level 1 **d_read( )** routine.

The first two and the last two extent descriptors are chosen to reside in the File Header so that easy access can be made to the front and the back of the file data. Likewise, the next two elements of the Short FEL are descriptors which refer to lists of extent descriptors (contained in "File Extent Continuation" (FEC) records) which apply to the front part and the back part of the file data. Finally, additional FEC records may be referred to indirectly through a single "File Extent Root Continuation" (FERC) record, whose descriptor is stored in the seventh position of the Short FEL.

The FECD and FERCD elements contain a Record Handle (RH) and a Record Length (RLen). However, the Length field of these descriptors contains the sum of the lengths of user file data described by subsidiary data structures.

In the current implementation, records are limited to 2046 bytes. Each FEC and FERC record contains a 14-byte header. Therefore, the maximum number of 8-byte elements is (2046 - 14) / 8 = 254 per record. The maximum number of Extents in a file using the current Short FEL structure is then calculated as follows:

First Level Extent Descriptors: 4

Second Level: 2 FECs x 254 ED/FEC = 508

Third Level: 1 FERC x 254 FECs/FERC x 254 EDs/FEC = 64,516

Total = 65,028 extents

In the case of very small fixed-size Extents of 512 bytes, this would lead to a maximum file size of 33,294,336 bytes. Much larger file sizes are possible for larger average Extent sizes.

In case the 65,028 Extent limitation is a problem, a simple extension can be made by allowing the FERC to become an Extent rather than be limited to a single record. This would require using the length field of the FERCD to describe the FERC extent length so that some efficiencies in locating a particular byte in the file might be lost.

Level 3

Level 3 provides the functions needed to implement a hierarchical directory, single-user file system. Multi-user and multi-tasking environments are expected to be supported by extensions to be added in later versions.

The on-disk structure is expected to be constant across operating systems. Where there are data type and functional incompatibilities in the various operating systems, Level 4 functions will provide the operating system specific adaptations. The initial target operating systems are MS-DOS, SunOS, VAX/VMS and Macintosh.

These Level 3 function definitions are modeled in part on Unix System V [AT&T, 1985; Bach, 1986] and on the variants of Unix defined in the Posix standard [IEEE, 1986], the Minix file system [Tanenbaum, 1987], and SunOS [Sun Microsystems, 1987].

Unique Aspects of the ODFS Level 3

Level 3 implements files and directories using the data structures defined in Level 2 and the functions defined in Level 1. In addition, it uses a Journal (whose control records are defined in Level 2) to record directory update information during normal operation.

One major difference between the ODFS and a typical hierarchical file system is that all internal (stored) references to files must be done by fully-qualified pathnames. This is because upward references (references from one directory to its parent by physical location) would lead to references to obsolete File Headers. Instead, each directory contains its own fully-qualified pathname and the names of each file (or directory) contained in it.

When a file is to be opened, the directory tree is always searched starting from the root directory. While this sounds like a lengthy operation, it is amenable to caching in RAM, i.e., the physical location (or even the contents) of the File Headers in one or more frequently-used path or paths can be kept in RAM.

Since every search descends the tree, there is an opportunity at each open to cross-check in the Journal for any updates to the directories being traversed. In fact, it is efficient to inspect the Journal first to see if there is an updated directory entry for the particular file which is the target of the search.

When a file is closed after being modified or extended (or deleted), a new File Header record is written followed by a Journal Record indicating the update for the directory entry referring to this file. (The directory entry contains the file name, a reference to the File Header location, and copies of selected information from the File Header.) The Journal Record is also saved in RAM in a Journal Buffer.

When it is time to remove the optical disk or to shut down the system, an **unmount( )** operation is made. This causes the ODFS to examine the Journal, update each directory that has been logically modified, and write a new Unmount Record. Contained in the Unmount Record are: a pointer to the High Water Mark, the File Header of the Root Directory, the Volume Name, and other parameters.

The **unmount( )** operation must be performed carefully; each directory update is done as a separate operation, with an appropriate Journal record being written at the end of the update, to indicate the pending update to this directory's parent directory. The order of the updates is important — they must be done from the bottom (farthest from the Root Directory) up, requiring (at most) one update pass to each directory in the tree. At the end of an **unmount( )** operation, the optical disk may be removed. The **sync( )** function performs the same Journal processing functions but the disk remains mounted.

A table large enough to hold at least 50 Journal entries (directory updates) should be provided in RAM. This table contains all of the Journal records (directory updates, deletions and insertions) which have occurred since the last Unmount Record was written.

At Mount time, any directory modification records which exist beyond the High Water Mark indicated in the latest Unmount Record must be read into the Journal Buffer. New modifications are added both to the Journal (on disk) and to the Journal Buffer until an **unmount( )** or a **sync( )** is performed.

Level 3 Directory Implementation

Only the distinctive aspects of the ODFS are detailed below. The other portions of the ODFS are substantially similar to traditional file systems or have not been defined as of November 1988.

A directory is a data file which contains the following (lengths in bytes are shown in parentheses following each field name):

Directory Header - one per directory:

File System Generation Number (2)
File Serial Number of this directory (4)

Length of Directory File Name (2)
Fully-qualified Directory File Name (variable, 1 to 32767)
Null byte (1)

Directory Entry - zero or more per directory:

Record Handle of the File Header (4)
File Serial Number (4)
File Type and Permissions (2)
Length of File Name (2)
File Name (variable, 1 to 32767)
Null byte (1)

A file is an ordered collection of data bytes stored on the volume. In the ODFS implementation the data bytes are stored in one or more Extents. The collection of Extents which are associated with a file are stored in a File Extent List which is stored in a structure originating from the File Header (see Level 2).

A File Name is a variable-length (but not null) string which is associated with a file. Association of a file name with a file occurs in (and only in) a Directory Entry, where the File Name and the Record Handle of the File Header record for the file are contained together.

The Default Root File is a Root Directory placed on a volume at the time of Formatting. It contains no directory entries.

A data structure called the Directory Dictionary (DD) is maintained in memory during normal operation of the ODFS. It contains information about every directory that has been seen since the last previous **mount ( )**. It includes the File Serial Number of the directory, a reference (in the DD) to the parent of the directory, and an "updated" flag. The parent structure is known because of the context in which a directory is encountered. The flag is used to mark directories for later update, i.e. when **sync( )** or **unmount( )** is called. (See the Sync Algorithm on page 45.)

Level 3 Functions

Only the distinctive aspects of the ODFS Level 3 functions are noted in the following descriptions.

format( )

This operation, if successful, causes a Default Root File (Directory) to be written at the lowest-numbered blank sector on the volume and a Unmount Record and RFH (Root File Header) to be written at the highest-numbered blank sector on the volume. The RFH written is the File Header of the Default Root File (Directory), and the Unmount Record written contains the Volume Name specified in this function call.

Note that it is possible to "reformat" a used optical disk cartridge using **format( )**. The resulting volume appears the same as a new formatted cartridge except for the number of blank sectors.

mount( )

To **mount( )** a volume means to make known to the system the file structure contained on an optical disk. The disk remains locked in the drive while it is mounted.

This function reads the last written Unmount Record and Root File Header and retrieves the Root Directory. It then checks to see if there are non-blank sectors at sector numbers higher than the High Water Mark given in the Unmount Record. If so, it performs Journal recovery. At the same time it rebuilds the Directory Dictionary.

Multiple logical volumes on a single cartridge may be supported in future versions.

unmount( )

This function causes all directories to be updated on the volume so that the optical disk contains a complete, consistent and independent file system. The disk is then unlocked so that it may be removed from the drive. (See **sync( )** below.)

sync( )

This functions causes all directories on the volume to be made consistent and up to date. (See page 45 for an algorithmic description of this function.)

This operation may take a long time. It is interruptible in that it consists of a series of individual directory updates, each of which is noted by a journal entry to update a directory entry in the parent directory.

open( )/create( )

At the time of a file **open( )** call, the latest File Header must be located for the desired file. Normally, a file system would simply locate the parent directory of the file and then go directly to the equivalent of the File

Header. However, since there may have been an update which has not yet been entered in the parent directory, the Journal must be searched for an applicable entry. The Journal entry will contain a reference to the parent directory and the file. The search of the Journal may be performed before retrieving the parent directory's File Header. It is only necessary to verify that the parent directory exists before searching the Journal. When a new file is created, it is necessary to verify that a file of the same name does not yet exist in the same parent directory. Again the Journal must be searched to verify the non-existence of the file to be created.

close( )

If the file being closed has been written or modified, a new version of the File Header is written. Then a Journal record is written to effect updating the directory entry for this file. The Journal entry information is also copied into the memory Journal Buffer. In the current implementation, the write buffer is flushed at the end of this function.

read( )

Normal file systems must deal with blocks of data which are fixed in length. When a file is to be read starting at an arbitrary byte offset, it may be necessary to read a block and discard some of the bytes preceding the requested portion of the file.

In the ODFS, Data Extents are variable length. It may be necessary to read an Extent and discard some of the bytes preceding the requested portion, just as in block-oriented file systems.

No difficulties occur in the ODFS unless the buffer provided for the read operation is shorter than the longest of the extents to be read. In this case, it is necessary to be aware of the record boundaries in the data extents. To deal with this possibility, the Level 1 **d_read( )** function returns the value of the "excess" length in the last record read (the number of bytes truncated from the last record in filling the read buffer). **d_read( )** also allows specification of an "offset" so that the subsequent read can skip the bytes already read. The Level 1 **get_rrh( )** function provides the balance of the information needed for Level 3 Read to perform the proper sequence of **d_read( )** calls of partial Extents without performing additional buffering at Level 3.

write( )

The current implementation of the ODFS permits only writes which append data to a file. This simplifies the tactics of buffering and memory management. However, there are no inherent limitations in the design of the ODFS which make it difficult to do generalized file updates. When existing extents are allowed to be updated, the tactical difficulties arise from attempting to balance a policy of not copying data when it is unnecessary against a policy of minimizing the number of Extents created.

recover( )

A special Recover function will be defined for the ODFS Level 3 which allows old states of the file system to be accessed (in a read-only mode). This function will locate prior states by stepping back through old Unmount Records and then stepping forward through the Journal Records.

Retrieval will be made using the **unmount( )** function or by date and time. The state of each file at the time of each **close( )** is available.

Sync Algorithm

STEP 1: Select next directory for update.

Starting at the lowest directory level (furthest from the root directory), choose directories which are marked for update, one at a time, performing update of all directories at a given distance from the root before moving on to any directory at a shorter distance from the root directory. The order of selection within a level is not significant.

STEP 2: Retrieve the File Header for the selected directory.

Read the File Header for the selected directory and prepare to read the directory file.

STEP 3: Allocate space in memory for and initialize an "Update List" for the selected directory.

The Update List will consist of condensed information extracted from the Journal Records written since the latest **sync( )**.

STEP 4: Build the Update List.

Scan the Journal. (The Journal may be read from the optical disk volume or, if a copy of it is kept in memory, the copy may be read.) Each Journal record which refers to the selected directory (as the "parent" of a file which has been created, updated or deleted) is added to the Update

List. However, some Journal records refer to an event which obsoletes a previous Journal record. Each such record replaces the old record in the Update List. Examples of pairs of Journal records in which the second record replaces the first are: create file X followed by update file X; update file X followed by update file X; and update file X followed by delete file X.

STEP 5: Apply the Update List.

Read the directory file, one Extent at a time. For each extent, scan the Update List and apply each matching File Update Record, in order, to the directory element it matches by replacing the information in the directory with the update information in the journal record. Each File Delete Record is applied by removing the corresponding directory element and scrolling up the other directory elements in the extent. After all Extents in the directory have been processed, new directory elements represented by file create records are appended to the last Extent or to a new extent. Each revised Extent is rewritten to the optical disk.

STEP 6: Rewrite the directory's File Extent List.

Applying the Update List to the selected directory has caused one or more Extents of the directory to be rewritten. The directory's File Extent List (FEL), maintained in memory as a linear array during file operations, is now repackaged into a File Header structure and into any required File Extent Continuation (FEC) records needed. The FECs are written to the optical disk.

STEP 7: Rewrite the directory's File Header.

The selected directory's revised File Header is written to the optical disk.

STEP 8: Write a Journal record.

A Journal record is written containing the file update information related to the update just performed on the selected directory. The parent directory of the selected directory now needs updating because the selected directory has just been modified.

STEP 9: Mark the parent directory.

A memory data structure (the Directory Dictionary) contains information about all directories which have been seen by the system since the latest **sync( )**. The entry in the Directory Dictionary for the parent of the selected directory is marked for update because one of its entries is now obsolete.

STEP 10: Repeat steps 1 through 9 until the Root Directory is selected.

Update of any directory ultimately causes the Root Directory to be updated. This is because the parent of each modified directory must also be modified, and the Root Directory is the ultimate parent of all other directories. Steps 1 through 9 are repeated until the Root Directory is selected in Step 1.

STEP 11: Perform steps 2 through 6 for the Root Directory.

STEP 12: Flush the write buffer.

Data and control records remaining in the ODFS write buffer (including the FEC records for the Root Directory) are written into the normal write area of the optical disk, i.e., starting at the High Water Mark.

STEP 13: Write the Unmount Record.

Transfer an Unmount Record into the ODFS write buffer. Set the target sector of the write to the appropriate place on the optical disk for the next Unmount Record sector.

STEP 14: Write the File Header of the Root Directory.

Transfer the Root File Header (the File Header of the Root Directory) into the ODFS write buffer.

STEP 15: Flush the write buffer.

The Unmount Record and the Root File Header, currently in the ODFS write buffer, are written to the next Unmount Record sector on the optical disk.

STEP 16: Clear the Journal.

The copy of the Journal that is in memory, if any, is cleared. All "marked for update" indications in the Directory Dictionary are cleared.

Level 4

Level 4 is a layer that is intended to permit adaptation of the file system for any operating system environment. Data format adjustments, function calling sequences and other apparent incompatibilities are dealt with in this level.

Example Operations

The following sequence is typical of the operations that may be made on an ODFS volume. See Figure 9 for a diagram of the files and directories presumed to exist on the volume.

In the following list, each numbered line represents one or more file operations invoked by the user or application program level. The steps shown indented under each numbered line are schematic of the operations performed at Level 3 of the ODFS. Each line that causes one or more records to be written on the optical disk has a record designator such as "R1" at the end of the line. These records are shown in Figure 10 and Figure 11 as they would appear assuming the High Water Mark value was 299 just before the beginning of this sequence. Figure 11 also shows the Unmount Record sectors, assuming that the highest numbered sector on the volume is 202145.

Figure 9. Example Directory Arrangement

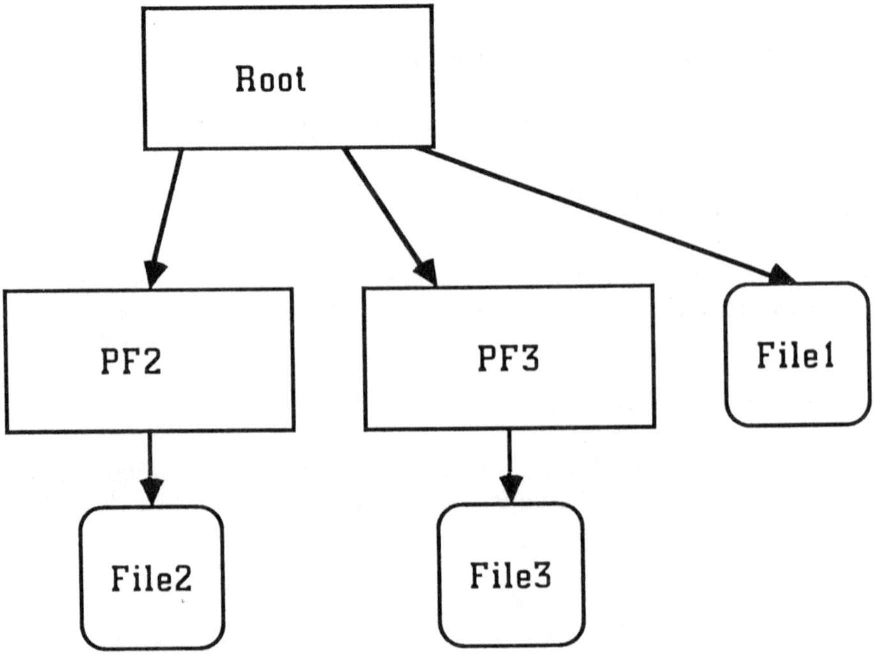

1. MOUNT
   lock cartridge in drive
   read_record(UR**)**
   read_record(RFH**)**

2. OPEN File1 for read
   check Journal for "Root/File1" updates
   d_read(directory**)**
   locate "File1" in Root Directory
   read_record(FH of "File1"**)**
   create LongFEL in memory (read FEC)

3. LSEEK, READ, CLOSE File1
   position to a byte in File1
   d_read(file data**)**

4. OPEN "PFs/File2" for write
   locate "PF2" in Root Directory
   check Journal for "PF2/File2" updates
   read_record(FH of PF2**)**
   d_Read("PF2" directory**)**
   locate "File2" in directory PF2
   read_record(FH of "File2"**)**
   create LongFEL in memory

5. WRITE to File2
   d_write(File2**) R1**

6. CLOSE File2
   c_write(new FH of File2**) R2**
   c_write(Journal "update"**) R3**
   mark directory "PF2" as modified

7. CREATE "File3 in directory PF3"
   close PF2
   locate "PF3" in Root Directory
   check journal for "PF3/File3" non-existence
   read_record(FH of PF3**)**
   d_read(directory PF3**)**
   verify "File3" not already in PF3

8. WRITE to File3
   d_write(File3**) R4, R5, R6, R7**

9. CLOSE File3
   c_write(FH of File3**) R8**
   c_write(Journal "create"**) R9**
   mark directory "PF3" as modified

10. UNMOUNT
    close all open files
    select directory PF2 for update
    d_read(PF2**)**

d_write(PF2**)** updated File2 entry **R10**
c_write(FH of PF2**) R11**
c_write(Journal "update"**) R12**
mark Root Directory as modified
select directory PF3 for update

d_read(PF3**)**
d_write(PF3**)** new File3 entry **R13**
c_write(FH of PF3**) R14**
c_write(Journal "update"**) R15**
mark Root Directory as modified

select Root Directory for update
d_read(Root Directory**)**
d_write(Root Directory**)** updated PF2, PF3, **R16**
c_write(FEC for Root Directory**) R17**

flush(normal write stream**)**
c_write_UR( ) R18
c_write(RFH**) R19**
flush(unmount record sector**)**
unlock cartridge in drive

Figure 10. Records Generated by Steps 1 – 9 of Example

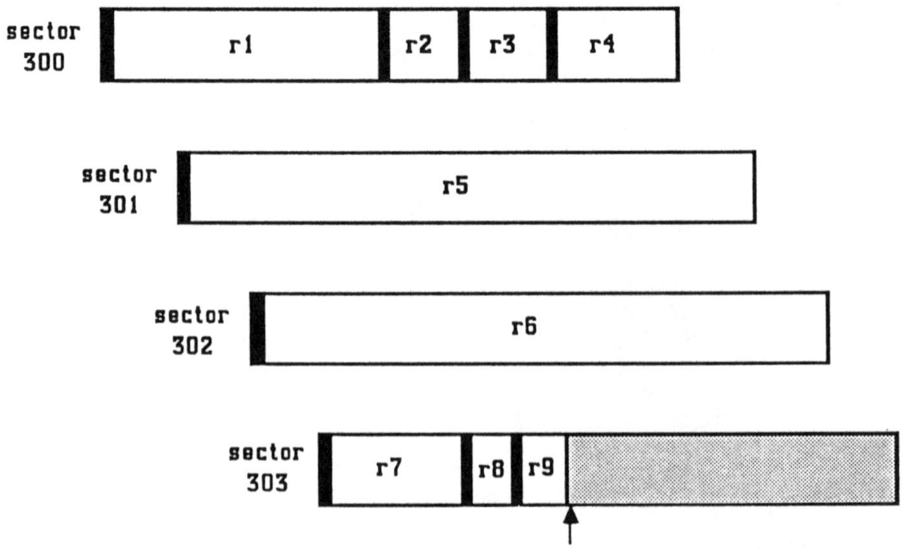

Figure 11. Records Generated by Step 10 of Example

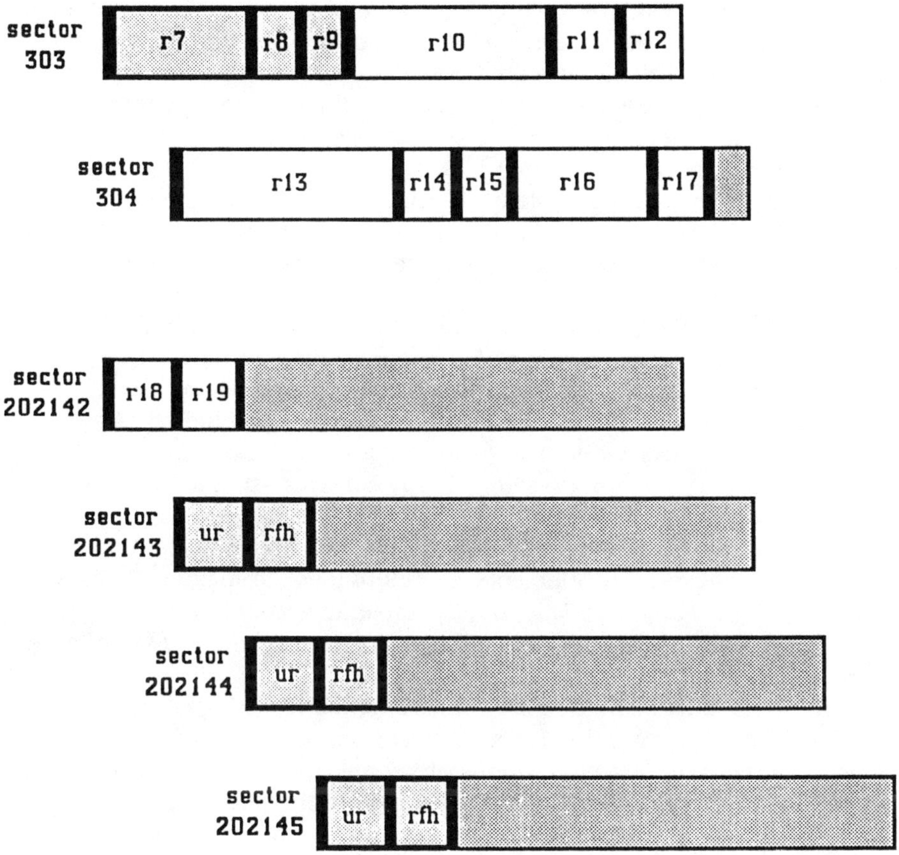

Comparison with the Optical File Cabinet

A recent paper by Jason Gait of Tektronix (1988) describes a file system called the Optical File Cabinet (OFC). The OFC allows the generality of block-by-block updating of files on the optical disk, without requiring copying of unmodified data blocks. It also implements a copy-back cache in which modified data blocks may reside for a time before being rewritten to the disk. The key data structure for accessing the disk data is the File System Tree (FST), a B-tree which maps all of the logical blocks of the volume to their actual locations on the optical disk. The key issue for the OFC is the management of the FST. This section compares some of the features of the ODFS with the OFC and its FST structure.

The chief difference between the OFC and the ODFS are that OFC interfaces with the operating system at the block management level. This allows the optical disk to appear like a normal block device and to be accessed by a normal device drive. This decision greatly simplifies the interface because a disk block is the basic unit of physical and logical storage. By contrast, the ODFS takes over the allocation of space on the optical disk and therefore cannot allow the operating system to manage space at the block level.

The OFC manages the system's block access by remapping the logical blocks into physical blocks. This requires building the FST which maintains the remapping information. The FST must then be stored and buffered in much the same way that file directories must be stored and buffered. In the ODFS, the decision was made not to duplicate this effort, but instead to implement only one directory/remap structure. In effect, this takes advantage of knowing what a file is while managing the allocation of space for both files and directories. The OFC, on the other hand, must manage blocks without knowing which blocks belong to which files because the operating system does not disclose that information at the device driver level.

The OFC requires the size of the FST to be chosen at the time the volume is formatted. The element size determines the maximum size of the file system. The ODFS as currently implemented has chosen Record Handles and Extent lengths large enough to allow an entire disk surface to be subsumed in the file system.

The OFC must make decisions regarding the rewriting of the FST to the optical disk because the disk's integrity is vulnerable to power loss as long as the latest information is not stored on it. Because of this, the OFC must choose a time interval at which to rewrite the FST. The ODFS, on the other hand, is vulnerable only to the extent that write buffers have not been written out yet. These buffers are the same for both data stream and the control stream — the Journal entries and file headers — because they are embedded in one write stream.

In the OFC, the block map must be available at memory speed for reasonable performance. The ODFS relies instead on access to directories and their File Extent Lists, which need to be cached.The OFC uses the device driver interface at the block level, which allows for a more standard o.s. interface. The ODFS takes on much greater responsibility for the files by building the entire file system. It is also necessary for the Level 4 interface to filter references to the optical disk volumes from references to files on magnetic media volumes, which are processed by the normal file system.

The ODFS reduces the "granularity" of access below the block level by breaking up the sectors into records. The OFC allows the operating system to manage a block cache in the usual way. This saves a lot of effort in implementation. The ODFS, to be most efficient, must reimplement caching at Level 1. Countering this disadvantage of the ODFS, there should be somewhat less rewriting of data because the ODFS manages the Extent maps of each file and can make choices about copying versus creating additional Extents whenever a file is rewritten or partially updated.

The ODFS can retrieve all past versions of every file because the journal contains a complete history for every directory entry. OFC is dependent on the writeback interval for finding old versions of the FST.

Conclusion

What follows is a brief discussion of the lessons learned thus far in the development of the ODFS.

It takes a long time to complete the definition of a file system. In the ODFS, a layered approach was chosen in order to separate the record access from higher-level functions. The interface and functions at each level much be defined and then refined. Ongoing implementation and testing are essential to the refinement process.

The ODFS allows very large Extents to be created. In practical implementations, however, it is best to define a reasonable maximum Extent size and record this maximum as a parameter of the file system or volume in the Unmount Record. This allows reasonable memory buffer management implementations. While it is possible to manage the reading of Extents which are larger than the available memory buffers, the record structure of Level 1 introduces an awkwardness that is not present when whole Extents can always be read into the buffers.

Operating systems are generally built with the assumption of fixed-size blocks in their file systems. Since the ODFS changes that assumption, it was necessary to redesign some mechanisms that are typically available as part of the operating system. These include memory buffering, file and directory caching and some of the file control information.

Data structures which are unique to the ODFS are the Directory Dictionary (containing directory "tree structure" information for all directories so far "seen" by the system) and the Memory Journal (a compact copy of the Journal which is the optical disk).

The most significant result of the ODFS design and implementation should be the demonstration of a practical use of a Journal. Since the natural allocation method for write-once media is sequential, the Journal Records fit into the spaces between Data Extents with very little overhead.

The chief advantage of the ODFS is avoidance of updates to directories during normal operation. As a consequence, however, the Journal must be searched on every **open( )** or **create( )** operation. Also, the

unmount( ) operation becomes complex. Whether the speed and storage space advantage of the Journal justifies the searching and the complexity of **unmount( )** will only be known after more experience with the ODFS system in actual operation.

Bibliography

Bach, M. J. *The Design of the Unix Operating System*. Englewood Cliffs, NJ: Prentice-Hall, 1986.

Gait, Jason. "The Optical File Cabinet: A Random-Access File System for Write-Once Optical Disks." *IEEE Computer*. June, 1988:11-22.

IEEE, Trial-use Standard 1003.1 ("Posix standard"), Institute of Electrical and Electronics Engineers, April 14, 1986.

Levy, John V. and Wayne Wang. "A File Structure for Non-erasable Media." *Digest of the Ninth IEEE Symposium on Mass Storage Systems.* (Monterey, CA, October 31, 1988), Institute of Electrical and Electronics Engineers, 1988.

Maxtor Corporation, *RXT-800S Product Specification and OEM Manual.* Document 1013040, Revision E, September, 1987.

Sun Microsystems, Inc., *SunOS Version 3*, 1986.

System V Interface Definition. Indianapolis, IN: AT&T Customer Information Center, Spring 1985: 1.

Tanenbaum, A. S. *Operating Systems: Design and Implementation.* Englewood Cliffs, NJ: Prentice-Hall, 1987.

5

Implementing WORM Storage in the MS-DOS Environment

ROB G. ZWICK

Since both magnetic and optical disk drives are random access devices, it seems logical to treat a WORM device as a magnetic disk look-a-like. However, it is also reasonable to treat a WORM device as a tape drive look-a-like since its write-once nature suggests that data should be written sequentially. Different approaches to implementing software to support WORM disks in the MS-DOS environment are discussed in this chapter.[1]

Design Issues and Approaches

The most important aspect of creating a WORM software product is the creation of an efficient data organization scheme for the maintenance of file and directory pointers. Since WORM devices have slower access times than their magnetic counterparts, it is necessary to minimize the number of seeks required to access data files.

Some designers have taken the approach of storing directory information on the outer tracks of the disk and file data on the inner tracks. As new files are added, the two grow toward each other. This concept was adopted by IBM for the software supporting its Model 3363 WORM drive.[2]

A problem with this approach is that it requires a great deal of head movement between opposite extremes of the disk surface to support file access and update. If this problem is not rectified, the interface to the WORM disk can become so slow that it may be deemed unusable. One way to help rectify this problem is to cache the file system's directory in memory or onto a magnetic disk.

However, a more efficient directory storage method can improve the overall usability of the WORM drive. One such scheme borrows from

[1]This discussion is based on the Optisys WORM magnetic emulation product.

[2]See Appendix 1 for an overview of the 3363's published specifications.

tape technology and writes information sequentially from the start of the disk. Since both user data and directory information are interspersed in the information stream, they are physically close to each other on the disk surface. Using this method, write operations only require forward head movement. However, a read operation requires a sequential scan of the written area starting at the beginning of the disk until the desired data is located.

As in the previous example, caching the directory can improve performance dramatically. Nevertheless, creating this cache requires the entire written portion of the disk to be sequentially scanned when the disk is mounted.

A Modified Tape Approach

Combining aspects of both tape and disk data storage methodologies can produce a magnetic emulation directory structure for which data is written sequentially and read randomly. With the use of limited directory and file allocation buffering either on magnetic disk or in memory, data access speeds can be increased.

Under MS-DOS, a directory and space allocation scheme must be designed which emulates the File Allocation Table (FAT) and directory entries. The MS-DOS FAT retains the chain of sectors used to store the contents of a file and keeps track of unused sectors on the disk. Each file on a disk has a directory entry, and each entry contains information which pertains to that file such as filename and extension, date created, starting location and attributes. The FAT and directory entries are very dynamic, and a good WORM design must be careful not to consume inordinate disk space in effecting updates to the FAT and directory entries.

One approach to this problem is a modified tape solution in which a certain number of sectors are pre-allocated at the start of the disk for directory use. If the active directory entries are kept in memory, the optical head rarely has to move any considerable distance on the disk to read requested data.

This method also allows for easy data manipulation. Erasing and copying files becomes a simple task. To read a file, the file's first data pointer must be located in a directory entry. Writing a file requires knowing the location of the first unwritten sector on the disk. After all data has been written sequentially from this point, the directory is updated.

A limitation of this approach is that it only allows for a flat directory structure, i.e., subdirectories are not supported. Since the data and directory areas are kept in separate areas, interspersing data and hierarchical directory structures in the data area is very difficult.

In addition, this approach does not allow files to be updated, appended or modified. The number of files which can be written to the disk is also limited based on the size of the pre-allocated directory area at the start of the disk. Unless this is of sufficient size, it could fill up before the data area fills up.

An Emulated Magnetic Disk Approach

Realizing that a modified tape approach is functional but not very useful, a magnetic disk drive emulation design is appealing. By using interspersed data and directory structures, tree-like directories can be built and pointers for updating and modifying files can be included.

With this approach, the directory and data information is interspersed. This allows inclusion of a control structure for each file written to the disk. If a user wants to modify or append a file, a new directory entry is created to reflect the changes in the file. This method is very beneficial in that it is device independent and allows the support of true hierarchal directory structures to allow easy data manipulation and the ability to update and append files.

Conclusion

The problem of allowing efficient storage and retrieval of general purpose user data on WORM media under MS-DOS can take many approaches. Magnetic tape-oriented designs are fairly straightforward to implement but they do not allow reasonable random data access. Although a magnetic disk emulation approach is more difficult, an efficient scheme can be implemented using sequentially written file directory structures interspersed with file data.

6

Implementing WORM and Erasable Optical Storage in the OS/2 Environment

CHOI T. KWOK

The use of optical storage with personal computers has opened up different realms of applications which require tremendous amounts of online storage. The OS/2 environment provides a more consistent and logical base for development of such large scale applications than does MS-DOS. Thus, it seems reasonable that OS/2 and optical storage should together form a powerful workstation.

The basis for developing optical storage software drivers under OS/2 is similar to MS-DOS since the device can be treated as a block device, i.e., in a manner similar to a magnetic disk drive. This should be considered a requirement since this is the only manner in which optical devices can be readily used by existing applications software packages.

In order to achieve this goal, the optical device driver must accept commands from the operating system such as read and write sectors, check the media and reset the drive without forcing the operating system to make special considerations for the device. This is particularly important for WORM devices because, although WORM media cannot be re-written, both MS-DOS and OS/2 treat all block devices as if they can be re-written.

Another factor in the design of device drivers for MS-DOS Rev. 3.X and OS/2 Rev. 1.0 is the logical disk size limitation of 32MB. This is due to the fact that the sector size is 512 bytes, and the maximum number of sectors is 65,520 (FFF0 hexadecimal). There are two methods of overcoming this barrier.

First, the media may be logically divided into multiple partitions, with each partition's size being 32MB or less. This makes a single physical disk look like multiple disks. Since each hard disk is referenced by a single letter of the alphabet starting with "C:", these 24 partitions allow access to 768MB. However, since optical disk surfaces can be well in excess of 1GB is size, this is often not an acceptable solution. A second method of overcoming this barrier is to use an undocumented feature of

MS-DOS that allows the disk sector size to be variable, i.e., not necessarily the default size of 512 bytes. Increasing this size increases the partition size, thus lessening the impact of the first approach's limitation.

OS/2 Limitations

Since OS/2 was designed to handle large storage devices, it would seem that writing device driver software for OS/2 would not be a difficult procedure. However, OS/2 turns out to have more limitations than advantages for this task when compared with MS-DOS.

With regard to the partition size limitation issue, OS/2 is not as flexible as MS-DOS because it only supports a sector size of 512 bytes. This can certainly be considered to be a design flaw since it is unreasonable to assume that all block storage devices will have 512 byte sectors. This limitation is particularly inappropriate for applications dealing with very large files. This restriction also opposes the existing trend of optical devices which often have sector sizes of 1024 or 2048 bytes.

OS/2 Rev. 1.1 allows storage devices of capacities up to 512MB. This was accomplished by increasing the size of the sector number field from 16 to 32 bits. The 512MB limit is an arbitrary value since the designers of OS/2 wanted to limit the size of the File Allocation Table (FAT). If all 32 bits were used, this field could support logical devices up to 2TB in size. Since the sector size under OS/2 is fixed at 512 bytes, devices with other sector sizes must be handled in the device driver. Operations can be used which read or write physical sectors, but extract requested bytes for read operations and merge new bytes with old for write operations.

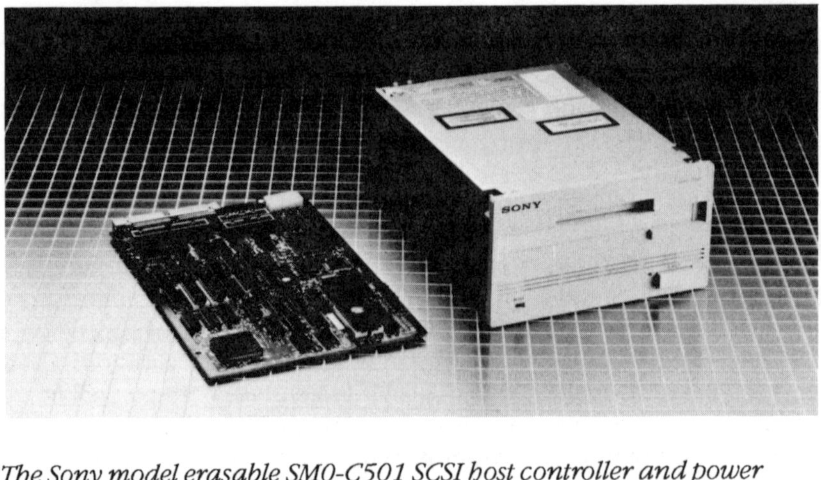

The Sony model erasable SMO-C501 SCSI host controller and power supply (Courtesy Sony Corporation of America)

Memory Caching

In light of the above restrictions, device driver performance can be improved by using a memory cache. The caching of FAT sectors removes the extra read cycle needed to write a smaller logical sector into a larger physical sector. However, since a FAT under OS/2 may be as large as 4MB, it is often unreasonable to cache the entire FAT. In this case, it would be preferable to maintain a partial cache and use a pre-fetch method of loading sectors which the driver would expect to use later. Hence, the driver should attempt to predict which sectors may be needed by upcoming requests and load these into the cache in advance of their being needed.

This method of pre-fetching sectors works best when files are stored in a contiguous set of sectors. This will be the case if few deletions and rewrites have been performed to the file system, or if a disk optimizer has been run on the disk. (It should be noted that OS/2's disk protection mechanism does not allow an application to access physical sectors directly. Thus, present MS-DOS utilities which re-order disk sectors to make files contiguous cannot be run or be easily converted to run under OS/2.) Caching has a definite downside when it comes to write requests. When OS/2 requests a write, it stops the application program which generated the request and passes control to the device driver. The device driver then performs the operation and reports it as "done" as soon as possible. With caching, however, the data may not necessarily have been written to the platter even when the 'done' status is returned. Thus, OS/2 and the application may believe that the data was written to the disk when in fact it was not. A system crash could cause unrecoverable data loss.

The trick is to determine the proper amount of information to write to the disk, and when to write it. It may be advantageous to write just the bare minimum, localize it to small areas to waste platter space, and to perform housekeeping at a later time so that the operating system and application programs remain responsive. This later time could even be the next time the system is booted.

With regard to WORM devices, caching can reduce the number of sectors used up on the write-once media when only a few bytes are changed at a time in a particular sector. With a magneto-optic erasable drive, caching can improve writing performance by reducing the number of times that the drive's necessary erase-before-write operation must be performed. Once again, these improvements will be best realized in updates to the FAT and directory sectors.

Multi-Tasking Issues

Because MS-DOS is a single-tasking operating system, its device drivers need only handle one request at a time. No useful work can be performed while a program is waiting for a data transfer request to complete. This often means that hardware status is polled until all I/O has completed.

OS/2 is a multi-tasking operating system, and its device drivers must be capable of handling requests from a number of applications simultaneously. Hence, the code must be re-entrant and be as efficient as possible. It would be grossly inefficient to poll devices because this could hold up other processes. In the world of WORM drives, where an average seek may take 100 or 200 milliseconds, processor time should not be used for waiting.

OS/2 contains a set of functions which allow a device driver to "go to sleep" while it is waiting for an I/O request to complete. Upon its completion, the driver can be woken by a hardware interrupt, and control can return to the requesting process or task.

OS/2 includes a set of queue management utility functions for handling device requests. Although requests come in from different applications, the device driver deals with them as separate atomic units not related to an application. Certain requests do not need to be queued because they can be processed immediately. I/O operations should be queued because they take a significant amount of time.

It is also desirable to have I/O operations processed not in the order in which they were received, but in the most efficient order. Hence, they should be sorted and placed in another queue. Multiple queues can and should be maintained for multiple physical drives, but queues for two logical drives which map to the same physical drive should be merged.

Conclusion

Using optical storage devices in an OS/2 environment would seem to be an appropriate match because many OS/2 applications will probably require the high-capacity storage provided by optical devices. However, OS/2's artificial limitations on sector size and logical capacity forces the device driver to perform extra functions such as disk caching and file optimization. OS/2 was developed with applications in mind, but the storage devices the operating system expects are just larger versions of floppy and hard disk drives. Considering the advanced application programming interface of OS/2, its limited support for high-density storage devices leaves something to be desired.

7

Implementing WORM Storage with Jukebox Support on the Macintosh

JAMES G. LANFORD

This chapter focuses on several aspects of the Macintosh operating system relevant to the integration of WORM technology. Specifically, this chapter addresses how the WORM implementation supplements the Macintosh's file management capabilities while capitalizing on its many strengths.[1]

Macintosh Environment Considerations

In the user-friendly Macintosh operating system, hierarchically stored information is represented as icons on the Macintosh screen's "desktop" in a fashion conceptually similar to that of a paper file system. On the desktop, icons exist for hard and floppy magnetic disks, folders, and files. When a disk or folder is opened by double-clicking on its icon with the mouse, its file and folder contents are displayed in a window. Thus, the end-user navigates through the hierarchically organized information of a disk simply by opening the appropriate nested folders until the file or files of interest are located.

A second method of locating a file is available if an end-user has left the desktop and is in an application program. This method involves selecting the file from the Macintosh's standard open dialog box. The open dialog box displays the contents of disks and folders in list form, and presents various options for acting on them such as open and cancel (see Figure 1). For this particular implementation, a Macintosh dialog box was used as the interface standard for actually selecting a file to be read from the optical disk (see Figure 2). A way to limit the files that appear in the dialog box was added.

For the files that are typically stored on magnetic media and single-user implementations of small WORM drives, finding files by clicking on

[1]This discussion is based on Micro Dynamics' MARS™ (Multi-user Archival and Retrieval System).

Figure 1. Macintosh Open Dialog Box and Desktop Volume Icons (Courtesy Micro Dynamics)

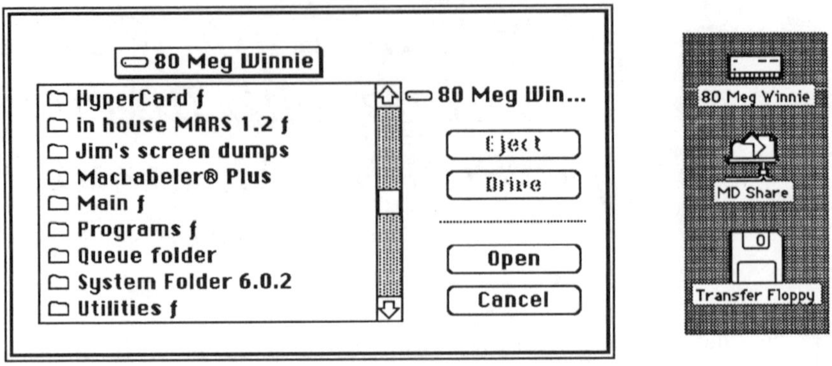

Figure 2. MD MARS Dialog Box (Courtesy Micro Dynamics)

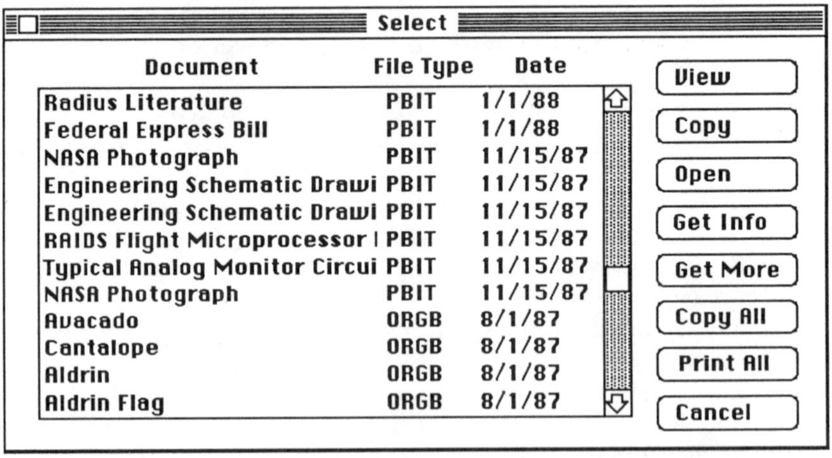

icons or selecting from a list works well enough. However, for the thousands or even millions of files that a large-scale multi-user WORM-based system is designed to store, the desktop becomes hopelessly inadequate. It may be reasonable for a user to want a small WORM drive to appear as just another drive icon on the desktop, but if all of the contents of a WORM jukebox were to appear, the desktop would surely breakdown under the load, both figuratively and operationally. This would occur because the Macintosh operating system would probably bog down before the first 12-inch WORM disk was filled. Thus, an approach that can handle the quantity of information involved without sacrificing the Macintosh's ease-of-use is required.

Supplanting the Macintosh File System

Sophisticated database software employing two dedicated servers makes information stored on the WORM disk available to an entire network of Macintosh workstations. The Optical Server efficiently controls read and write access to multiple WORM drives including jukeboxes; the Directory Server provides fast, flexible keyword searching on millions of files.

Software supplements some aspects of the functionality of the Macintosh operating system and replaces others. All of the software operates using standard Macintosh operating system routines. For example, the various modules of the application program itself including Input, Retrieve, Directory Server, and Optical Server are launched from the desktop. These modules incorporate most standard Mac features such as consistently organized pull-down menus. This particular system takes this feature one step further by allowing routine keyword data entry to be accomplished by simply selecting appropriate choices from pop-up menus of choice that appear when the user points at the field in question.

The purpose for this software is to replace aspects of the Macintosh's operating system involved with locating files with a more efficient way of handling large numbers of files (or "documents").**The Directory Server is actually nothing more than a replacement for the Macintosh file system environment (including the "Finder").** It provides a powerful special purpose database that allows a network of users to use

Figure 3. MD MARS WORM Data Structure for Directory Server (Courtesy Micro Dynamics)

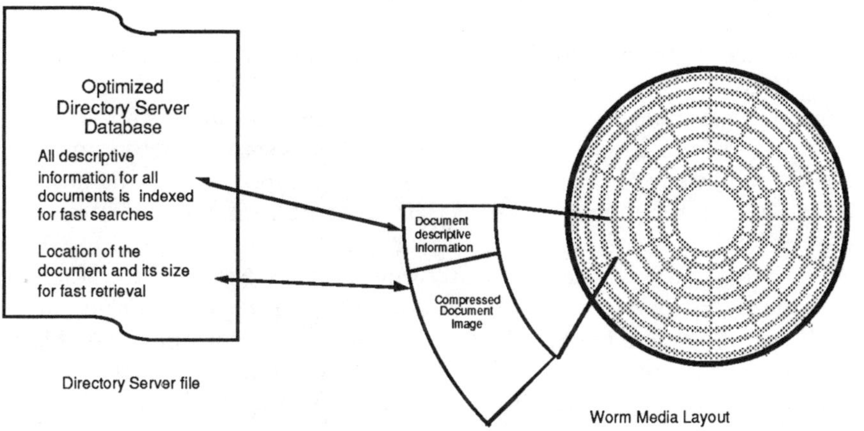

keyword searches for file descriptions including the use of any combination of fields, relational operators, and wildcards. The Finder was never intended to be able to handle this demand; it was designed for a relatively small number of documents on a magnetic disk, and can only locate documents based on file name searches.

The Roles of the Directory and Optical Servers

In this design, the Directory Server is only required to maintain the keyword directory information about the documents. The Optical Server's function is to know where a given document is on any WORM disk that has been introduced to the system (regardless of online/offline status) and control the actual reading and writing of the disk. The reason for distributing these two file management functions is to increase performance. The working directory information is maintained on magnetic media to allow the Directory Server (see Figure 3) to respond to any query from a network user quickly. Since the document files themselves are maintained on the WORM disk, it is advantageous to minimally involve the WORM disk and Optical Server.

Figure 4. Jukebox Control Dialog Box (Courtesy Micro Dynamics)

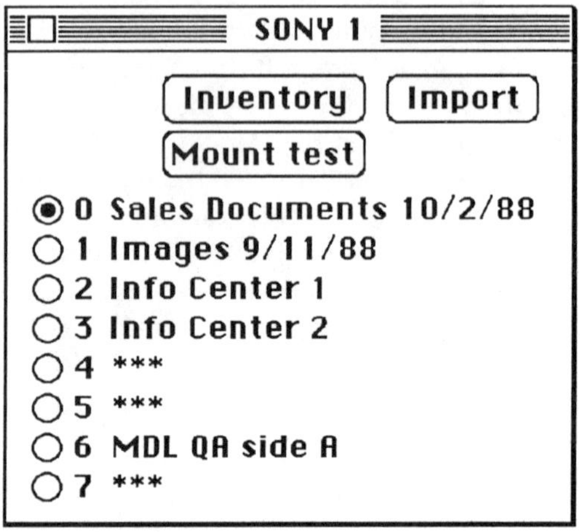

A backup copy of the directory information is also saved on the WORM disk. A Directory Server rebuild utility is used if the Directory Server's magnetic media information is lost or, when adding WORM media, transported from another Micro Dynamics' MARS system. Before moving the WORM disk to another system, the end-user simply selects the desired cartridge with the mouse and clicks the "prepare for transport" button in the optical server and then the "eject from jukebox" button.

When a jukebox is used, the software must keep track of the slot and the side orientation of each WORM disk. After a service call or any unusual occurrence, the media might end up in different locations. The Optical Server contains an inventory button (see Figure 4) which mounts each side of every WORM disk in the jukebox and updates the slot and side orientation list. The inventory process usually takes about 15 minutes. The information available for each volume is shown in the Volume Information dialog box in Figure 5.

Figure 5. MD MARS Volume Information Dialog Box (Courtesy Micro Dynamics)

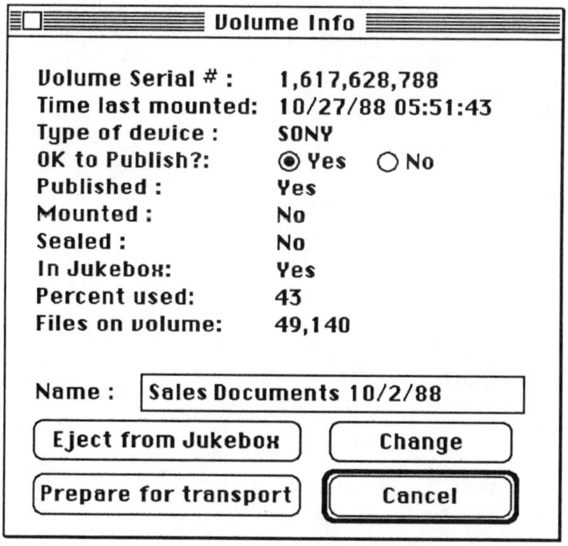

In this system, a request goes to the Optical Server to read a document from the WORM disk only when the search (which has thus far only involved the Directory Server) has allowed the user to exactly specify a particular document. The result is that the system can support a large number of heavy end-users before there is any noticeable degradation in performance.

Conclusion

The vast storage afforded by optical devices creates new file management problems. The Apple Macintosh's icon-based end-user interface can be used to run new programs which can more conveniently handle the descriptors for a large number of files stored on an optical disk. The management of many optical disks in a jukebox can also be handled in this manner.

8

Implementing WORM Storage in the Unix Environment

BRIAN A. BERG

This chapter describes two implementations of WORM storage under the Unix operating system. These implementations are considerably different from each other since they each had distinct requirements. Each implementation consisted of adding a block mode and raw mode device driver to the Unix kernel. A set of utilities was also created.

Neither implementation required modifications to operating system code. As a result, neither allows access to a mountable read/write Unix file system on the WORM disk. However, each implementation allows an existing file system or a portion thereof to be moved to the WORM disk and accessed in a read-only manner.

The most difficult problem that optical software developers face is allowing a WORM-based file system to be dynamically updated, and much of this book describes how this problem is attacked. This chapter describes two implementations that satisfy somewhat simpler system requirements. It also describes a system based on one of these implementations which can be used to store a mixed-mode (text and images) database.

Arix Implementation

This implementation runs on the Arix Corporation (formerly Arete Systems Corporation) multiprocessor super-minicomputer. In late 1985, Arix received a contract to develop a Unix-based WORM product. A major stipulation in this contract was that the Unix file system be supported on the WORM disk without modification to the Unix kernel code itself. Arix concluded that this would result in an implementation that would only allow the Unix file system to be accessible in a read-only manner. Hence, block device access would be read-only, but raw device access could be read/write.

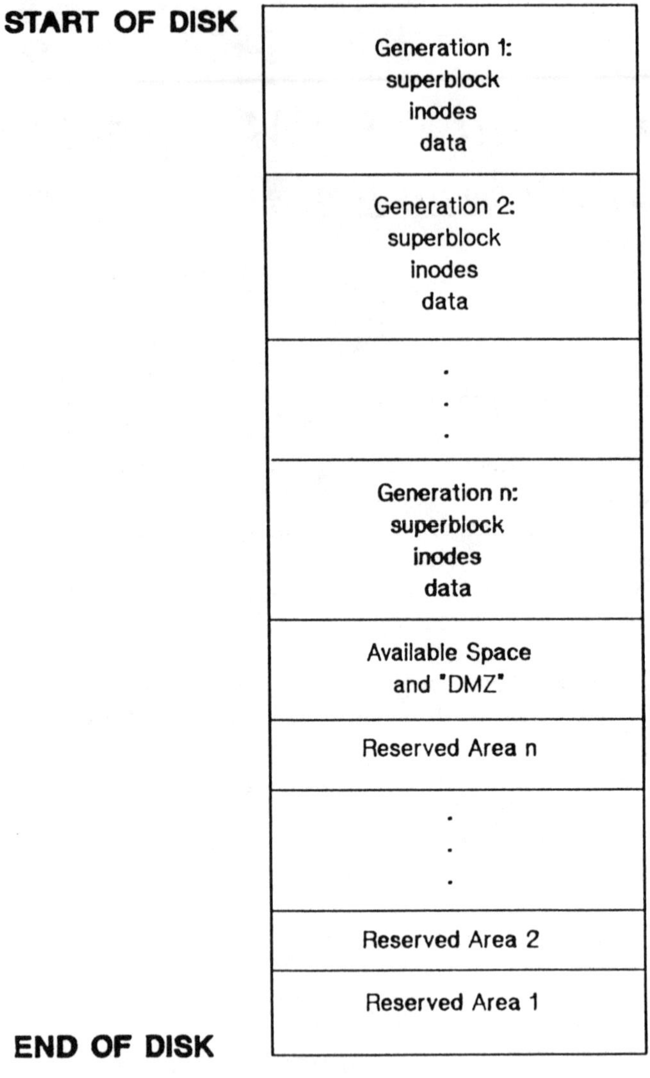

Figure 1. Arix Unix File System Implementation (Courtesy Berg Software Design)

Released in mid-1986, the resulting system allowed the following Unix file system functions:

1. The ability to add, delete and replace files and directories.
2. The ability to supersede a previously-created file system.
3. Support of all commands which require only disk read access.

The implementation involved the creation of utilities to support the following functions:

1. Create and update the file system as described above.
2. Display disk status information.
3. Make the disk usable after a system crash.

The first utility was implemented by copying a directory hierarchy from magnetic to optical disk. This approach allows data to be created on magnetic disk exactly as desired before being committed to optical disk.

The layout of the WORM disk to support the Unix file system is shown in Figure 1. In this implementation, "Generations" of file systems grow sequentially from the start of the media while "Reserved Areas" grow reverse-sequentially from the end. A file system Generation is a set of files, their associated inodes (file sector pointers) and the latest superblock (a special Unix file system sector). This idea of two areas growing toward each other from each end of the disk is a commonly used technique for WORM implementations.

The inodes and superblock on a Unix magnetic disk file system are located at the very start of the disk. However, since the WORM file system is updatable, the inodes and superblock must be updatable as well. This is accomplished by remapping these entities to other than the first few sectors of the optical disk. Any attempts to access these sectors are intercepted and mapped to the appropriate place on the disk. The code to perform this remapping was embedded in the driver and did not require a Unix kernel modification.

If an inode sector is updated for the latest file system Generation, it will reside within the confines of that Generation's sectors. If it did not get updated, it will still be valid even though it resides in an earlier Generation area. Pointers are maintained for all inode sectors, and are updated only when necessary.

The remapping process is accomplished by saving all the current pointers in the latest Reserved Area. These values are read at mount time and used by the driver for read operations. Since the disk can only be mounted as a read-only device, these values are valid the entire time the disk is mounted.

Files can be added, removed and replaced, and untouched files from previous Generations will still exist in subsequent Generations. Hence, files can carry forward from any number of previous Generations. Previous Generations may be superseded by ignoring the file pointers in the latest Reserved Area and starting with an empty set of inodes. This is also what is done the first time a platter is written.

As the Generation areas and Reserved Areas grow toward each other on the disk, the unwritten area between them gets smaller. A platter can be updated as long as this unwritten area (known as the "DMZ") remains

Figure 2. Plexus Unix File System Implementation (Courtesy Plexus Computers

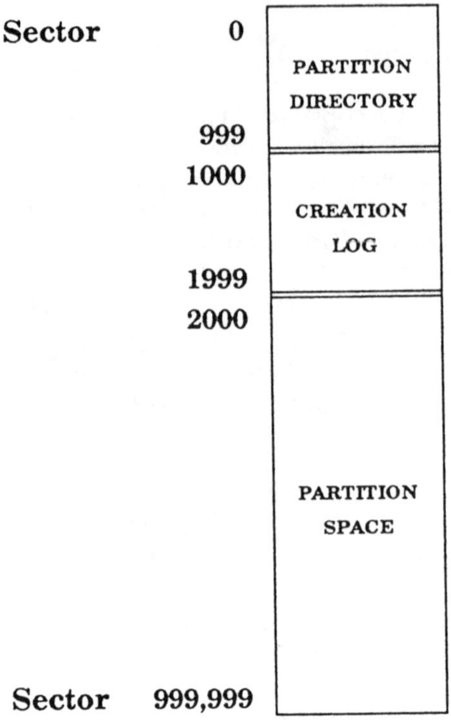

at least a certain number of sectors in size. This is necessary in order to find the latest Reserved Area on a platter. The process of mounting a platter includes searching backwards from the end of the disk for the latest Reserved Area. The latest Reserved Area is preceded by the last unwritten sectors of the DMZ. The ability to distinguish between written and unwritten sectors is a basic characteristic of WORM media, and is exploited by the code which mounts a platter.

Plexus Implementation

This particular implementation runs on the Plexus Computers super-minicomputer. This WORM product can support storage of a mountable Unix file system although it cannot be updated like Arix's. While this restriction exists, the Plexus implementation allows for any other kind of Unix entity (e.g., the output from any program) to co-exist with a file system or other entities on the same optical surface. Hence, any program can send its output to optical disk for permanent storage.

The WORM disk surface is divided into three areas: (1) the Partition Directory, (2) the Creation Log, and (3) the Partition Space. Each data entity is contained in a "partition" in the Partition Space. The total number of entities that can be created on a disk is determined when the first partition is created in the Partition Space. Figure 2 shows the layout of a platter configured to support up to 1000 partitions.

A partition is opened and accessed by way of a Unix minor device. It may be opened in either of two ways: with a fixed size, or indefinitely. A fixed size open will allocate a specified number of sectors to a partition, and the sectors can be written randomly and after any number of subsequent partition **open( )** operations. An indefinite open allows only sequential sectors to be written, but the only limit to the number that can be written is the number of unwritten Partition Space disk sectors remaining on the disk. Only one indefinite partition may be open on a disk at any one time.

When a partition is first created, an entry is made in the Creation Log. When it is closed, an entry is made in the Partition Directory. The Partition Directory and Creation Log contain information like the partition name, creation date, starting address, etc. For fixed size partitions, these entries are identical. For indefinite partitions, these are also identical with one exception: the size field in the Creation Log is zero, but this field in the Partition Directory is accurate. **The Plexus design includes these nearly identical data structures for one important reason: to allow recovery from a crash occurring while an indefinite partition is open.**

When a WORM disk is first accessed after being loaded into a drive, the Creation Log and Partition Directory are scanned and verified to have the same number of entries. If the Creation Log is determined to have one more entry than the Partition Directory, a crash occurred while an indefinite partition was open and the disk must be "repaired" before it can be used. Repairing consists of determining the number of sectors written to the last indefinite partition and making an appropriate entry in the Partition Directory to effect a **close( )** operation. This design guarantees that the Partition Directory contains an accurate record of partitions in the Partition Space.

A Unix file system could be moved to a WORM disk by way of the Unix **dd** utility. The file system's raw device would be the **dd** input file, and output would be sent to the WORM partition creation utility. This utility would create an indefinite partition containing the magnetic disk file system. Once the file system was copied, the partition could be mounted as a read-only file system. It would be a snapshot of the magnetic file system as it existed at the time of the copy.

A System Built on the Plexus Implementation

The Plexus WORM subsystem product was released in mid-1986. It proved to be an essential element of the Plexus XDP™ (Extended Data Processing) product which was released in late 1987. XDP is a "mixed-mode" data processing system which allows database management software to access large non-traditional database entities such as digitized images, large text files and any form of unstructured data. The WORM disk is used to store these basic large objects, or "blobs".

The Informix relational database product was modified so that while traditional entities were still stored on magnetic disk, a column in a database table could contain a pointer to a blob on optical disk. Blobs are typically two to three orders of magnitude larger in size than their traditional database counterparts, and storing these two different sized objects on the same peripheral device would allow the blobs to use a disproportionate amount of the magnetic storage space. In addition, magnetic storage space would be quickly used up. Although blobs can be stored on magnetic disk, it makes more sense to store them on a large capacity device such as a WORM disk.

This approach created two problems as a result of the removability of WORM media:

1. An XDP database could not be guaranteed to be totally accessible at any one moment.
2. Each WORM disk had to be uniquely identifiable to guarantee data integrity.

The first problem was partially solved by using a jukebox to manage a large number of WORM platters. However, since disks are removable from jukeboxes, the problem of a partially inaccessible database remained and special error codes had to be defined.

The second problem was solved by labeling each WORM disk when it was first used. A unique label could be created based on the date, time, drive number and system installation serial number.

When a blob was included in a database, its magnetic disk pointer could be created by concatenating this unique label with the blob's starting sector number on the WORM disk. Thus, this pointer could uniquely identify the one place in the world where the correct data existed.

Conclusion

WORM software implementations vary greatly in their capabilities. A dynamically updatable file system is a complex undertaking. Less complex implementations can still be integrated with other software elements to create powerful data storage and retrieval systems.

9

Implementing WORM Storage in the VAX/VMS Environment

IAN MACRAE

WORM software products use two basic design approaches: magnetic tape emulation and magnetic disk emulation. This chapter touches briefly on magnetic tape emulation, but focuses primarily on magnetic disk emulation implementations which run under the DEC VAX/VMS operating system.

Magnetic Tape Emulation

Some vendors support WORM devices by using magnetic tape emulation in an attempt to address the archival backup market. These products were amongst the first to appear because although WORM devices are random access, writing a write-once medium in a sequential fashion as is done by tape drives is straightforward to implement. Examples of such products include Aquidneck Systems International's Optical Archiving System (OAS) software product and Qualogy's QLC-1000 optical disk controller board.

Tape emulation products are often not cost-competitive with magnetic tape systems themselves. In particular, the current generation of helical scan tapes can record several gigabytes on a standard VHS videocassette tape or about 1GB on a Digital Audio Tape (DAT) with error rates comparable to those of WORM media. DAT tapes and short VHS tapes can be quickly scanned and rewound. As a result, the slow access times which tape drives have traditionally exhibited are no longer a serious problem.

Magnetic Disk Emulation

In spite of efforts to make WORM convenient for online access, many firms prefer to implement the technology as a backup device. This is a practical use since current media prices range from $100 to $500 per disk. WORM disks are now perceived by a growing number of companies and organizations as appropriate for archival backup applications.

Figure 1. WORM Disk Partition Scheme 1 (Courtesy KOM, Inc.)

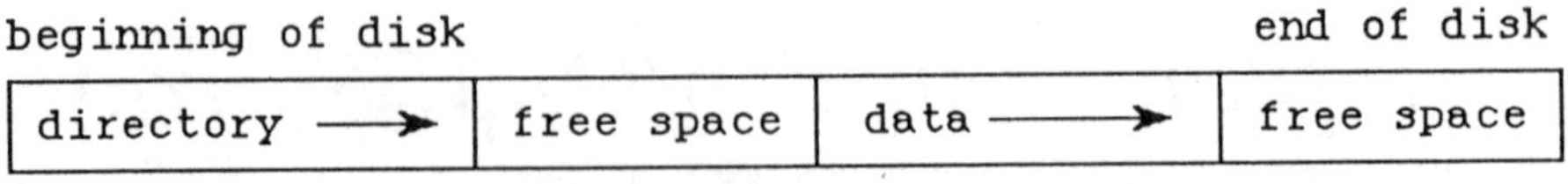

If used as online random access devices, extra features are essential for the overall acceptance of WORM technology. For reliability, the WORM system must be self-contained (no magnetic disks needed) and consistent at all times (no chance of power failures). Also, it should work just like a magnetic disk so that software written for magnetic storage is directly usable with the WORM system.

Standalone File Systems

The first WORM implementations created standalone file systems accessed by specially written applications. A typical example of a standalone file system is a large database of images or other large files on a WORM disk.

Sometimes I/O functions were provided by a subroutine library that was linked into the application under development, but the most common practice was to write new programs which were specifically designed to use WORM. These programs directly manipulated the disk and thus required intimate knowledge of the properties of the particular disk drive chosen.

The WORM disk was often partitioned into areas as shown in Figure 1. This format mimics that used by traditional magnetic disk file systems in which data is recorded on the disk followed by a directory update. Some very popular systems such as Perceptics' LaserWare currently use this format. A drawback to this approach is that the number of files to be stored must be estimated before the disk can be used so that the amount of directory space can be pre-allocated.

Some systems such as the OptiDriver from Optisys, Inc. allow the "deletion" of files by using a variance of the standard directory structure to indicate that a file is to be ignored when a subsequent file search is performed. However, some simple systems do not allow files to be deleted at all.

Another approach uses only one free area on the disk (see Figure 2). Although this solves the pre-allocation problem, it introduces a much larger problem. Since the speed of WORM disks is quite slow compared to magnetic disks, performance degenerates to unacceptable levels when

Figure 2. WORM Disk Partition Scheme 2 (Courtesy KOM , Inc.)

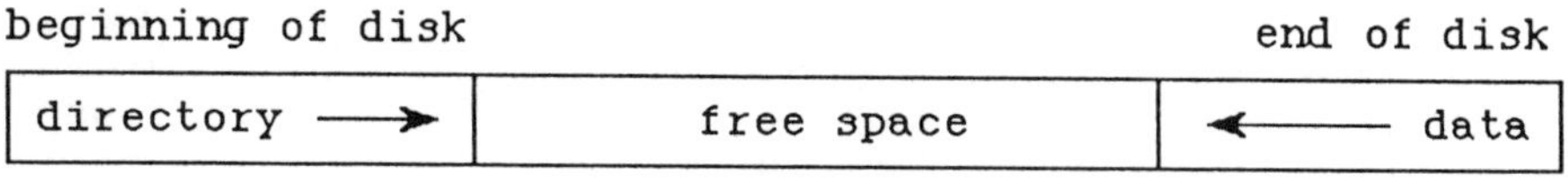

Figure 3. Remote File Server Architecture (Courtesy KOM, Inc.)

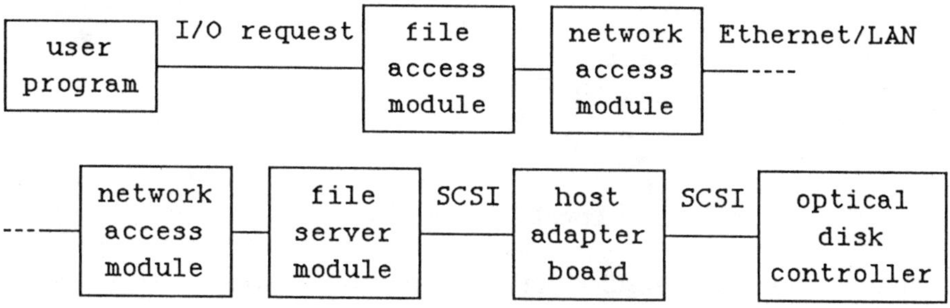

small files are stored due to the head seek time between access of the directory area and data area.

Remote File Servers

In an attempt to make system integration simpler for other software developers, some early products were released as file servers.[1] Networked file systems are supported by a number of operating systems including Unix and DEC's VMS and RSX. These operating systems can be easily made to support optical storage by creating a software module (usually a standalone program located at a remote node on the network) which recognizes the standard file system messages, but interprets them in terms that are appropriate to a WORM file system (see Figure 3).

However, an application is required to call appropriate I/O routines supplied in a library. The actual format of the WORM disk was irrelevant to the application since the file server was responsible for maintaining the integrity of the file system structures. However, every I/O request from the user program had to be queued first by the operating system and then by the network access module, transmitted onto the network, interpreted at the remote node, and then sent to the drive. Due to the additional overhead incurred by the magnetic emulation software, performance was often very poor.

[1]The OPTIFILE I developed by KOM, Inc. is a file server for DEC's RSX-11M/PLUS.

Figure 4. Local File Server Architecture (Courtesy KOM, Inc.)

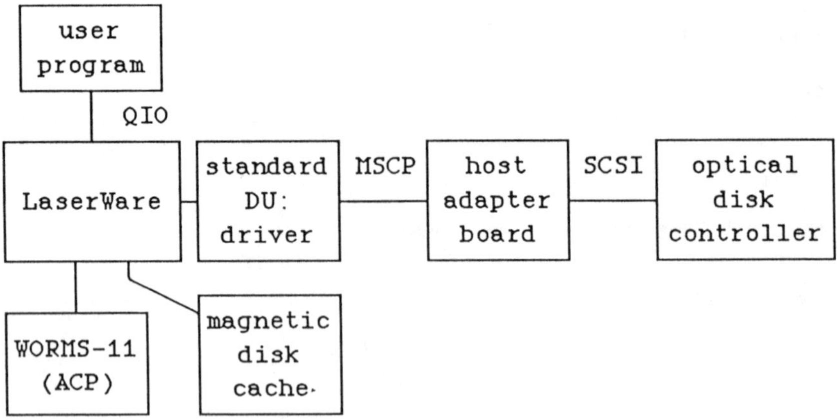

Local File Servers

Other attempts to make disk operations transparent to users (e.g., Perceptics' LaserWare file system) required that developers have intimate knowledge of the file system so that its internals could be fully emulated. With this method, I/O requests to a device driver from an application program were intercepted and handled as either normal magnetic disk operations or optical disk operations.

File functions (such as opening and closing files) were interpreted by an ACP[2] which emulated the appropriate disk structures in order to maintain file headers, allocation maps, and directories (see Figure 4). Data I/O operations occurred either directly with the WORM disk or by way of a temporary cache on magnetic disk.

ACPs provide the powerful file system features of VMS such as data security and disk quota checking. Unfortunately, it is a difficult task to completely emulate a magnetic disk, i.e., to implement all of the features provided by the DEC file system. In addition, since direct I/O operations such as writing the boot block do not use the ACP, a special utility program to initialize the disk must be written.

Using part of a magnetic disk as a cache can provide throughput benefits since WORM I/O is much slower than magnetic disk operations.

[2]ACP (Ancillary Control Process). In DEC's RSX and VMS operating systems, an ACP is a privileged program responsible for maintaining the file system structures on a disk device. The standard DEC RSX and VMS ACPs implement a file system structure named "Files-11." Perceptics provides their own ACP which implements a file system structure named "WORMs-11."

Figure 5. Standard SCSI Device Driver Architecture (Courtesy KOM, Inc.)

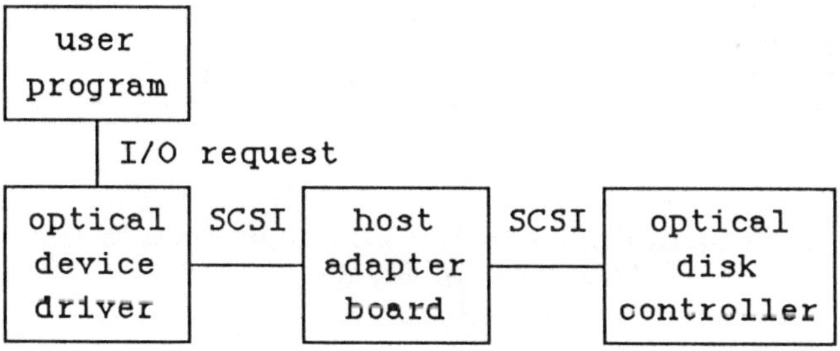

However, the gains may be illusory since it may eventually be necessary to wait for the system to save data onto the WORM disk before it can be dismounted. There is also a risk that the system will crash before data has been safely written to the WORM disk.

The Device Driver

Most of the overhead in remote file servers was due to the layers of applications and system software between the user and the disk drive. Since local file servers only intercept **some** I/O requests, they cannot properly emulate a magnetic disk file system. An obvious solution to this problem is to remove as many layers of software as possible and intercept **all** I/O requests.

The natural place to handle WORM devices is clearly in a device driver (see Figure 5). Special application software is thus eliminated since the application can use the WORM device driver just like any device driver. In addition, control of the WORM disk is centralized since I/O requests from any application pass through the driver.

Unfortunately, while adequate documentation describing how to write a device driver is usually available, information about file system structures and ACPs is harder to obtain. The main disadvantage of writing a device driver is that the resulting code is rarely portable.

From time to time, new versions of the operating system are released. If the manufacturer follows its own software guidelines, upgrading to a new version is often trivial. Unfortunately, some users have encountered serious problems since VMS version 5.0 has been released. Networking software ("clusters") applications have been most vulnerable.

Figure 6. WORM Disk Partition Scheme 3 (Courtesy KOM, Inc.)

Figure 7. Customized SCSI Device Driver Architecture (Courtesy KOM, Inc.)

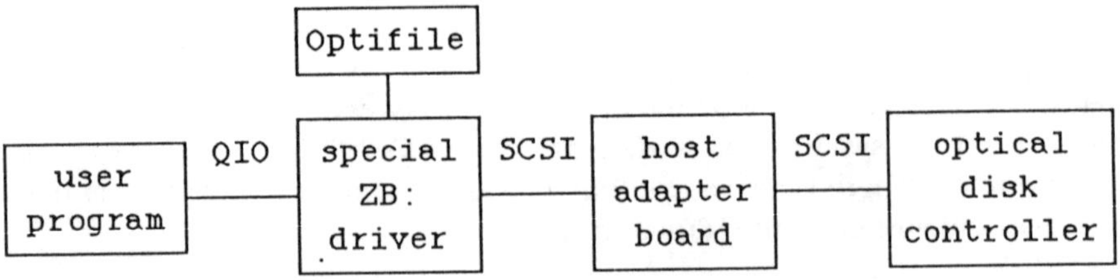

Figure 8. Externalized Magnetic Disk Emulation Architecture (Courtesy KOM, Inc.)

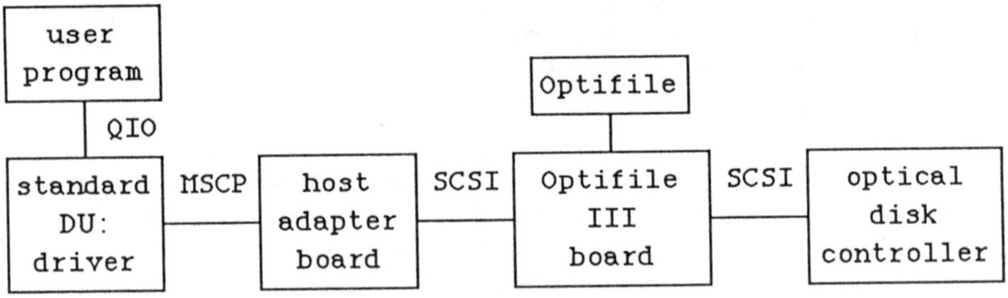

A New Emulation Approach[3]

The basic idea involved in the newest generation of implementations is the creation of a filter between the user and the optical disk. If this camouflage is successful, it will appear to the user that a magnetic disk is being used. To support this "fiction", the user must be able to write any block on the disk any number of times and to read back the data that was last written.

To implement this approach, a "map" is kept for every single block on the magnetic disk that is being emulated.[4] Whenever data is written, it

[3]This discussion is based on KOM's OPTIFILE II and III products.

[4]A "map" is simply an array of optical disk block numbers indexed by block number.

is saved to the WORM disk and the location on the optical disk is updated in the map. Bad blocks on the WORM disk are automatically eliminated by rewriting data whenever the drive reports an error. Data is read by consulting the map and accessing the appropriate block on the disk.

The map is kept up-to-date in memory and stored on the disk along with the user data. The map is flushed to the WORM disk whenever dismounted, and periodically during write operations (often one block for every 256 blocks of user data), leaving the disk consistent at all times. There is a slight risk of data loss if the system crashes during a write operation. However, this is the same danger that exists with a magnetic disk since the operating system updates the directory after the data is written. Hence, data may exist on the WORM disk that is inaccessible.

The WORM disk format consists of interleaved sets of user data and map data, stored in the order it was written from the beginning of the disk (see Figure 6). The disk space overhead for this design is often about 0.5 percent.

This software approach is built on top of the standard WORM device driver, interpreting all I/O requests (see Figure 7). It requires no knowledge of file system structures since the standard ACP also uses the device driver to maintain the file system structures. However, the device driver must be maintained whenever new releases of the operating system appear. In addition, some administrators do not like "foreign" software (especially privileged programs or drivers) installed on their system.

One way to avoid these problems is to get away from the operating system entirely and use standard device drivers. Doing this successfully requires a hardware solution. Instead of being embedded as part of a device driver, a special board is inserted between the host adapter and the WORM drive. Some recent implementations of this approach such as the ISi 525GB WORM drive have implemented the necessary firmware in the disk controller itself. This option appeals to users who do not like third-party software or who are concerned with security.

With the appropriate host adapter board (typically one that converts standard disk requests into SCSI commands), the WORM drive is simply cabled to the board. Under VMS, the standard MSCP disk driver can be used as if it was accessing a magnetic disk: all block numbers in SCSI commands are mapped to the correct block on the optical disk. The disk emulation is performed by firmware residing on a board available via the SCSI bus. The only operating system update is the inclusion of support for another magnetic disk drive (see Figure 8).

This example used a VAX as the host computer and VMS as the host operating system. However, with the appropriate host adapter, virtually any host would be able to use the drive.

Conclusion

The current trend in WORM software products under VAX/VMS is toward complete magnetic disk emulation and operating system independence. Both of these goals are achieved by an architecture which implements the necessary algorithms outside of the host system. This design can be effected in firmware on a board which resides between the drive and the host adapter, or in the firmware within the drive itself.

Bibliography

Heinemann, D. D. "Optical Controller adds WORM to DEC." *Computer Technology Review* (January 1988).

"Hit Single." *Digital Review* (November 10, 1986).

LASAR - Laser Archival Storage and Retrieval. Knoxville, TN: Perceptics Corp., March 1986.

Mallery, D. "Optical Allusions." *DEC Professional* (April 1987).

OPTIFILE Technical Reference Manual (for DEC RSX-11M/PLUS) v1.0. KOM Inc., February 1986.

Steinberg, J. A. "Light Wars II." *Digital Review* (March 23, 1987).

SECTION III
JUKEBOX SOFTWARE

10
Evaluation of Optical Disk Jukebox Software

DR. SANJAY RANADE AND FONALD YEE

Jukeboxes are now commonly available as mass storage devices for a number of computer systems. Software to drive and access these units poses interesting challenges to the software designer. Although the basic jukebox robotics functions can be readily implemented, the efficient management of data files access presents a much more complex problem.

Under the general category of "Jukebox Software" come a variety of products whose only commonality is the use of an optical disk jukebox for data storage. The market segment at which these products are directed, their implementation approaches, the intended applications and the functions they support vary greatly. Therefore, rather than attempt to compare the different products against each other, it is more meaningful to categorize them into broad types and applications to which each type is best suited.

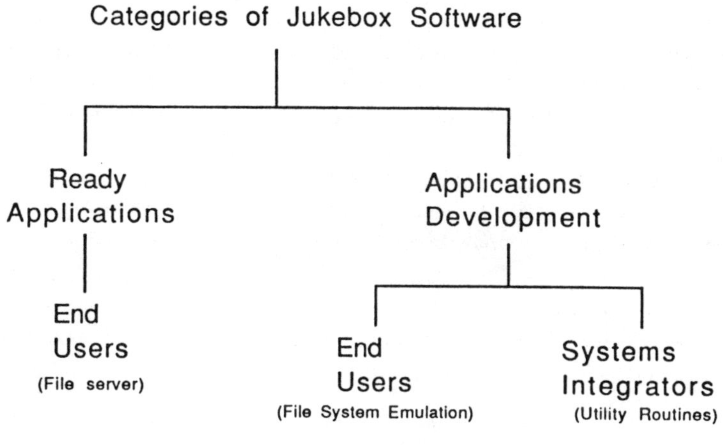

Figure 1. Implementation Approaches (Courtesy ST Systems Corp.)

The three main approaches to implementing jukebox software are shown below. The general problem is to retrieve and display the record N stored in a file F. F is one of many files residing somewhere in the jukebox. Different combinations of vendor-provided software routines, programs, or explicit user commands perform jukebox operations.

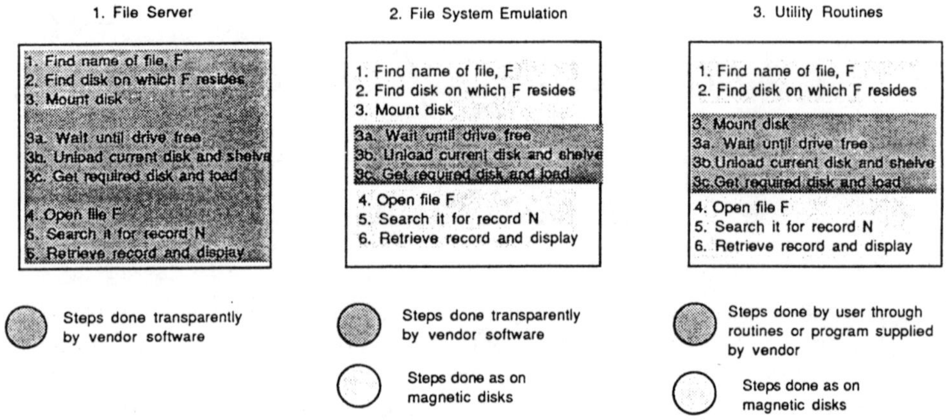

Software Categories

Commercially available optical jukebox software falls into three distinct categories, each corresponding to a particular type of application. The implementation approach used for each category differs, and the data access steps performed explicitly by the user and through the vendor software also differ in each case (Figure 1).

In the first category belongs software provided as part of an integrated or turnkey product which includes all necessary hardware, systems software, *and* applications software. In this category, the jukebox and the controlling software act as a central file server catering to requests from different user-developed or vendor-supplied applications. The user is presented with an independent subsystem and is not expected to alter its software.

Software in the second category is intended to let the user view individual WORM disks in a jukebox as disk volumes which can be mounted in the same manner as conventional magnetic disks. The major goal here is to emulate the host's file system on WORM disks as transparently as possible. In response to user commands (e.g. Mount and Dismount), the software generates the necessary jukebox commands and executes them to perform the desired operation. Software in this category is particularly suited for end-users who want to increase available storage with minimal impact on existing applications.

The third category is software for integration with user-developed applications. It is sold in the form of utility routine libraries or separately executable programs. This approach is particularly suited to the systems integrator whose general interest is to tailor a system for a given application. By allowing full access to jukebox functions, the user gains a great deal of flexibility. Operating system dependent routines can be isolated into a "portability library" which the user can re-define for each new computer and operating system.

These three categories present different problems for jukebox software evaluation. Because the products are so different and because they are targeted towards different market segments, they cannot be compared against each other. The following discussion will therefore focus on characterizing the advantages of different product types, examining the implementation approaches, and relating them to different types of applications. Since the emphasis in this chapter is on evaluating jukebox software rather than applications, this chapter will concentrate on the functions and features available through the software and implementation approaches rather than applications.

User Categories

For evaluation or comparison purposes it is important to look at the different categories of jukebox users. Each type of user has a different view of the jukebox storage, stressing some jukebox features or capabilities and perhaps ignoring others. Accordingly, different evaluation criteria are relevant to each type of user. For our purposes here, it will be helpful to distinguish between four user classes.

The first user class is the **general user** for whom the computer system is purely a tool and who is not interested in its internals. The second is the computer manager who views the jukebox as an important resource which adds to the capability of the total system. The third is the systems or applications programmer whose concern is to ensure efficient use of the jukebox. The last category is the computer operator responsible for the day-to-day operation of the jukebox in the same way as any other peripheral requiring some degree of operator interaction.

The main interest of a general user will be to access data as rapidly and simply as possible. This class of user sees the jukebox as a huge disk offering online access to large amounts of data. This general user does not care about features such as loading, unloading or exchanging volumes, or algorithms for moving platters to reduce swap times. This user certainly does not care whether the software is easily portable. Ease of access to large amounts of data, powerful indexing and search facilities, and remote access are the primary concerns.

The second user, the **computer manager**, looks at the jukebox primarily as a resource shared by many users. Features for data security, growth or expansion capabilities, different access paths to the data, ease of integration into an existing system, cost and performance are all important. Report capabilities which show disk usage by individual users or projects are also important.

The third user, the **systems programmer**, has quite a different view of the jukebox. It is seen as a complex new peripheral requiring software over and above a device driver and utility routines. Interested in supporting the jukebox efficiently and cleanly, the systems programmer may need to change or add a function, or be required to port the software to another system. Ease of modification and portability are key issues for the systems programmer.

The fourth and last user, the **computer operator**, is interested mainly in operating the jukebox easily. Careful attention is paid to features for error recovery, exchanging platters, changing priorities, or message facilities.

Software Functions and Features

This section is a checklist for the four user classes described above. This checklist is composed of criteria which may be used to determine the suitability of jukebox software for a given application. These criteria are not of equal importance to the different user classes. Accordingly, the checklist is based on the features and functions that are of particular interest to the four identified user classes.

Features of Primary Interest to General Users

1. *File system.* Does the software support the file system used by the operating system of the computer? If it does, then can data be accessed using standard utilities? If not, a comprehensive set of utilities to read and store data in the jukebox must also be available.

2. *Data catalog.* Does the software provide a catalog feature allowing users to query for the presence of and location of particular files? Can users obtain a snapshot of the jukebox including a list of pending requests?

3. *Data availability.* What are the steps required to access data in the jukebox? Besides the data filename, the user may need to know the name of the disk volume on which data is stored. On the other hand, an archive identification number may be sufficient. Is the user's data present in the jukebox? If not, how is the operator notified to load the disk containing the user's data?

4. *Remote access.* Can data in the jukebox be accessed through a network? What kind of additional hardware and software is required?

Features of Primary Interest to Computer Managers

1. *Data security.* How is the data in the jukebox box secured? Are there any security features over and above those provided by the operating system? Can individual disks be allocated to particular users or projects? Is a volume shadowing capability available?
2. *Capacity.* Is there a limitation on the number of jukeboxes supported? Does the software allow easy expansion?
3. *Technology refreshment.* What provisions have been made in the software to anticipate technology changes (e.g., increases in disk capacity or new mass storage technologies)?
4. *Availability.* With which computer systems can the software be used? Which of the available jukeboxes and WORM drives does it support?
5. *Cost.* What is the cost of the jukebox software?

Features of Primary Interest to Systems Programmers

1. *Source language.* Is the software written in a high-level language such as C? Is the software written to be easily modifiable?
2. *High-level language interface.* Is there a high-level language interface to the software? This means that a comprehensive set of routines should be available to the user allowing the full use of the low-level functions supported by the software.
3. *Portability of software.* Is the software written to be portable? Has the same software been ported to another computer and operating system? Are the operating system dependencies clearly isolated? How will the vendor support porting?
4. *Response time.* How does the software handle multiple requests? How long does the user have to wait before data becomes available? Are there sufficient provisions to share the optical drives fairly?
5. *Performance tuning.* Is it possible for the user to lock in the disk for a given period so that it will not be swapped out to accommodate another request? Can the user direct physical placement of the disk to minimize swap time?
6. *Logical volume to physical location mapping.* How is this implemented? Is there a volume name for each side of the optical disk?
7. *Jukebox communication.* What type of interface is available to the jukebox robotics and the optical drives in the jukebox? Possibilities are RS-232 and SCSI.
8. *Multiple jukebox support.* Will the software support multiple juke-

Figure 2. Category 1 Jukebox Software (File Servers) (Courtesy ST Systems Corp.)

Feature	FileNet (DIMS)	Kodak (KIMS)	FileTek SM/1
Type	Integrated turnkey system	Integrated turnkey system	Intelligent storage subsystem
Target Market	Document storage, processing and retrieval	Document storage, processing and retrieval	Data Archive (image or non-image)
Computer	Sun,VAX,IBM-PC,PS/2, FileNet (turnkey)	VAX, IBM-PC	Micro VAX
Jukebox	FileNet	Kodak, Cygnet	Filenet, Cygnet
Drives	Hitachi, LMSI	Kodak, Hitachi	Sony, LMSI
Remote Access	Ethernet, T1 line (56 kb/s)	SNA Gateway bimodal. Protocol converters	Hyperchannel. Require host software
User interface	Provided. Can be tailored to user by vendor	Custom. Vendor support for custom forms.	Custom. Program interface.
Operator Interface	Unix/Custom	VAX/Custom	VAX/Custom
Other software	Commercial DBMS (Oracle) + Utilities	Commercial DBMS (VMS/RDB)	Custom utilities
Approximate cost for 1 jukebox system + peripherals	$0.35M	$0.5M	$0.5M

boxes? How much disk space and memory is used to support each jukebox?

9. *Multiple user support.* Can several users access the jukebox concurrently? How are such requests resolved?

10. *Request management.* How are data requests handled? Can priorities be assigned to individual requests? How many requests can be queued?

Features of Primary Interest to Computer Operators

1. *Operator interface.* What kind of operator interface is available? Which operator commands are available? How is the jukebox placed offline and online?

2. *Disk spin up and spin down.* If necessary, will the software perform these functions when disks are mounted and dismounted?

3. *Jukebox status and configuration.* Will the software provide a snapshot of the jukebox configuration in response to an operator command?

4. *Error logging and recovery.* What provisions are there to track and recover from errors? Is there a report or error logging facility?

5. *Optical drive management.* How are drives allocated? Is status information returned to the user?

6. *Slot management for platter load/unload.* How is the movement of disks into and out of the jukebox handled?

7. *Volume verification.* How does the software ensure that incorrect volumes are not inadvertently loaded?

Figure 3. Category 2 Jukebox Software (File System Emulation) (Courtesy ST Systems Corp.)

Evaluation criteria	Perceptics LaserStar	KOM Optserver	U.S.Design JukeVOS
File system	Near ODS-2	ODS-2	Near ODS-2
Data catalog	Utility	Utility	Utility
Jukebox snapshot	Utility	Utility	Utility
Data availability	FIFO queue	User queue	User queue
Volume load/mount	Transparent	Explicit	Explicit
Remote access	As host	As host	As host
Host data security features	Most	All	Most
Source Language/Access to code	Inaccessible	Inaccessible	Inaccessible
High-level language interface	Yes	Yes	No
Portability	No	No	By vendor
Coupled Optical Disk Software	LaserSystem	Optfile	VOS or other
Performance tuning	Utility	Utility	Utility
Jukebox communication	SCSI, RS232	SCSI	SCSI
Multiple jukebox support	Yes	Yes	Yes
Multiple user suport	Implicit	Yes	Yes
Request management	FIFO	FIFO	User
Request priorities	Yes	No	No
Jukebox Management	Utility	Utility	Utility
Robotics commands	Transparent	High level	Menu options
Security	Volume-level	Volume-level	Volume-level
Capacity growth	Yes	Yes	Yes
Technology update support	No	No	No
Computer System	VAX/VMS	VAX/VMS	VAX/VMS
Jukeboxes supported	Cygnet, LMSI	Sony	Sony
Drives supported	Optimem,LMSI	Sony, LMSI, others	Sony,Optimem and others
Operator interface	Command set	Command set	Command set
Operator message facility	Yes	Yes	Yes
Disk spin up.down	Transparent	Transparent	Transparent
Jukebox status, configuration	Yes	Yes	Yes
Error logging and recovery	Yes	Yes	Yes
Optical drive management	VMS&Package	VMS&Package	VMS&Package
Slot management	Automated	Automated	Automated
Volume verification on mount	Yes	Yes	Yes
Initialization	Various modes	Various modes	Various modes

8. *Message facility for operator.* Is there a message facility to notify the operator when the jukebox needs to be attended?

9. *Initialization.* How is the jukebox initialized and brought online to the host computer? Can the jukebox database be rebuilt on initialization?

10. *Robotics commands.* Does the software support individual robotics commands issued by users or operators?

Implementation Approaches

The main challenge for a systems designer is how to represent and manage the jukebox resources to provide efficient and reliable access to data stored in the jukebox. A variety of design options are possible, but most of these fall into three main groups: (1) file server, (2) file system emulation, and (3) utility routines. Each group is particularly suited to one type of application.

Approach 1: File Server

The first approach views the jukebox as a large data store. Access to this data store is channelled through a single "server" program whose function is to translate file requests into appropriate jukebox commands. This program maintains a database relating files to jukebox slots and disk surfaces. Applications programs supply a filename to the server. The server examines the current state of the jukebox and executes whatever low-level commands that may be necessary to access the requested file and move it to a location specified by the application.

Because this approach centralizes all jukebox accesses, it is well-suited to a multi-user environment. It also removes the need for applications to control jukebox robotics. The main disadvantage of the file server approach is that it does not support record-level operations efficiently. More seriously, existing applications designed to access conventional magnetic storage devices must be modified to use the jukebox. The cost of products in this category is also much higher than products in other categories.

Approach 2: File System Emulation

The second approach is also the most general one for integrating the jukebox robotic and drive controls. The jukebox appears to the host operating system as one or more standard magnetic devices. Control of the jukebox is hidden from the user with this "transparent" approach, and the user accesses the device through standard operating system functions and utilities.

The most important advantage of this approach is that only minimal user training and code modifications are required to use the jukebox. Products can be readily integrated into an existing system with ease. Standard I/O request scheduling, security and resource management functions already present in the operating system can be utilized. Because of its generality, this approach also allows the jukebox to be used as a general storage peripheral in a multi-user environment or as a dedicated device for a given application. The major disadvantage of this approach is that the software is difficult to implement since the code is closely coupled to the operating system. As a result, it is not easily ported to another operating system.

If portability is important and if functions such as request scheduling can be left to users, a simpler variation of this approach is possible in

Figure 4. Category 3 Jukebox Software (Utility Routines) (Courtesy ST Systems Corp.)

Evaluation criteria	Cygnet - Jukebox Interface Management System (JIMS)
File system emulation	Not supported
Data access procedure	Application
Data availability	Application
Response time	First-In-First-Out (FIFO)
Network access	Handled through host facilities
Data security	Volume level
Status and index service	Yes
Source Language	C
High-level language interface	Extensive subroutine library
Portability	Rewrite 'portability' library
Logical - physical mapping	Yes.1 disk = 2 volumes
Jukebox communication	RS-232 (juke) ; SCSI (drive)
Multiple jukebox support	Yes. 300K memory per jukebox
Multiple user suport	Yes
Request management	FIFO queue/relative priorities.
Jukebox Management	On-line, Off-line commands
Operator interface	User written application
Disk spin up/down	Provided where necessary
Jukebox status, configuration	Yes. Each jukebox, drive , disk
Error logging and recovery	Magnetic disk log file.
Optical drive management	Allocates drive, returns unit no
Slot management	Import and export of disks
Volume verification	At import, export and mount
Message facility	Sent to applications and operator
Initialization	3 modes. Can rebuild tables
Robotics commands	By translating user functions
Security	Volume-level
Growth	Can reconfigure or add jukebox
Technology refresh	No. Optical disk only
Ported to	Sun/Unix ; VAX/VMS

which the optical disk software and jukebox software are completely decoupled. Jukebox functions can be provided through a single program which is run by users prior to using a jukebox. Because of the decoupling, any optical disk software package can be used for reading and writing to optical disks.

Approach 3: Utility Routines

The third and the simplest approach for jukebox software design is to provide a set of subroutines that can be called by an applications program to directly control individual functions supported by the jukebox hardware. In this approach, responsibility for the optical disk software is entirely up to the user and the question of coupling does not even arise. In effect, the vendor provides a set of software tools which can be used to tailor the jukebox to a given application.

Software which is implemented in this fashion is suited for modification and porting to another computer and operating system. The operating system dependencies can be isolated in a separate library which the user can modify for a new environment. The major disadvantage of the utility routine approach is that each application is allowed an equal level of jukebox control and must be aware of the state of the jukebox, e.g., which drive is loaded with which disk. However, additional inter-task communications and request coordination facilities can also be provided in a multi-user environment. Depending on the operating system, these may result in significant overhead.

Candidate Products

This section is an overview and comparison of representative products belonging to each category described above. Figures 2, 3, and 4 summarize the main features of each product.

Category 1: File Servers

All three products in this category use the file server approach and present a data archive capability to the user. File level access of data is the most efficient mode of operation. WORM as well as other mass storage technologies may be easily accommodated in this approach. Disk drives, jukeboxes, tapes or any other type of storage used in this approach is completely transparent to the user.

FileNet Corporation's Document Image Management System. This is a turnkey, document processing system driven by a distributed client/server architecture running the Unix operating system. It uses Hitachi or LMSI WORM drives in a FileNet jukebox for data storage. A variety of high resolution scanners and printers can be purchased with the system to allow digitization and storage of documents. Software tools and utilities are provided as part of the total system. The system is accessed by the user and operator through interface software and utilities written to run under Unix. The interface or the utilities can be customized using the WorkFlo™ high-level programming language. All necessary software to begin processing of document images is standard with the FileNet system. Access over an Ethernet link or a T1 (56kb) line is available. The necessary protocol conversion software must be available on the user's computer.

Eastman Kodak's Information Management System (KIMS). KIMS is an integrated turnkey system using WORM disks and jukeboxes geared to the document storage and retrieval application. Of the three versions

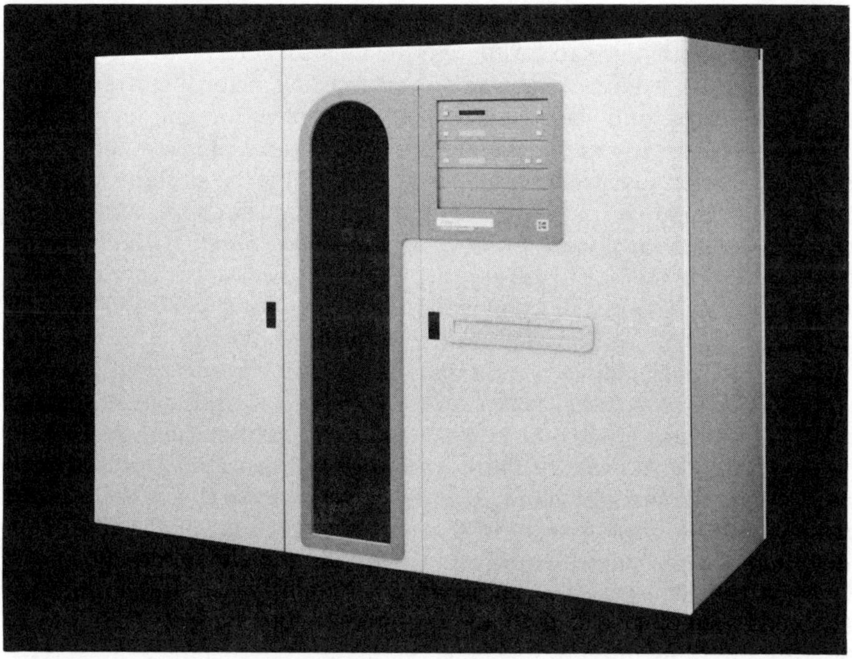

KIMS 6800 Optical Disk Library (Courtesy Eastman Kodak Company)

of the basic KIMS system, two run on a VAX, and the third on a IBM-PC. They are available in a variety of workstation configurations or as a standalone system. Document scanners, laser printers and display terminals are part of the packaged system. Eastman Kodak-developed and other commercial software layers executing under the computer operating system provide a number of services including data indexing, data summary, and data retrieval.Access to the two VAX-based systems is available through other hosts using Ethernet. IBM 3270 terminal emulation is also supported. The system uses image databases stored on optical disk; the larger configurations can also use microfilm. In the DEC-based systems, an optional System Network Architecture (SNA) gateway allows bimodal communication between the KIMS system and an IBM host. This option allows KIMS users IBM 3720 terminal emulation and access to data stored at the IBM host, and IBM users access to KIMS. Communications support through protocol converters is also available.

FileTek, Inc.'s Storage Machine/1 (SM/1). The Storage Machine/1 (SM/1) is an intelligent mass storage and retrieval system integrating special storage management software and off-the-shelf hardware. Unlike the FileNet and Eastman Kodak products, the SM/1 is targeted towards storage of non-image (document) data and also contains a flexible and powerful program interface. Although the user sees the system as a large one-level store, it is implemented in layers using magnetic and optical disks, jukeboxes, and shelf storage. The concept of the one level store, stressing uniform access to data without regard to the media and manner in which it is stored, was originally introduced by the designers of the early Atlas computers. Since then the concept has materialized under various guises and at various levels such as paging, segmentation, virtual and hierarchical memory. The approach used in the SM/1 is very promising and will very likely be enhanced in future systems, perhaps through special additional hardware for improving access efficiency.

The hardware pathway to the data in the SM/1 is a communications link (NSC HYPERchannel) rather than a bus interface. Both multiple users and hosts can access the SM/1. Each host computer is required to have a network adapter for the network connection and interface software. The system architecture is modular and allows the system to be configured with varying levels of storage capacity, functionality and performance. Storage capacity can be increased transparently to users.

Although file level access of data is the most efficient mode of operation, individual records within files can also be retrieved and updated. However, existing applications must be modified to include calls to special program callable interface routines. Other available software provides data catalog and operator interface functions.

Category 2: File System Emulation

Each of the products in this category provide a single interface that integrates a jukebox with VAX/VMS host computers. In each case a separate software package is provided to emulate the existing magnetic disk media file system. Each jukebox software package manages the host computer interface with varying degrees of transparency, and does not interfere with the operating system or applications programs.

Perceptics Corporation's LaserStar. This package allows the user to view the jukebox as multiple disk drives; each drive corresponds to a media surface in the jukebox. For example, a jukebox containing 16 double-sided optical disks will appear to the user as 32 WORM disk drives. When access is requested to an optical volume not currently in a drive, the software automatically queues the request and places the selected volume in the first available drive. Explicit commands from the user to load and unload optical drives are not necessary. Transparency of the jukebox and WORM disk to VMS is achieved to a high degree.

If a disk volume is swapped out of a drive, it remains software mounted. This means that every volume in the jukebox may be software mounted concurrently for read-only operations. An I/O request to a mounted volume will cause the software to automatically place that volume in a drive to complete the request. A separate utility allows the user to insert or remove disks from the jukebox and to specify volume-level access parameters.

KOM, Inc.'s OptiServer. OptiServer is a single interface that integrates optical disk jukeboxes with a host computer. It manages jukebox functions without interfering with the host operating system or applications programs. The OptiServer provides four simple commands to control jukebox operation. These commands can be entered at the operating system command level or called as routines from within an applications program. The software keeps track of all these operations and is able to generate status reports on file directories, optical disk volumes, and disk drives. In addition, it maintains a database of all files in the jukebox and allows specific file requests by a user. It also maintains a database of all files in the jukebox and allows specific file requests by a user. Requests to access files in the jukebox are queued and serviced automatically by OptiServer in a First-In-First-Out (FIFO) manner.

OptiServer is coupled with KOM's optical disk software product OPTIFILE which uses a device driver to handle physical I/O requests made to the jukebox optical disk drives.

U.S. Design's JukeVOS. Like the KOM product, JukeVOS provides the user with a set of commands to manage jukebox operation. However, these commands are only available through a single program which is activated at the operating system command level. Subroutines to perform the same functions through applications programs are not available. Although the software keeps track of volume, disk, label and slot correspondence, no file database is maintained. The user must know the volume name of the disk on which a file resides and explicitly load this disk into a drive for data access. The problem of resolving access conflicts due to multiple users is not addressed by the software.

JukeVOS operates in conjunction with the companion VOS product which supports the DEC Files-11 volume format. These two products are not coupled and it is possible to use JukeVOS with optical disk software from other vendors (e.g., the Perceptics LaserSystem). JukeVOS is written in C. Because it is not coupled to the file system software, it can be readily ported to another operating environment. A Unix implementation in forthcoming. A board-level version of JukeVOS which will treat optical disks in the jukebox as separately mountable volumes is under development.

Category 3: Utility Routines

Software in this group is intended to provide a set of routines or tools allowing a user to customize jukebox operation for a specific application. This is the only category which requires the integrator to have developed or purchased a separate software package to handle the logical format of

Figure 5. JIMS Implementation Overview (Courtesy ST Systems Corp.)

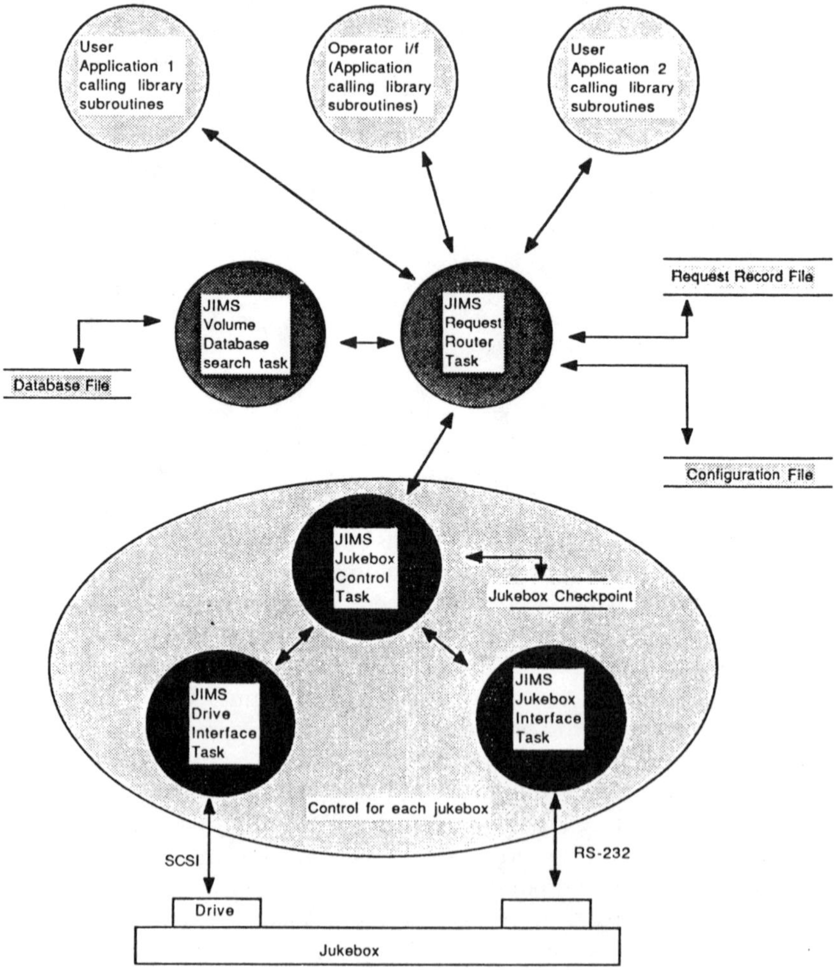

the WORM media. The only product in this category is marketed by Cygnet Systems, Inc., an OEM. The software, Jukebox Interface Management System (JIMS), is a collection of routines and programs that allow easy integration of Cygnet jukeboxes into user computer systems.

Cygnet Systems, Inc.'s Jukebox Interface Management System (JIMS). The main function of the software is to allow access to optical disk volumes by reference to volume names rather than location inside the jukebox. For example, if an applications program requests a particular volume mount, the JIMS package uses internal tables to generate the necessary jukebox robotics commands to perform the operation. The applications program can then use the disk as if it were manually inserted into the optical drive.

JIMS provides facilities for modifying the software so that it can be easily integrated into a wide variety of computing environments and applications. This means that JIMS can be used with the user's existing optical disk software with very little modification. Portability exits allow operating system dependencies to be isolated and resolved before integration, or changed entirely if porting to a different system. User exits can be modified by the user to suit particular applications.

JIMS is implemented under Unix as a set of communicating processes which handle requests issued by user applications using the subroutine libraries provided. Figure 5 shows an overview of the JIMS implementation.

Cygnet's Series 5000 Jukebox for 5.25-inch Optical Drives and Media (Courtesy Cygnet Systems, Inc.)

Conclusion

New jukebox software products and new releases of existing optical products are constantly appearing on the market. Board-level implementations of jukebox and optical disk software will figure prominently in the near future.

It is likely that the product characterizations included in this chapter will be rapidly out-of-date. What is unlikely to change is the implementation approach and the overall functionality of a given product line because each is targeted towards a particular market segment. Similarly, the evaluation criteria and their breakdown by user classes will continue to be useful to determine whether or not a particular product is suitable for a given application.

Other major software enhancements will occur with the introduction of the "second generation" of jukeboxes. Physical partitioning of the jukebox according to projects or applications, dynamic load balancing to reduce swap times and some level of self-tuning (transparent and intelligent shuffling of certain file types) are just some of the innovations likely to appear with the new products. As mentioned previously, these basic techniques have been known to computer systems designers since the early 1960's. It is only a matter of time before they find their way into the jukebox software arena.

Bibliography

Carringer, M.W. "Real World Jukebox Implementation for Digital'sVAX/VMS." *Computer Technology Review*, Summer 1988.

Della Torre, M. "Using HYPERchannel in a Mass Storage Environment," presented to NEXUS User's Group At FileTek, Inc. (Rockville, MD), Fall 1987.

JIMS Product Description Revision A. Sunnyvale, CA: Cygnet Systems, Inc., August 1988.

JIMS Functional Design Specification. Sunnyvale, CA: Cygnet Systems, Inc, October 1988.

JukeVOS User's Guide Revision C. Lanham, MD: U.S. Design Corporation, August 1988.

KIMS System 4000 Specifications. Rochester, NY: Eastman Kodak Comny, October 1988.

LaserStar Production Description. LaserStar Product Description. Knoxville, TN: Perceptics Corporation, August 1987.

OptiServer User's Manual. Ottawa, Canada: KOM, Inc., August 1988.

11

The Universe Online: A Case Study of a Jukebox Implementation

PETER M.B. SHAMES AND EVA C. MARSH

The Hubble Space Telescope (HST) will be the first large optical observatory to be permanently stationed in space. It will be launched aboard the Space Shuttle this year (1989). Positioned high above the earth's distorting atmosphere, it will yield unprecedented detailed views of the universe. The HST, a cooperative venture of the National Aeronautics and Space Administration (NASA) and the European Space Agency (ESA), will function in space as a remotely-controlled observatory into the 21st century. Although the size of a highway bus, the Telescope is an instrument of incredible precision. If its mirror were enlarged to the width of the continental United States, the highest "mountain" on the mirror's surface would rise less than 4 inches above the deepest "valley". The Telescope can identify 30 million different stars and hold steady on a target equal to the size of a star on an American flag seen from 3000 miles away.

Operated by the Association of Universities for Research in Astronomy (AURA) for NASA, the Space Telescope Science Institute (STScI) is responsible for conducting the Telescope's scientific operations. A large part of STScI's operations responsibility involves management of the data acquired by HST that is available to local and remote observers.

DADS (Data Archive and Distribution Service) is a major system expected to augment the tape archives originally planned. However, it will not be available until about two years after launch. In the interim, the Data Management Facility (DMF) has been developed to support archive and distribution functions during the launch and post-launch era. The DMF takes advantage of current WORM and networking technologies.

A full copy of the data archives will be provided to the ST-ECF, a European Coordinating Facility (Garching, Federal Republic of Germany). Developed in cooperation with the ST-ECF, the DMF will be used there and can be installed at other archive centers even after DADS is made available. Contributions to the DMF were also made by a staff member of the Canadian Astronomical Data Center (CADC) located in the Dominion Astrophysical Observatory.

Data from Space Telescope will be transmitted to the ground by satellites in geosynchronous orbit. The scientific information will be relayed by NASA's Goddard Space Center to STScI in Baltimore, MD for study by astronomers around the world.

Design Criteria for the DMF System

Since a primary requirement of the DMF was to efficiently archive data and distribute it to both users and archive sites, considerable effort was put into designing mechanisms that would permit easy and secure data transport. Full data portability and independence from operating system or proprietary formats were also important design goals that have been achieved. WORM technology was chosen as the storage device since today's optical disks offer roughly a twenty-to-one reduction in storage volume when compared to magnetic tape; a single volume will store approximately two days of observation data. The need for a distributed architecture that would support different local workstations and a modular system that would evolve over time also determined a number of design choices. [1]

Portable Optical Disk and Data Formats

Use of standard disk structures and standard data formats are keys to supporting the STScI data portability and distribution requirements. To achieve secure data transport, a disk format has been defined that permits data to be transported between operating systems. This feature has been successfully demonstrated at STScI, and data has also been exchanged between STScI and the ST-ECF with either site acting as a transmitter. The WORM disk structure also permits secure handling of incremental updates since directory header information is updated when each file is written and the occasional bad disk sectors are smoothly processed.

Use of FITS for Local and Remote Data Delivery

In addition to the portable disk formats, STScI has adopted the use of the FITS (Flexible Image Transport System) data standard which supports general data portability. [4] Astronomy is one of the few science communities where a standard self-descriptive data format and a relative few portable data analysis environments (IRAF/STSDAS, AIPS, IDL, MIDAS) are extensively used. Although data is generally archived in the FITS format in DMF, other formats are used where needed.

Interfaces Ease Integration of Networks and Databases

DMF users may be local or remote, located at VAX clusters or on SUN workstations, and may use TCP/IP or proprietary DECnet protocols. Application interfaces that provide standard client-server access mechanisms from different host systems over different networks have been defined [6]. These interfaces, along with others that support a choice of database technologies, serve to provide a layer of insulation between applications and services [7]. These interfaces also assist in the migration of services and user agents across different system and network architectures.

Modular Architecture Design

The STScI strategy to provide portable systems that can gracefully evolve as the underlying hardware and systems are upgraded relies on the DMF's modular design and the application interface concepts. These features facilitate hardware changes and help distribute functions to different processors if necessary.

The FH (File Handler) has been designed to be re-configurable and expandable since it must serve a number of different sites and because WORM technology is dynamic. The modular DMF design has already permitted the accommodation of different 12- and 5.25-inch WORM drives, and has allowed changing from a single network protocol to two alternate protocols.

The modular FH architecture also supports the optional use of a WORM jukebox. Although the Cygnet Systems, Inc. 12-inch model has been integrated by using the firm's Jukebox Interface Management Software (JIMS), other interface software could be used for this or any other manufacturer's jukebox.

Portable Software

Until DADS is completed, the interim DMF system will assume the overall archive and distribution responsibilities. However, DMF software will be used on a continuing basis at the ST-ECF and possibly at other HST archive centers such as the Canadian Astronomical Data Center. The availability of a system such as DMF that can be installed and operated on a modest budget is of critical importance to ST-ECF and other HST archive centers.

Although much of the DMF software was originally developed on a SUN workstation, it was ported to the VAX/VMS environment where it now operates. Building on earlier experience with portable systems, the DMF has been designed to be modular and re-configurable with the intent of being able to be ported back to a Unix system. In order to enhance portability and maintainability, the entire system is written in C, and any operating system dependencies are carefully isolated in appropriate interface libraries and system dependent "include" files.

Overview of the DMF

The DMF consists of two major pieces: the File Handler (FH) and the User Interface (UI). The FH, a server running on its own host system, can screen all service requests and validate requestor user IDs against the list of those permitted to access the data. Only service interface requests are permitted, and no users may log into the host system. Valid archive requests are filled by transferring the file back into the user's home (or working) directory on the local system. Although this mechanism is somewhat more complicated than simple schemes that typically require the user to copy retrieved files from the WORM disks or local staging disks, it does permit a level of protection and resource management that would otherwise be difficult to achieve.

The FH is responsible for both the management of the actual optical disk archives and for limiting access to any proprietary data stored in the archive [2]. It consists of several cooperating processes: the main driver process (FH main), a process that maps file names to optical disk locations, and a process for each type of WORM drive and for each type of jukebox in the system. Note that the jukebox module is optional since a jukebox may not be part of the system. Another module provides an operator interface for handling system management and maintenance functions.

The User Interface (UI), called STARCAT, is designed to provide a portable interface that can support access to the archive catalogue and to other databases from distributed users [5]. The DMF uses a client-server architecture in which the clients (copies of STARCAT) are distributed and the server (FH) is accessed using local or wide-area network links. While many copies of STARCAT may be distributed to local workstations or remote user sites, there will usually be only one copy of the FH located where the data is actually archived.

Responsible for managing all of the user interactions with the system, the UI handles user queries to various databases including the DMF observation catalogue [3]. The UI also provides utilities for handling responses to these queries. The results of a user query to the catalogue appear as ASCII files that can be edited or stored in a local table management system. They may be edited and/or modified and then passed along to the FH file as an archive retrieval request.

Current Uses of the DMF

Major portions of the DMF capabilities are operational at the Institute and are being actively utilized. Currently, the largest use of the DMF is for storage of the Guide Star Support System (GSSS) digitized plate scans. These were generated as part of the processing of the Guide Star Catalogue (GSC), an accurate database of "guide stars" which was created in preparation for the HST launch. The GSC contains around 20 million stellar objects and will be soon published on CD-ROM. The catalogue was created by scanning 1500 photographic survey plates of the northern and southern hemispheres, and then processing this digitized data using specialized feature extraction algorithms. The GSC will be used for fine guidance of the HST during actual observations.

The GSSS scanned plate data is of considerable operational and scientific interest and is now being copied to WORM media. The digitized data occupies more than 6000 magnetic tapes, but is being transferred to approximately 400 LMSI 12-inch WORM disks. A portion of this data will be stored online at any given time in a jukebox. This data is used with a software package GASP (Guide Star Astrometric Support Program) which provides astrometric assistance to HST researchers. The combination of the archived scans, the Guide Star Catalogue and the GASP software provides the equivalent of a "digital measuring engine" generating precise pointing positions.

The early use of the DMF system for GSSS plate data has allowed the software to be tested and fine-tuned. It has also been possible to demonstrate the functionality of the system for handling the volumes of data required to support HST observations. A daily archiving input rate of 2.0GB (5 GS plates) has been achieved. Since the GS plate archive processing included a complete verification pass that compared the archived data to the original files, the actual data flow was 4GB per day or nearly the total expected load on the operational HST archive.

Evolution of the DMF System

The DMF was originally conceived in late 1984 as a modest facility that could archive the HST data and distribute that data to the ST-ECF. The actual construction of the DMF system began in July, 1985.

In an earlier exploratory project, key parts of the system were prototyped using a SUN 2/120 workstation and an Optimem 12-inch WORM drive. Various options for device interfaces and disk formats were explored. Since no standards for 12-inch WORM media or for disk structure formats existed at that time, a system independent format was defined to allow easy portability. The design allows data to be sent to sites and individuals who may be running on different systems and using WORM drives other than those employed by STScI. The disk structure formats have also been proven by writing data on the SUN under Unix and reading it back on the VAX under VMS.

When formal DMF development began, the prototyping approach moved into full-scale activity with three full-time programmers. The tasks under development were divided into the File Handler portion that managed the optical disks and the archive itself, and the User Interface that provided the necessary user services and handled query processing, screen updates, and other user functions.While the basic design concepts in the DMF have remained much the same over time, the Institute's system architecture has evolved and a large VMS cluster with a significant number of SUN workstations is now in use. The ability to support a variety of networked systems became a requirement.

The data and disk structure portability showed immediate payoffs in this environment, but other modes of heterogeneity also were also identified. In particular, the systems use two incompatible network protocol suites (TCP/IP and DECnet). An application interface called NET, cut at the logical session layer, sits on top of both current protocol suites, while providing a single portable interface. The need for a database server and the ability to access it from many systems has driven the development of a database interface called STDB. STDB provides a standardized database interface that supports access to one or more databases such as Sybase on the SUNs and Britton-Lee on the VAXs.

By layering a version of STDB on top of NET, and using the screen management features in the STARCAT user interface, distributed access is provided to all of the DMF services from any of the local systems. Because the STARCAT has been designed to be portable and runs on top of standardized network interfaces, copies of this user interface can be distributed to other sites for remote access to our services. A similar, modular approach has also been taken in the internal structure of DMF itself. The system now accommodates three kinds of WORM drives, and adding new ones is not a major task.

Using a jukebox to provide access to the bulk of the expected data was considered a part of the DMF design and operations concept. Minimizing the need for operator intervention to access commonly used data was another factor. Cygnet was chosen as the jukebox vendor.

The DMF design included a jukebox process that required direct interface to the jukebox robotics. Although an in-house implementation was planned, Cygnet offered the option of using their JIMS package in early 1988. However, JIMS was developed on Unix systems for OEM use, and the DMF was running on a VAX/VMS system.

Choosing to Use JIMS in the DMF

In March, 1988, STScI was given a copy of the Unix (System V) version of the JIMS code to examine. After reviewing the JIMS design and source code, it appeared to be portable in the same amount of time that it would have

Figure 1. DMF System Architecture after JIMS Integration (Courtesy Space Telescope Science Institute)

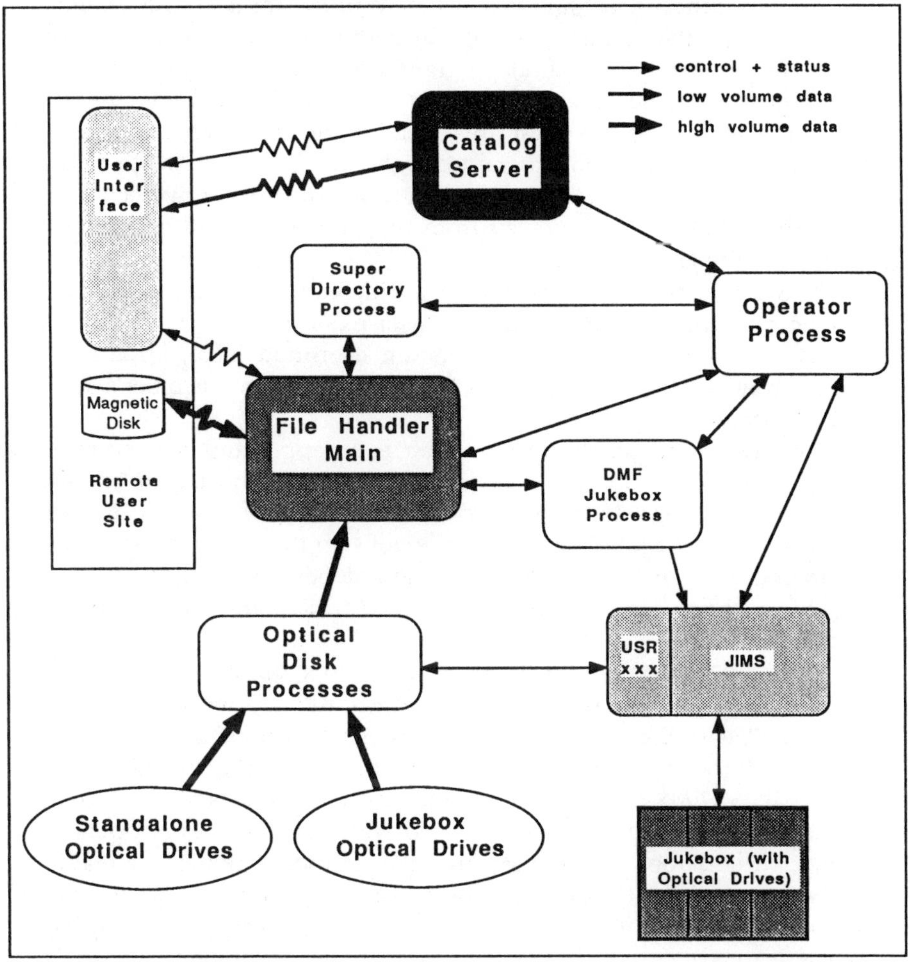

taken to write the originally planned minimal jukebox system interface. After porting, JIMS provided a powerful jukebox management system.

A considerable number of functions built into JIMS such as disk labeling, disk initialization and operator interface were already provided in the DMF software. Integrating JIMS into the DMF was a matter of moving these functions below the JIMS interface level.

The greatest benefit for the DMF was the ability to have a subsystem that already talked to the jukebox, managed both the jukebox interface and the media within the jukebox, and could easily be integrated into the existing structure. As a result, the most significant advantage of JIMS was ease of integration.

JIMS Functionality

The primary function of JIMS is to allow access to optical disk volumes by reference to the volume name rather than its location in the jukebox. For example, if the application program asks JIMS to mount a volume, JIMS generates the necessary commands to the jukebox to move the disk from a storage slot to a WORM drive, load it into the drive, and spin up the drive. The application program can then read from or write to that disk as if it were manually inserted into a standalone drive. Figure 1 shows how JIMS is the gateway from the operator on an applications program to the jukebox.

JIMS can also be easily ported to a wide variety of computing environments or applications. Portability "user exits" permit o.s. dependencies to be easily resolved. User exits are user-modifiable, application-specific routines that allow JIMS to be customized to a customer's application environment.

JIMS allows the jukebox to function as an application service rather than as a low-level robotics device. High-level function calls are translated into the appropriate robotics commands for moving media into and out of drives in the jukebox. Another benefit of JIMS software is reduced integration time; once the operating system dependent routines are written, the package can be integrated into the target environment by the customer.

JIMS can be configured to run in many operating system environments by use of portable design techniques. At the low-level, the software controls to the jukebox robotics via ASCII commands over an RS-232 line. At the high-level, function calls permit a programmable interface to JIMS. JIMS software is offered in object code and C language source code, for selected machines and versions of the Unix operating system. In addition, customers provide their own routines for reading and writing volume labels. This is important because labels must be unique for each volume to insure data integrity at any installation, and the user can best determine the necessary labeling technique.

JIMS monitors system operation and will not allow the jukebox to function in an unknown state. An inventory function is invoked implicitly at system initialization, or explicitly by an application if discrepancies are detected in the location of volumes within a jukebox.

JIMS Functions

1. *Interface at the program level.* An application program interface is provided at the volume name level, providing routines to perform mount, unmount, import and export functions.

2. *Logical volume to physical location mapping.* JIMS satisfies a volume request by mapping the volume name to a specific side of a WORM disk as stored in a specific slot in a jukebox.

3. *Request management.* Although requests are placed in a FIFO (First-In, First-Out) queue, mount requests can be given a relative priority to affect the order in which they are handled in this queue. Each jukebox control task within JIMS has a queue for holding requests.

4. *Disk spin up and spin down.* JIMS performs disk spin up and spin down operations under software control for drives in which spin functions are not RFPI-controlled. This is part of the mount and unmount functionality.

5. *Jukebox communication.* JIMS supports an RS-232 communications path to the jukebox robotics and a SCSI communications path to the WORM drives.

6. *Jukebox management.* JIMS supports taking a jukebox offline and later putting it online to allow jukebox maintenance.

7. *Jukebox configuration.* Configuration information (jukebox, drive, and disk status) on all managed hardware and media can be provided.

8. *Multiple jukebox support.* The number of jukeboxes that JIMS can manage is limited only by available system memory.

9. *Multiple user support.* The software supports requests from multiple applications by way of its FIFO queue.

10. *Error logging.* JIMS logs error and warning messages to a magnetic disk file. It is the operator's responsibility to manage this file.

11. *Optical drive management.* When processing user requests, JIMS allocates drives and returns information to the caller describing the drive in which the requested volume has been mounted.

12. *Import/export slot management.* JIMS manages the movement of disks into and out of jukeboxes. The mailbox door remains in a closed position until an import command is issued, and is returned to a closed position when an exported disk is removed. Imported volume names (one for each side of a disk) are verified as part of the "import" command. The imported disk is assigned an arbitrary storage slot location.

13. *Volume verification.* Each time a disk is imported into a jukebox, the volume label is read and verified. JIMS supports volume labels eight bytes in length. Volume labels are normally read each time a volume is mounted in a drive or when a volume is exported from the jukebox, although the user can disable verification at mount and export by modifying the configuration file. A user exit routine is responsible for the actual read operation. If the volume label does not match that which is provided by the user, an error is returned and the operation aborted. When an uninitialized disk is imported into a jukebox, JIMS requires that volume names be provided for each side of the disk before it can be stored in a jukebox slot.

14. *JIMS messages.* After mounting a disk, JIMS reports the drive being used to the application. If a request is made for an unknown volume, JIMS will report that the volume is not found. Applications making requests of the software will receive a message if the parameters passed to JIMS are invalid. Completion of jukebox or drive online/offline requests and import/export requests are reported to the operator interface.

15. *JIMS startup.* There are three startup states. The first time JIMS is started, a cold start is performed to inventory[1] all disks in all jukeboxes in order to build a mapping table. Later restarts of JIMS can use a warm start to bypass the inventory operation. If for some reason JIMS terminates abnormally, it can be restarted hot to perform any pending requests.

16. *Robotics management.* The user-requested functions are translated into low-level robotics commands that are sent over an RS-232 line to the jukebox.

17. *Operator interface support.* JIMS supports operator interaction by providing a message facility for notifying the operator when a jukebox requires attention.

The Case Study: Integrating JIMS with the DMF

The DMF jukebox interface was designed in a generic manner to allow it to use any jukebox. When the Cygnet jukebox was selected, JIMS did not exist. When JIMS was released, it was only available in a Unix version. However, the DMF required a VMS jukebox software package. Due to JIMS' modular design, though, the porting job was estimated to be a modest two to three man-month job.

Since STScI has had considerable experience with Unix and VMS ports, problem areas were easily identifiable. The major areas that needed work were process initiation, signal handling, and Inter-Process Communications.[2] These are important in JIMS because JIMS is a set of processes that communicate with each other. The other area of effort was expected in the network interface.

Most of these areas were well-isolated in the JIMS code since Cygnet had clearly addressed porting considerations in its software design. However, some of differences between Unix System V, the BSD libraries, and the VMS libraries were not so obvious. A total of twenty-four routines, in addition to the portable interface library routines, had to be slightly modified.

[1] Inventory refers to the compilation of a mapping table indicating the storage slot location of each volume by reading a volume label from each disk surface in a jukebox contained therein.

[2] Inter-Process Communication (IPC) is an operating system level scheme for message passing between programs.

In addition to building the standard set of user customizable routines and modifying the standard portability routines to match the system interface, STScI also added several new portability routines. These routines, which Cygnet has now incorporated into its standard portability set, include routines to handle process startup, termination, signals, and alarms.

Summary of JIMS Port and Recommendations

The total effort to integrate JIMS into the DMF took about two man-months. About 75 percent of this time was the port from Unix to VMS, and the remainder was integration with the DMF itself. Writing a VMS version of JIMS from scratch would have probably taken at least six man-months.

The original estimate for the minimal jukebox interface was two to three months. Although this interface was not intended to have as much functionality or flexibility as JIMS, it would have taken more advantage of the capabilities already in place in the DMF to save redevelopment time. While the planned development for the DMF would have met the immediate requirements, JIMS offered the added functionality of multiple jukeboxes, multiple queues, and request prioritization that the minimal design would not have included.

As far as STScI is concerned, providing JIMS along with Cygnet's jukebox products makes good sense. A jukebox can be a complex peripheral to integrate into a system, and having JIMS facilitates a quick integration.

There are, however, several problems that need to be resolved.

One of the implementation choices that was made in JIMS was to use a large data structure to describe the jukebox and optical disk status. This structure is passed from module to module to handle requests. This method of Inter-Process Communication is more time-consuming under VMS than Unix. JIMS could be more efficient by possibly using an object-oriented, message passing interface with some additional restructuring of the code. This type of change would clean up the inter-module interfaces and reduce the overhead under both VMS and Unix.

STScI has also identified a problem with error recovery and task signaling among the several modules that comprise JIMS. This is now being discussed with Cygnet's software staff and the problem should be resolved in the next release of the JIMS software.

Conclusion

The Hubble Space Telescope Data Archive and Distribution System (DADS) uses WORM and jukebox technology to handle a daily data transfer flow of many gigabytes. A jukebox management software subsystem was needed, and the Cygnet JIMS package was ported from Unix to VMS to fulfill this requirement. Although the inefficiency of Inter-Process Communication under VMS made JIMS less efficient as compared with Unix, JIMS' modularity made the porting task straightforward.

References

1. "DMF Design Guide." DMF/STScI Internal Document. May 1987.

2. "DMF File Handler Design Specification." DMF/STScI Internal Document; March, 1987.

3. "Design of the DMF Catalog." DMF/STScI Internal Document. April 1986.

4. "FITS: A Flexible Image Transport System." *A&A Supplement Series* 44, (1981) 363-370.

5. Pirenne, B., L. Hunt, A. Richardson, G. Russo. *STARCAT— Complete Database Front-End.* Presented at the Astronet Conference on Databases and Archives. December 1988.

6. "NET Interface Specification Document." Version 2.0. DMF/STScI Internal Document. March 1988.

7. "The STDB Interface." DMF/STScI Internal Document. July1987.

SECTION IV
OPTICAL DISK EVALUATION AND PERFORMANCE ISSUES

12
Benchmark Testing of WORM Drives: A Systems Integrator's Perspective

DR. SANJAY RANADE

Three major issues immediately face integrators whenever a new technology product is introduced into the computer marketplace: (1) compatibility with and ease of integration into existing systems, (2) cost, and (3) impact on system performance and capacity. In the case of WORM technology, the first two issues have been effectively addressed by drive manufacturers by the adoption of the popular SCSI interface protocol and pricing these products generally below conventional magnetic tape drives. The performance issue is a relative "unknown" and requires further investigation.

Performance information provided by optical disk drive manufacturers is generally incomplete and valid only under certain conditions which may seldom prevail in the actual product use. In particular, data transfer rates can vary greatly depending on data characteristics, software interfaces and the application. In order to use optical disks as a reliable component in new computer systems, their performance and operational characteristics must be thoroughly tested. Benchmarking these products, therefore, becomes an important preliminary step for systems integrators who may use WORM technology.

Benchmarking Goals

The general goals for benchmark testing of WORM drives are:

1. *Performance measurement.* In the case of new or developing technology products, parameters such as data transfer rates and error rates are not well-established and may vary considerably between applications and the hardware interfaces chosen. WORM technology falls into just such a category. Although drive manufacturers quote various performance figures for these products, experience shows that these differ from those obtainable in practice. Consequently, these parameters must be verified through benchmarking. Data transfer rates depend to a very large extent on the type of data, software techniques used to arrange the read and write operations and on the hardware configuration utilized. Systems using WORM drives, therefore, must be carefully designed using performance figures that have been measured using configurations similar to those intended for operational use.

2. *Software interface evaluation.* Various types of software interfaces have been developed for interfacing write-once systems to different host computers. The study described later in this chapter addressed only interfaces developed for VAX/VMS. Its goal was to identify a product that would allow the DEC Files-11 data format for the optical disk and allow full access to it by "hiding" its write-once nature as effectively as possible.

3. *Hardware evaluation.* Another goal was to evaluate the hardware itself and verify that various specifications regarding error rates, operating temperature, and reliability were satisfied. It was also important to gain experience in physically handling the drive, media and, if possible, a jukebox in order to record the times taken for operations such as loading and unloading drive media and exchanging disks in the jukebox. These considerations were important because many copying, shelving, duplicating and restoring operations were planned over the anticipated long life of the target system.

4. *Life cycle costing.* The life cycle cost of the entire archive system depended to a large extent on the number of optical disks used in storing data. The storage capacity of each disk, in turn, varied somewhat depending on the software interface. Another goal, therefore, was to determine the number of overhead blocks that were actually used in recording data to calculate the efficiency of disk usage.

This chapter focuses on performance measurement. A detailed description of other goals is outside the scope of this paper and are only briefly addressed.[1]

[1] A fuller discussion of these issues will appear in *WORM Optical Disks: A Systems Integrator's Perspective* by Dr. Sanjay Ranade, to be published by Meckler Corporation in 1989.

Figure 1 (Courtesy ST Systems Corp.)

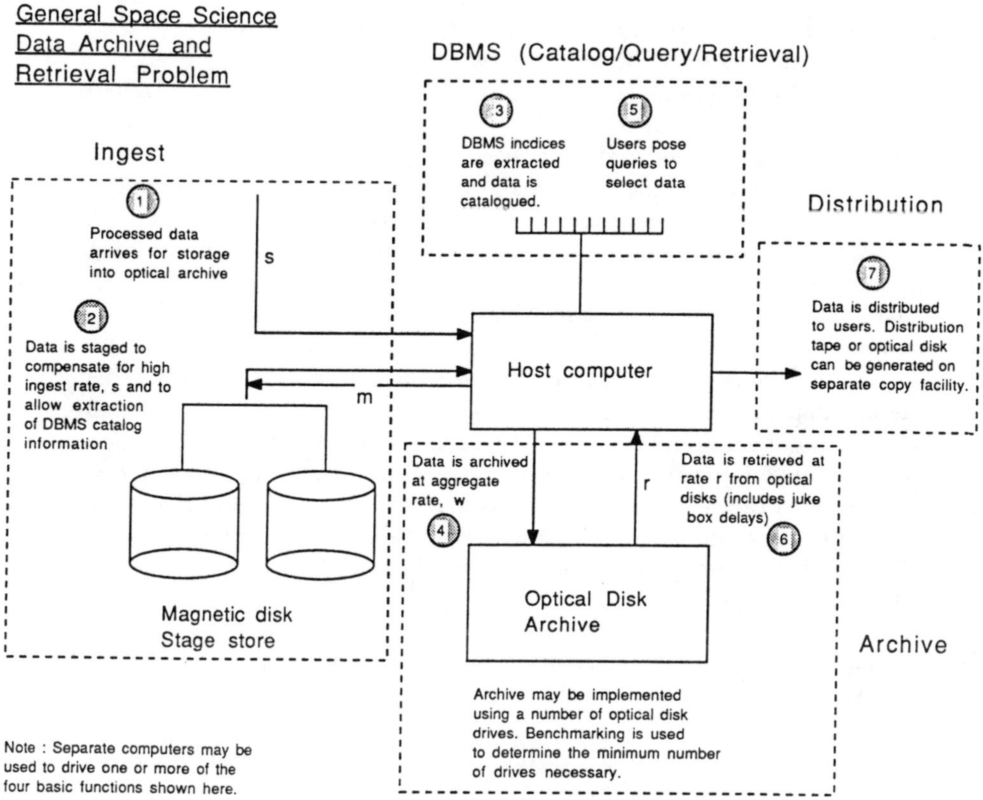

Space Science Data Archive Application

Advances in WORM technology have made possible new application areas and new computer system capabilities. WORM technology is particularly significant for space science data archive applications since storage and efficient access to huge volumes of data has always presented a problem. The data must be stored in a DBMS to allow its efficient search by way of user queries. Once data has been identified, it must be retrieved from the archive and distributed to the user.

Satellites typically transmit data at rates which result in a storage requirement of several gigabytes per day, or roughly the capacity of a single 12-inch optical platter.[2] With current technology, it is quite practical to store one years' data in a single jukebox, and to store several years' data online in a series of daisy-chained jukeboxes driven by a single computer.

Figure 1 illustrates the basic archive/distribution problem. Recorded satellite data arrives into the host memory via its bus, at a rate *s*. It is then staged on conventional magnetic media at a rate *m*; next, DBMS indices are constructed and inserted into the DBMS with blank pointers to data files. After further processing, the data is moved to the optical platters in the archive at a rate *w*. Data is later retrieved from the archive at a rate *r*. These activities are typically implemented as four separate processes. These separate processes are:

Data ingest receives data from the satellite and places it on the staging store (magnetic disk).

Data process and catalog further processes the data and enters a record for data items in the DBMS catalog.

Data archive moves the data from the stage store into the archive store and updates the DBMS entry to point to the archive location.

Data retrieval moves the data from the archive back to the stage store and then to the user via tape, disk, or through a network. If no re-formatting is necessary, the data need not be staged during retrieval.

These processes each result in a certain data traffic on the computer bus. The overall traffic is limited by the maximum capacity of this bus. The real problem, then, is to arrange the software tasks and select read/

[2]The projected data rate for the proposed Earth Observation System (EOS) is about 2TB per day.

Figure 2. Test Results for Drive D1, Controller C1 (Courtesy ST Systems Corp.)

Block Size (KB)	Number of Transfers	Read - Total Time (secs)	Write -Total Time (secs)	Read Rate KB/sec	Write Rate KB/sec
1	1000	86.7	253.1	12	4
4	1250	121	328.9	42	16
8	1250	137.5	345.6	74	30
16	1250	171	378.9	120	54
24	209	34.3	86.3	150	60
32	157	29.9	69.2	172	74
42	120	26.9	77.6	192	67
52	97	25.2	67	205	77
63	318	93.6	214	219	96

write strategies to make the most efficient use of the bus, thus allowing the best possible archive and retrieval rates. Among the major parameters which constrain the archive performance are the rates *s*, *r*, *w* and *m* described previously. If these parameters are known, it is possible to construct a queuing model of the entire archive and estimate its overall performance. The rates *s* and *m* are generally well-established, although it is still possible to improve them using various software techniques. The rates *r* and *w*, however, are not well-established and must be determined experimentally.

The following section discusses experiments carried out to determine typical values of *r* and *w* for a data archive application.

Case History

A recent project required the design of a data archive that would be capable of storing data at a maximum rate of up to 16GB/day and retrieving data at about 12GB/day. This translated into an overall retrieval rate, *r*, of 170KB/sec and an overall archive write rate, *w*, of 195KB/sec. These rates were within the maximum advertised capabilities of some of the WORM drives considered. For all of the reasons mentioned previously, however, it was necessary to verify these figures by testing in an environment similar to that proposed for the archive. Two WORM drives, one dedicated to reading and the other to writing, were considered sufficient for implementing this portion of the archive.

Accordingly, benchmark tests were performed using a variety of drives and interfaces. DEC VAX computers (VAX 11/780, VAX 11/750 and Micro VAX II) were used in these tests since these machines had been chosen to drive the archive on the basis of other selection criteria. Each machine used the VMS operating system. Test programs were written in Fortran, system services provided by the operating system were used, and the U.S. Design VOS optical disk file system emulation software was employed.

The lowest software layer, the device driver for the optical disk, was a modified version of the DEC DU driver. This driver is the standard DEC driver used for a certain class of magnetic disks. All of these software layers contributed to some overhead with a corresponding effect on the drive performance. Since this overhead was essentially the same for each of the drive and hardware combinations tested, no effort was made to quantify it. Therefore, it is possible that similar tests for the same hardware components with a different computer, operating system and optical disk file system emulation software may provide somewhat different resul ts.

In order to estimate drive performance, a large number of data transfers representative of the intended applications must be performed. Each type of transfer must be repeated many times using different combinations of drives, hardware interfaces and software techniques. One of the easiest ways to accomplish this is to transfer increasingly larger amounts of data for a given drive, hardware interface and software technique and to note the transfer time in each case. The times required for the transfers can then be plotted against the size of the data blocks transferred. These plots can be compared and evaluated to determine the best combination of drive, interface and software strategy.

Figures 2 through 4 illustrate some of the benchmark results that were obtained through these tests. Figure 2 shows the performance of drive D1 using controller C1. Notice that the write rate is roughly half the read rate and reflects the extra revolution required to verify the data. Figure 3 shows the results for drive D2 using controller C2. Here, the read and write rates are similar and reflect the DRDW (Direct-Read-During-Write) method for verifying data. The maximum read and write rates (about 160KB/sec) is roughly 35 percent less than the advertised maximum sustained rate for this drive.

Similarly, the maximum read rate for drive D1 (about 219 KB/sec) is about 27 percent lower than the advertised maximum sustained rate. Both the 160KB/sec and the 219KB/sec rates correspond to transfers using a block size of 63KB. In practice, the block size typically would be much lower and would result in even lower transfer rates. Figure 4

Figure 3. Test Results for Drive D2, Controller C2 (Courtesy ST Systems Corp.)

Block Size (KB)	Number of Transfers	Read - Total Time (secs)	Write -Total Time (secs)	Read Rate KB/sec	Write Rate KB/sec
1	2000	399.1	282.3	5	7
4	1250	183	221.6	28	23
8	625	102.9	135.5	50	38
16	625	126.2	142.3	81	72
24	417	109.5	111.3	94	92
32	157	39.1	42.7	132	120
42	239	73.7	77.5	139	133
52	193	66	67.2	156	153
63	159	63.9	64.1	161	160

Figure 4. Test Results for Drive D2, Controller C1 (Courtesy ST Systems Corp.)

Block Size (KB)	Number of Transfers	Read - Total Time (secs)	Write -Total Time (secs)	Read Rate K B/sec	Write Rate KB/sec
1	500	64.6	64.6	8	8
4	250	35.2	35.4	29	29
8	125	19.6	19.5	52	52
16	313	58.9	58.8	87	87
24	209	45.8	46	112	112
32	94	23.6	24.6	131	131
42	24	7	7	147	147
52	97	32	32	161	161
63	318	119.3	119.6	172	172

Figure 5. Test Results for Drive D1, Controller C1 (Courtesy ST Systems Corp.)

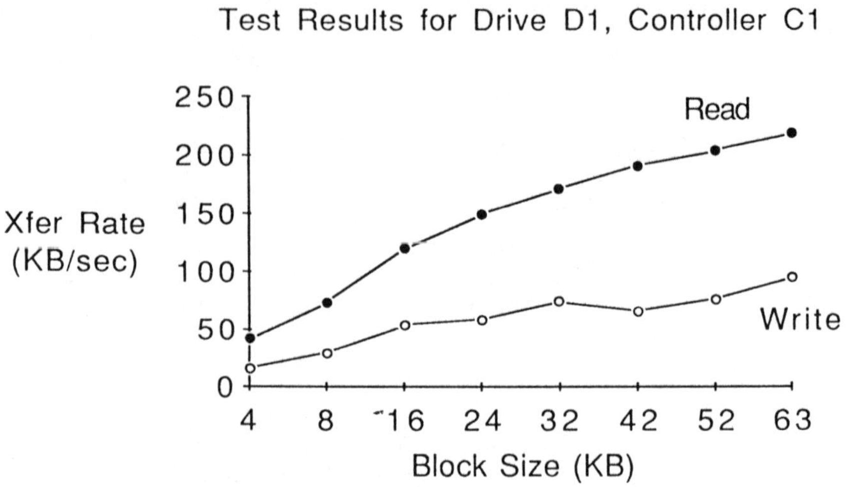

Figure 6. Test Results for Drive D2, Controller C2 (Courtesy ST Systems Corp.)

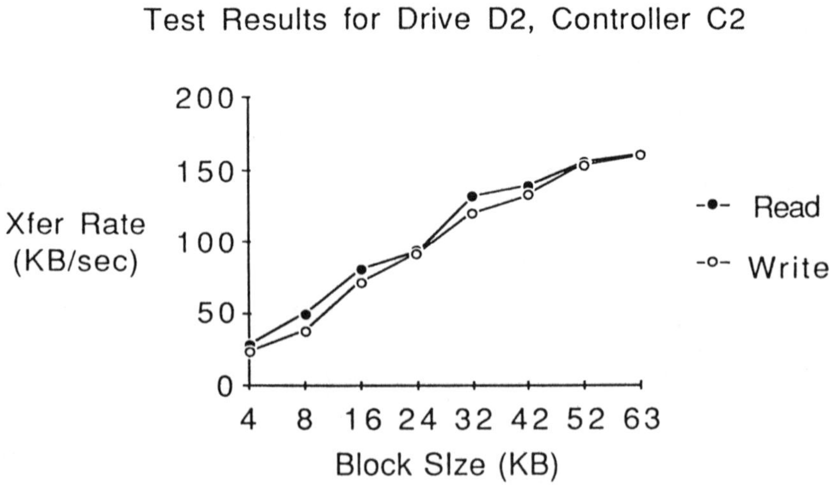

Figure 7. Test Results for Drive D2, Controller C1 (Courtesy ST Systems Corp.)

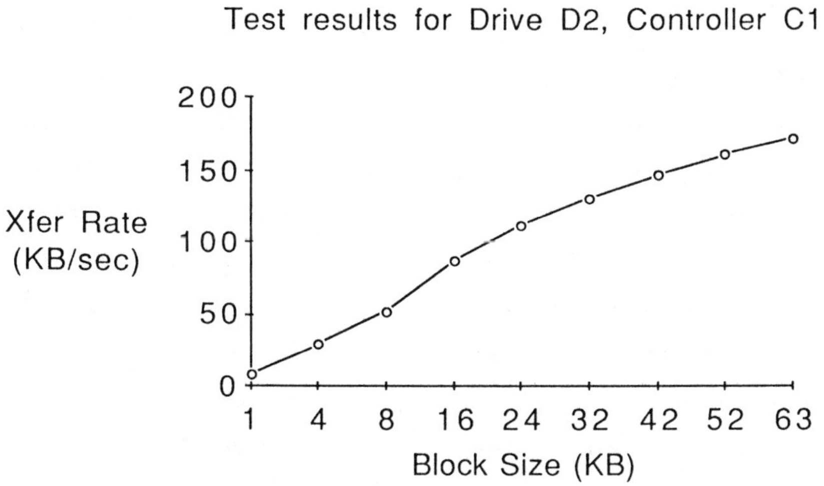

shows the results for drive D2 using controller C1. Notice that the change in controller increases the maximum read and write rates by about 5 percent. Figures 5 through 7 demonstrate corresponding curves for each set of results.

Analysis of Results

Why is there such a large discrepancy between the advertised transfer rates and the rates that were actually obtained in practice? To answer this question, it is necessary to consider how data is recorded on a WORM disk as well as the different factors that affect optical drive performance. It is also necessary to consider the individual steps involved in reading and writing optical disks. There are several factors that determine the rate at which optical drives can read and write data. Some of these depend on the characteristics of the WORM drive itself; others are influenced by the interface hardware, operating system and applications program software.

Hardware Limitations

Hardware limitations arise due to the characteristics of the computer bus and the interface (or host adapter), and from the characteristics of the drive hardware itself. The maximum data transfer rate for any of the optical drives used in our tests (467.5KB/sec; see Figure 8) is well within the

Figure 8. Optical Disk Drive Specifications (Courtesy ST Systems Corp.)

Drive Characteristics	D1	D2	D3	D4
Rotational Speed (rpm)	720	480	1122	600
Sectors per revolution	25	32	25	62
Bytes per sector	1024	1024	1024	512
Average seek time	0.25	0.15	0.145	0.25
Time per revolution	0.083	0.125	0.053	0.1
Kbytes per revolution	25	32	25	31
Data Rate (KB/sec)	300	256	467.5	310
Average latency	0.042	0.063	0.027	0.05
Max, bytes/transfer	63	63	63	63

known bus capabilities the VAX computers (1.2MB/sec for the Unibus and 1.6MB/sec for the Qbus). Bus limitations, therefore, are not addressed in this paper.

The controller overhead is due to the fact that data is transferred to the computer through use of DMA (Direct Memory Access) hardware. DMA hardware blocks CPU access to the memory and steals cycles to pump data directly into or out of the memory as required. This overhead is relatively small and difficult to quantify. It also depends on the particular SCSI host adapter used for the WORM disk.

The WORM drive hardware characteristics (Figure 8) which influence data access times are:

- the rotational speed of the disk, r (rpm)
- the number of bytes per track, N_t
- the seek time, t_s
- the average latency, t_l
- controller buffer size, B (bytes)

A "read data" command issued to an optical drive results in a sequence of steps that is somewhat different for each drive. Data is read from the disk sectors and transferred through the interface to a host computer memory buffer. The maximum (or "burst") rate at which the data can be read is thus $r * N_t$ KB/sec. This assumes that all the required data resides in the same track and that the reading head is positioned at that track. In practice, the required data may be distributed across tracks, incurring a seek time for each fragment. The total time, T_1, to access n bytes of data is given by:

$$T_1 = t_s + t_l + t_t$$

where t_t, the time to transfer n bytes of data is given by:

$$t_t = r * (n/N_t).$$

For write operations, since the disk's write rate cannot keep pace with the host's data transfer rate, data being written to the drive must be buffered. This relation assumes that $B > N_t$ and that the time taken by the optical drive electronics for error correction or checking does not affect the drive's ability to write data. If $N_t > B$, then $\mathrm{int}(N_t/B)$ rotations of the disk will be required to complete the data transfer.

For certain WORM drives, the simplifying assumptions described above are not valid and other factors need to be considered. For example, some drives provide two different modes of transferring data. To examine these it is necessary to consider how data is recorded on an optical disk.

The physical track on the optical disk is one continuous spiral from the center to the outer edge. A logical "track" is one complete revolution of the disk. Disk rotational speeds vary from 480 to 2160 rpm. With most drives, each track is preformatted into a certain number of sectors, and each sector contains 512, 1024, or 2048 bytes of data. To keep the read or write laser beam on one track for several revolutions, it is necessary for the beam to jump back to the original position once per revolution.

The two methods of transferring data are called sequential and interleaved. In the sequential mode, contiguous sectors are accessed sequentially. In the interleaved mode, sectors physically separated by k sectors are accessed sequentially, i.e., sectors are read or written in the order 0, k+1, 2(k+1), etc.

Each method results in a different data transfer rate which depends not only on k, but also on the size of the controller buffer, B. Choice of method depends on the characteristics of the data. In cases where the interleave factor k is larger than the buffer size B, it may be preferable to use the interleaved mode if it is available.

Application Program Overhead

Suppose that a large block of data is broken up into a number of smaller blocks, where each smaller block is less than N_t. A separate I/O request is made for each block. This strategy will result in an overall loss of performance. The time elapsed between the completion of one I/O request

Figure 9. Service Times for Read Requests (Courtesy ST Systems Corp.)

Request Size (KB)	Service time D1	Service time D2	Service time D3	Service time D4
1	0.30	0.22	0.17	0.30
4	0.31	0.23	0.18	0.31
8	0.32	0.24	0.19	0.33
16	0.35	0.28	0.21	0.35
24	0.37	0.31	0.22	0.38
32	0.40	0.34	0.24	0.40
42	0.43	0.38	0.26	0.44
52	0.47	0.42	0.28	0.47
63	0.50	0.46	0.31	0.50
64	0.59	0.59	0.36	0.61
75	0.62	0.64	0.38	0.64
99	0.70	0.73	0.43	0.72
125	0.79	0.83	0.49	0.80
150	0.95	1.06	0.59	0.98
175	1.04	1.16	0.65	1.06
200	1.20	1.38	0.75	1.25
225	1.28	1.48	0.80	1.33
250	1.37	1.58	0.86	1.41

Figure 10. Estimated and Measured Read Rates for Drive D1 (Courtesy ST Systems Corp.)

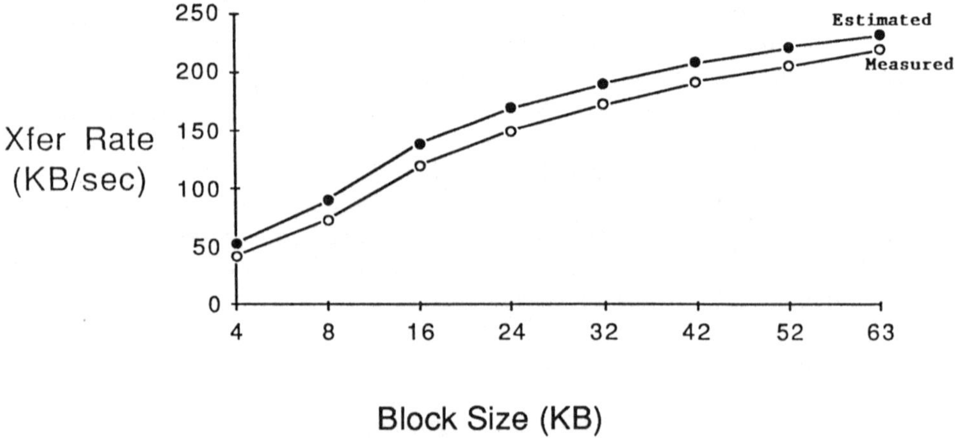

and the start of the next creates the likelihood that at least one extra disk revolution will be required before the disk is once again correctly positioned for the next I/O to commence. To estimate the resultant delay, it is only necessary to know the size of the largest disk block that can be transferred in one request. The total number of extra revolutions required to transfer n blocks of data is int(n/63) for all of the drives considered.

Thus, the total access time is:

$$T_2 = t_s + t_l + t_r(n/N_t) + [t_r * \mathrm{int}(n/63)]$$

where t_r is the time taken for one disk revolution. This relation can be used to estimate the read rates for different values of n. Figure 9 shows request service times for different values of n for each of the drives considered in this study. Figure 10 shows a comparison of the estimated and measured read rates for drive D1 using the track-to-track seek time rather than the average seek time. The small discrepancy between the estimated and measured values is within the tolerance of the operating system overhead discussed below.

Write-Verify Overhead

In the case of write-verify operations, the delays are more serious. In general, there are three techniques for data verification through hardware. The first is called DRDW (Direct-Read-During-Write) in which data is written and read immediately before the head moves on. In this case there is practically no overhead, although the disk's rotational rate is often slow.

The second technique is to read the data that has just been written and perform a byte-by-byte comparison with the intended data while it is still in the controller's buffer. This second method will require at least one extra revolution of the disk and more if $n > B$. If $n > B$, then in general, $1 + n/B$ extra revolutions of the disk will be required. This is the reason why a large buffer size B results in more efficient data transfers. With some drives it is possible to disable the write-verify option. In this case the read and write rates are virtually identical although data integrity is not guaranteed.

The third technique is "write verify with relocation". This is usually software-selectable and allows a data block to be relocated to a reserved area if a write error occurs. This method is often used to handle errors discovered by the first two techniques.

Operating System Overhead

The overhead contributed by the operating system arises from the service time for each I/O request and is, therefore, dependent on the number of separate I/O requests. This overhead may be quantified more easily. (For VAX/VMS, 10ms per I/O request is a generally accepted figure for this overhead.)

Other factors that reduce the effective data transfer rate arise because of the overhead incurred through multi-programming. In all of the results presented here, the computer was dedicated to running the benchmark test alone. In a multi-programming system, however, other tasks are likely to contend for the computer bus and levy additional delays as a result.

Systems Integration Considerations

The results obtained above and the operational experience that was gained through the benchmark exercise significantly influenced subsequent design decisions and component choices. The most important conclusions concerned the number of drives that would be required to support the required read and write loads. The following is a summary of the steps taken to arrive at the final design. Analysis for only two drives is presented below, although several were considered in this study.

1. *Performance.* In the case of drive D1, it was clear that a single drive could support the required read rates. A single drive would not support the required write rate, but two drives operating simultaneously would easily do so. With a data blocking factor of 16KB, two drives would suffice; with this factor further reduced to 8KB, a total of four drives operating concurrently would be required.

In the case of drive D2, it was clear that a single active drive would not be able to support the data storage function. Two drives could handle the write function providing that the data blocking factors were sufficiently high. Likewise, one drive would be able to handle the read function only if the blocking factors were about 32KB. Two drives would require these factors to be at least 16KB whereas three drives would permit blocking factors as low as 8KB.

2. *Software interface.* Although different software interfaces were not tested, it was verified that the interface which we had selected [1], was capable of performing all of the operations that were required of it. Its most important feature was to store data using the existing VAX/VMS Files-11 file structure and preclude the need for custom software.

The software interface performed exactly as described in its documentation. High-level routines (corresponding to DCL commands) were used for disk initialization, mounting, dismounting and closing. Low-level Fortran-callable routines were used for performing the benchmark tests. Since the time of the tests this interface has been significantly improved and now offers several additional useful features.

3. *Hardware evaluation.* Both the drives and controller hardware performed reliably throughout all of the benchmark tests.

4. *Life cycle costs.* As described previously, media cost and capacity are important factors that influence the total life cycle cost for the archive. If media M1 affords a storage capacity C percent greater than media M2, then 36.5 * 5 * C fewer M1 disks are required over a five-year lifecycle. In fact, 365 * C fewer disks would be required in our application since a "safe-store" copy of each disk was also needed. Using a figure of $250/disk, this leads to an eventual saving of about $250,000 over the 5-year life of the archive. Even accounting for higher storage capacities and decreasing media cost, the cost benefits of choosing M1 over M2 were considerable.

Jukebox cost was also a major factor in the drive selection. There were several jukebox devices on the market at the time of this study, but each was restricted in the kinds of WORM drives supported. Additional important characteristics for jukebox selection were cost, capacity, and software availability. [Editors' note: See Chapter 10 for an evaluation checklist of WORM jukebox software.]

Conclusion

This chapter has described benchmarking of WORM disk drives as a necessary first step in arriving at a reliable archive design. This study started out with the primary goal of measuring drive performance in order to validate an archive design. This design was originally developed on the basis of a comprehensive market survey and published drive specifications.

As the study progressed, it became clear that the number of drives that had been used in the design was deficient, although the bus structure and interface techniques chosen were adequate. Drive performance differences were outweighed by other factors such as media, drive, and jukebox cost.

It was also found that because of the commitment to using an existing file structure, it would not be possible to exploit the full performance capability of the WORM drive. Although additional performance could be achieved with custom software, the cost would be unacceptable.

The benchmarking effort enabled us to arrive at a reliable archive design whose performance could be guaranteed within certain clearly specified parameters. Although it was expensive, it was a step that could not be excluded in the application where performance and efficiency as well as costs were important factors. The exercise yielded valuable data which we used to accurately size and cost the overall system. Large life-cycle cost savings were made possible.

Bibliography

LASERWARE User Manual. Knoxville,TN: Perceptics Corporation, August 1987.

Optimem 1000 Optical Disk Drive Interface Manual. Mountain View, CA: Optimem, Inc., April 1987.

Thoma, George, J. Cookson, F. Walker, F. and S. Hauser." Interfacing Optical Disks to a Document Image Storage and Retrieval System". *Journal of Imaging Technology,* 12, No. 5,(October 1986).

Vaidya, N. and B. Lowery. *Software for Optical Archive and Retrieval.* STX/SAR Report NSSDC/WDC-A-R&S 88-8, August 1988.

VOS Software User's Guide. Lanham, MD: U.S. Design Corporation, August 1987.

13
Sector Striping Techniques for WORM Drives

EDWARD BESHORE

Without question, WORM data storage is becoming an accepted technology by a large number of users. Although the medium is ideal for many applications, WORM drives themselves often fall short. Frequently, those who would adopt WORM must reject it because of insufficient data transfer rates. Such applications might include:

- Telemetry from single opportunity events such as satellite transmissions and weapons tests. A high transfer rate to an archival, "hardened" media is required.

- Image processing for scientific, medical, remote sensing and engineering requiring high data transfer rates.

- Secure systems that require removable media but which need magnetic disk performance.

The transfer rate is fundamentally limited by rotation rate and sector interleave, and not bus bandwidth. The data transfer rate for a 5.25-inch WORM drive typically runs from 200 to 300KB/sec, while rates for 12-inch and 14-inch units are somewhat higher. In addition, most optical drives must perform write verify passes which further handicaps transfer rates by forcing an additional rotation during write operations.

The advent of higher performance processors also places a greater significance on the data transfer rate of a mass storage device. Processors and memory are now at least three orders of magnitude faster than disk storage. Without new techniques and technologies, the transfer rate bottleneck will only become more critical.

Sector Interleaving Versus Disk Interleaving

The concept of sector interleaving on disk drives is not new. By physically separating consecutive logical sectors on a disk cylinder with one or more sectors, slower disk electronics are given time to process the current sector and prepare for acquisition of the next logical sector. The negative aspect of sector interleaving is that more than one rotation is required to read a full cylinder or track of data. Newer, high-speed disk controllers feature so-called "1:1 interleaving" which means that logical sectors are physically adjacent on the disk, allowing a full cylinder to be read in a single rotation.

Disk interleaving, or striping, is the technique of distributing consecutive logical sectors, or groups of logical sectors, across two or more physical disk drives. This technique exploits the burst transfer rate of the controller, transferring enough data to just fill the controller's memory buffer in each disk drive (in the case of a write). While the drive is physically writing the data to the disk, the host may start the transfer of the next group of sectors to another drive. This is done repeatedly for each drive connected to the system. By the time the host gets back to the first drive, that drive has completed its first write request and is ready for another.

Sustained transfer rates approaching bus speeds are possible by properly selecting the number of disks to stripe across (sometimes referred to as the "striping factor") and the amount of data to transfer in each read/write request. This sustained rate can be as high as 4MB/sec in the case of a device with a synchronous SCSI interface.

Requirements for Effective Sector Stripping

In order for a disk drive to be effectively used for striping, it must meet some simple requirements. First, the disk must have an independent, onboard buffer memory capable of holding one or more physical sectors of data. A convenient buffer size is a full disk track. Such a buffer is typically available for most WORM drives manufactured today (it is also typical for SCSI devices in general).

The second requirement is that the drive must be capable of processing a read/write request without the constant attention of the host computer. For a SCSI device, this requirement would be satisfied by support of the disconnect/reconnect feature. For other devices, the drive/controller should provide an interrupt to signal a change in status or a register must be available to the host that can be polled for command completion.

In addition to requiring certain features from the disk hardware, disk interleaving demands that certain on-disk data structures be present to support the creation, reading and writing of files spread across the multiple platters. Special records to associate the members of a disk set as well as special File Allocation Tables (FATs) to group distributed physical sectors into a file are necessary.

Redundant copies of directories and FATs may be made for security purposes. Some commercial striping products implement cyclic redundancy checks and error correction schemes that can reconstruct data on missing or damaged platters. Without such measures, loss of one piece of media from a striped set could invalidate or severely cripple the entire set.

A Sector Striping Implementation Example

In the following example, it is assumed that a file system for the media has been defined. Such a file system will manage the organization, format and location of directories and sub-directories. Insertion time initialization of the media and location of the most recent directory data are also the responsibility of the file system. At mount time, the locations of the next blank sector available for writing (often referred to as the "high water mark") is determined for each piece of media in the striped set.

It is assumed that a file is located by finding its filename in a directory. A directory is a file of records that contain, in addition to the file name, additional information required by the system or the application. A directory will also contain a pointer to a sector where the FAT for the named file can be found. The FAT is sorted by logical sector number within the file. The FAT points to one or more physical sectors spread across the entire striped set, effectively linking those sectors to form a single file.

Structure definitions for both a directory record and a FAT record are as follows:

```
struct directory_record {
  char filename[8];           /* MS-DOS style name */
  char extension[3];          /*  and extension */
  long FATaddress;            /* sector address of FAT */

}

struct FAT_record {
  long logical_start;         /* logical sector in file */
  unsigned int count;         /* sectors in this extent */
  char platter;               /* platter number in set */
}
```

The FAT is a collection of one or more contiguous sectors, filled with **FAT_record**s sorted by **logical_start**. A **FAT_record** with an undefined **logical_start** value (such as -1) can be used to terminate the FAT.

When a file is open, an in-memory structure is initialized for the file. This structure is a File Control Block (FCB), and it is used to keep current information about the state of the file. One is required for each open file:

```
struct FCB_record {
  char modified;          /* set when file is changed */
  char next_platter;      /* platter to use in next I/O */
  long FATaddress;        /* address of start of FAT */
}
```

Each piece of media in the striped set should be initialized before use. Initialization consists of writing a base record that contains at a minimum the following information:

1. Volume name of the striped set.
2. Number of platters in the set.
3. Platter number of this platter.
4. Date and time of initialization, or some other data to uniquely identify the set.

This information should be used at volume mount time to ensure that all members of the same set are available for use. When a file is created, a directory entry for the file should be created, along with a NULL entry for its FAT.

When an existing file is opened, its directory entry and corresponding FAT is located. During the open process, an FCB is created or allocated and a pointer to it is returned as a file handle to be used in subsequent calls referencing the file. The **next_platter** field of the FCB is initialized to 0, the first platter number in the set.

Directories and FAT's can physically reside on a specific platter or can be duplicated across all platters for redundancy. Writing data to a file is performed through a call to **Write_data( )** (See Figure 1). The following constants are used to customize **Write_data( )** and "tune" its performance:

SECTORSIZE — The media sector size in bytes, e.g., 512, 1024 or 2048.

SECTORSPERXFER — The number of sectors to transfer at a time between the host and a drive. The resultant number of bytes should not exceed the size of the drive controller's onboard buffer cache.

NUMPLATTERS — The number of disk platters in the striped set.

Figure 1. Routine to Write Striped Sectors

```
Write_data(FCB_record, start, length, data)
    handle *FCB_record;          /* file handle */
    long start;                  /* file start byte for writing */
    unsigned int length;         /* number of bytes to write */
    char *data;                  /* data buffer to be written */
{
    /* initialization */
     numtransferred = 0;
     standard_xfer = SECTORSIZE * SECTORSPERXFER;

    /* loop until all bytes are transferred */
     while (numtransferred < length) {

    /* determine number of sectors to transfer */
       if ((length - numtransferred) < standard_xfer) {
         numsectors = length / SECTORSIZE;
         if (length % SECTORSIZE)
             numsectors++;
       } else
         numsectors = SECTORSPERXFER;

    /* get space to write on selected platter */
       location = next_free(FCB_record->next_platter,
              numsectors);

    /* write the data */
       WORM_write(FCB_record->next_platter,
              numsectors, location, data);

    /* update in-memory or on-disk version of FAT */
       update_FAT(start, numsectors, FCB_record);

    /* set up for next sector */
       FCB_record->platter++;
       if (FCB_record->platter == NUMPLATTERS)
         FCB_record->next_platter = 0;

    /* bump necessary pointers */
       data += num_sectors * SECTORSIZE;
       numtransferred += numsectors * SECTORSIZE;
     }
}
```

Write_data( ) effectively loops as many times as necessary, sending **standard_xfer** bytes to each drive in order until the number of bytes transferred is equal to the requested transfer length.

The first order of business in the **Write_data( )** while loop is to determine how many sectors to transfer to the next drive in sequence. It will be either SECTORSPERTRANSFER sectors or less.Next, a call to the routine **next_free( )** returns a sector address on the requested platter where **numsectors** sectors can be written contiguously.

Next, the sectors are written via a call to **WORM_write( )** which writes **numsectors** of data pointed to by data starting at sector **location** on drive **FCB_record->next_platter**.

Finally, the FAT is updated to reflect the write. It can be maintained in memory or can be immediately updated on the media. If the update is done to media, the platter holding FAT and directory data might best be separate from those platters holding data to prevent a time consuming seek on the data drives. The FAT should also be maintained in sorted order by **logical_start** at all times.

A read operation is performed in a manner similar to writing, except there is no need to locate free sectors, to write data or to update the FAT. Instead, the byte offset and length of the requested data must be converted to a sector offset and length. The FAT must be searched to find the proper starting sector (hence the need for a sorted FAT) and the read managed in a manner similar to that for a write as performed in **Write_data( )**.

When a file is closed, the FAT should be sorted and flushed and the FCB cleared if this has not already been done. The directory entry should then be updated to point to the latest copy of the FAT.

Conclusion

The transfer rates of WORM drives are often inadequate to meet the needs of certain applications. Sector interleaving or striping may be a viable solution to this dilemma. Users requiring high-performance can justify the necessary expenditure of time to implement striping algorithms similar to the one presented in this chapter.

A more general solution lies in standardizing a file system format that will accommodate striping in addition to multi-volume sets. This would allow data interchange between dissimilar systems. Such a proposal is being considered by standards committees in the United States and Europe. Interested parties can write to the author for additional information. [Editors' note: See Section VI for a review of currently proposed file system format standards.]

Acknowledgments

I would like to acknowledge the contributions of Jim Harper, Stephen Moraco, Margaret Sandor and Todd Putnam for many useful discussions and ideas. Also, my thanks to Don Crouse of Large Systems Consultants for educating me about striping.

SECTION V
STANDARDIZING SOFTWARE INTERFACES

14
The Role of the SCSI Interface

BRIAN A. BERG

The Small Computer Systems Interface, more popularly known as SCSI, is the most common interface for optical storage devices. This is partially because of timing, i.e., the emergence of both SCSI and commercial optical storage products around 1985. More importantly, however, increased intelligence to handle errors on the fly as required by WORM and other optical devices was most appropriately handled within the drive itself, and SCSI's system architecture lends itself directly to this concept.

In 1986, SCSI was formally adopted as ANSI standard X3.131-1986. This chapter will informally refer to this standard as "SCSI-1". SCSI was designed as a "system level" as opposed to a "device level" interface in order to hide the internal requirements of a device from the host computer. The controller is embedded in the device in this architecture, and hence the most complex details of its operation are handled within the device itself.

The SCSI Architecture

In a traditional device interface architecture, a host computer requires a controller board and software device driver unique to each device type (see Figure 1). Hence, a board slot and host memory for a software driver is required for each chain of disk drives, tape drives, etc.

By using a more generic interface such as SCSI, the host can use a single SCSI port and single device driver to gain access to a number of device types, including optical and magnetic devices, scanners, printers and even other host processors. These host processors can communicate with each other or share access to the peripherals resident on the SCSI bus (see Figure 2). It is even possible for a host processor to initiate a data transfer between two devices on the bus.

SCSI allows eight device types to co-exist on a SCSI bus at one time. Each of these has a unique device ID number. Just as a traditional

Figure 1. Traditional Device Interface Architecture (Courtesy Berg Software Design)

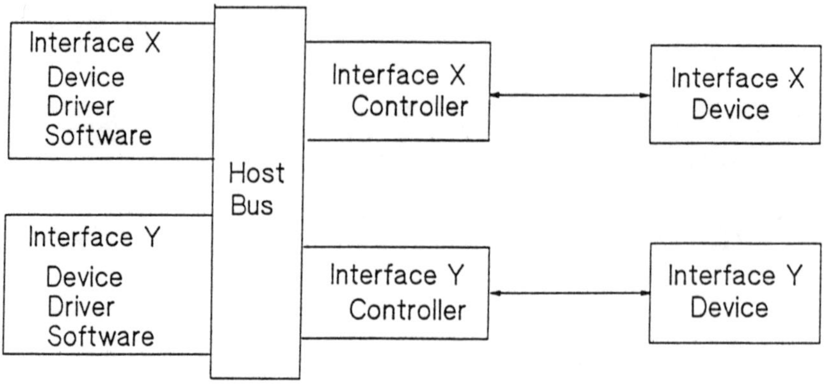

host-resident controller can have a number of devices chained to it, SCSI allows eight devices to be chained at each ID "node". Each of these has a unique Logical Unit Number (LUN) for its ID. Since there is at least one processor on the bus, and it requires its own ID, it can access as many as 7 × 8, or 56 devices by way of a single SCSI port. Although this many devices may not be practical, the flexibility of such an architecture can be easily seen.

SCSI Software Development

The SCSI architecture moves the intelligence necessary to control a particular device out of host memory and into the device controller's firmware, i.e., its ROM-resident software. As a result, peripheral manufacturers must have a software team to develop this firmware. This is a function which they are often not used to performing. However, the cost of developing this firmware can be amortized over a (hopefully) large number of units by the manufacturer. In addition, SCSI allows for a greater degree of device sophistication, and software algorithms to implement complex functions can remain proprietary.

Since the most difficult software development effort for a SCSI peripheral is handled by the manufacturer, this results in a cost savings for system integrators. Their job is made easier since the task of developing a SCSI device driver is more straightforward than developing a non-SCSI device driver for any particular peripheral.

Although the SCSI ANSI standard was a milestone, it was still possible for devices to be software incompatible, i.e., a single device driver could not necessarily easily handle a number of otherwise incompatible

Figure 2. SCSI Device Interface Architecture (Courtesy Berg Software Design)

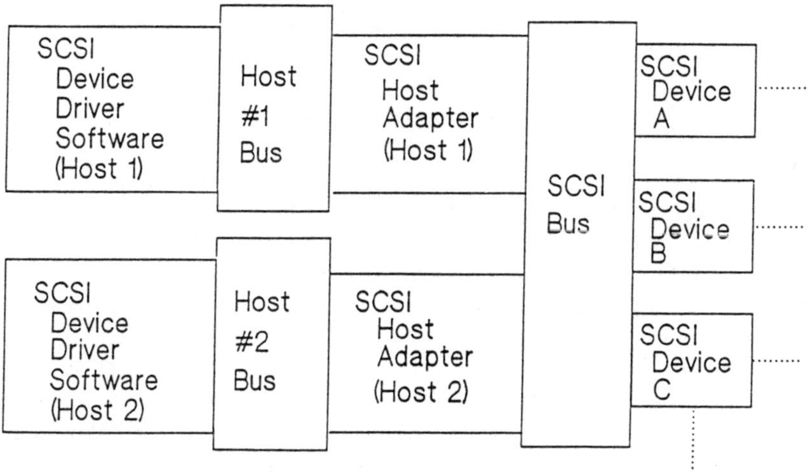

device types. It is this fact that caused the Common Command Set (CCS) document to become a defacto standard when it was released in 1986. The CCS defines a set of standard SCSI commands, and CCS-compliant devices must implement this set. A CCS device driver can be self-configuring, i.e., it can determine which devices are present and prepare for their use by way of the Inquiry, Read Capacity, Mode Sense and Mode Select SCSI commands.

Most CCS-compliant devices also implement some "vendor unique" commands to take best advantage of certain hardware features and to provide useful functions not defined in the SCSI spec. This approach makes SCSI an "open interface" since it allows the introduction of new device types which can still be called "SCSI-compliant". While this keeps SCSI flexible, it often makes a device driver contain code specific to the devices for which it was written. Hence, a "plug and play" capability is not necessarily true for some advanced device features.

SCSI Error Handling

The SCSI standard requires a SCSI device to automatically and transparently handle media errors. This implies that the media will appear flawless to the host. Hence, all error correcting codes (ECC), retries and defect management must be performed by hardware and firmware within a device. Addresses based on cylinder, head and sector number are replaced by logical block numbers which range from zero to some maximum value.

The result of this architecture is simple and generic error handling software in the device driver. This concept also makes it easy to add support for new SCSI devices. This is an important point if it becomes necessary to change optical device vendors and/or include support for other vendors' products.

SCSI Port Implementations

Some computers have implemented a SCSI port on a standard system board or on their motherboard. SCSI is available in this manner on the newer Sun Microsystems computers and on all but the oldest Apple Macintosh computers. SCSI is also available in the form of a host adapter. The latter is a plug-in board which adapts the computer's bus to the SCSI bus by way of a SCSI chip and usually some on-board firmware.

The recent availability of highly powerful second generation SCSI chips has simplified the job of implementing the hardware and firmware to handle the SCSI bus protocol. This is because much of what was always required to be implemented in software is now implemented on the chips themselves. Hence, the software to control each SCSI node is greatly simplified. In addition, performance is improved due to the speed of on-chip firmware and the reduction in the number of interrupts required for a SCSI command to complete.

Assessing SCSI Device Features

Because SCSI has so much potential for robustness in implementation, it is important to know what to look for when reading a SCSI specification, and how to understand the ways in which vendors mislead with statistics. The most confusing figures concern data transfer rates because they vary depending on how they are measured. Variables include:

- Burst vs. sustained
- Internal vs. external
- Writing vs. reading data
- With or without ECC bytes
- With or without bad blocks being remapped
- If media is formatted as M-CAV, inner vs. outer track

Today, all mature SCSI devices have firmware which is compliant with SCSI-1 and with CCS Rev. 4.B. Device features to look for include:

- Support of disconnect/reconnect
- A large data buffer (cache) on the controller board
- Sophisticated management of the SCSI bus
- ECC and seek and servo control via multiple microprocessors and/or second generation SCSI chips

In addition, the existence of a fully embedded versus a bridge controller often indicates a mature system design.

The extent of the optional features implemented is worth considering. The vendor's SCSI OEM manual should be obtained, and the presence or absence of the following features determined:

- Disconnect/reconnect control parameters
- Variable retry count
- Changeable SCSI ID
- Copy command (between SCSI devices)
- Start/Stop Unit command
- Prevent/Allow Medium Removal command

Assessing SCSI Host Adapter Features

Unless a SCSI port is already standard in your system, a SCSI host adapter compatible with your system bus will be needed. Features to consider in a host adapter include the following:

- Support of disconnect/reconnect
- Ability to be a bus target as well as an initiator
- Existence of an on-board buffer to allow use of the host bus only in bursts
- Multitasking capability via command mailboxes (this is not applicable to MS-DOS; it is important for multitasking operating systems such as OS/2, Unix, and VAX/VMS)

This list demonstrates that host adapter features deserve assessment just as optical drive features since there can be a great deal of variance in the robustness of the on-board firmware.

The Future of SCSI

SCSI is becoming highly popular. The number of vendors using SCSI is growing by 50 percent each year, and the number of products by 100 percent each year. Over 50 percent of the SCSI market is for the Macintosh, and Apple's SCSI CD-ROM drive is expected to have a tremendous impact on CD-ROM's growth.

IBM is expected to start shipping a high-speed SCSI host adapter for their PS/2 Micro Channel Architecture (MCA) bus this year. This board would mark IBM's first endorsement of SCSI. At the Fall 1988 Comdex Exposition, a prototype of this board was demonstrated with a number of SCSI devices including a Maxtor M-O drive and an Apple CD-ROM drive. This board is reportedly able to transfer data at a rate of 5MB/sec, the estimated upper limit of SCSI-1.

What makes this board particularly interesting is that it will be one of the first boards to take advantage of MCA's bus-master capability, its most advanced feature. This capability allows the main system processor to temporarily relinquish control of the system bus so that a processor on an expansion board can use the bus for high-speed data transfers. The board is said to use a second generation Adaptec SCSI chip. Adaptec itself has a board with similar capabilities.

In addition, the SCSI-2 specification is nearing completion. SCSI-2 is virtually a superset of SCSI-1 and the CCS. It defines a standard command set for magnetic disk and tape, printers, processors, WORM, CD-ROM, jukeboxes and scanners. SCSI-2 will make it possible for these devices to transfer data to each other over the SCSI bus without the need for intermediate host buffering with a standard Copy command. The Copy command allows for capabilities such as the transfer of data from a scanner directly to an optical disk. Such a capability will be immensely powerful since scanners are often used in optical storage environments.

SCSI-2 also allows for 16- and 32-bit wide data paths, permitting 20-24MB/sec transfer rates to be realized when integrated SCSI-2 chips hit the market. Access to these features, along with smarter firmware in vendor-embedded controllers, will allow device drivers to easily harness advanced capabilities in new devices, optical and otherwise, with minimal effort. The result of all this is the reduction of the traditional I/O bottleneck.

Conclusion

SCSI creates a standard interface for a multitude of computer peripherals. It removes the requirement for intimate knowledge of a device's characteristics by the device integrator. SCSI provides for savings in software development costs and required host board slots. It also provides a gateway to an ever more diverse and otherwise incompatible set of devices. The growth of SCSI is consistent with the industry's continuous trend toward miniaturization and distributed processing.

15
An Open Software Architecture for Storage Device Integration

LARRY W. HOLMSTROM

WORM data storage provides important new capabilities to the personal computer and offers significant new application opportunities to the personal computer user. Although WORM drives have been integrated into currently available systems, they have not received wide acceptance. Instead, WORM has been used in specialized turnkey applications. In order for WORM to receive wide user acceptance, three developments must occur. First, the WORM drive must decrease in price to a point approximately equivalent to a 100MB hard disk drive. Second, WORM media must be less than $50 for a 1GB disk. Third, new software is required.To achieve wide acceptance of WORM-based applications, new software must be prepared and standardized. Software required to support the WORM drive include new operating system functions, enhanced device drivers, file managers and applications support. Issues relating to these software developments are discussed in this chapter.

System Input/Output and SCSI

WORM technology is not likely to be the primary storage system in the personal computer, but will remain an auxiliary storage device. New operating systems and applications demand access to a resident, high-performance, read/write storage device. Normally, this device is a magnetic hard disk. Other data storage devices such as WORM are added to the personal computer as needed. These ancillary storage devices present an interesting challenge to system manufacturers.

The current trend for personal computer manufacturers is to lower the price and size or footprint of the system unit. This is often accomplished by minimizing the number of feature slots in the system unit. This approach saves both space and power. An example is IBM's PS/2

Model 50, a high-performance 80286-based system which has only three feature slots. One slot is used for the memory expansion necessary for OS/2 (which requires a minimum of 1.5MB of RAM). One of the two remaining slots is often used by the local area network adapter. This leaves only a single adapter slot to be used for all add-on peripheral devices such as a WORM drive. Thus, many new personal computers are effectively "single slot" systems.

In the past, each device attached to a personal computer required its own adapter. Peripheral expansion was made by using additional adapters. Personal computers had adequate slots for this expansion, but this is clearly not feasible on the new "single slot" personal computers. Fortunately, the Small Computer System Interface (SCSI) provides a ready solution. SCSI allows the daisy-chaining of up to seven devices on a single adapter. In this manner, many external devices may be attached to a small footprint, low-cost single slot system.

Many data storage peripheral devices developed in the past few years have been offered with a SCSI interface. All personal computers have access to a SCSI interface either through an onboard SCSI port as is the case with the Apple Macintosh, or through adapter cards on IBM-compatible PC's. Through SCSI, the user has access to a multitude of peripherals which provide expansion to the basic system configuration.

The SCSI Hardware Challenge

The electrical interface of the SCSI standard is well-defined. The SCSI signal lines, functional sequences and their electrical characteristics are standardized and well-accepted. Problems exist with the connector definition because of an inadequate connector which fits on the personal computer adapter bulkhead plate. Assuming agreement can be reached on the number of supported pins (50 or 60), this problem has been solved with the definition and availability of the SCSI-2 connector. While important, connector differences can be resolved using adapter cables. Therefore, clear solutions exist for a SCSI hardware standard which can support auxilliary devices such as a WORM drive.

The SCSI Software Challenge

Many SCSI peripherals are available to the personal computer. However, these peripherals have caused a significant problem in the creation of supporting software device drivers. A subset of the SCSI commands, the Common Command Set (CCS), was created to address this problem. While the CCS is well-defined, data and command content for the structure is very general and open-ended. The SCSI standard describes which commands are suggested for each class of peripheral, but the peripheral manufacturer has a number of options in deciding which commands to implement. Even the "standard commands" have vendor unique fields. In addition, vendors may create their own unique commands.

This flexibility in the SCSI standard has provided an elastic interface to the peripheral manufacturers. The architecture of the SCSI interface is sufficiently general to allow for the invention of new SCSI devices which have not been considered in the past. The acceptance of SCSI as a generalized interface provides a solid platform for growth into the 1990's. **However, the SCSI software problem remains: to create drivers with an architecture of sufficient flexibility to complement the flexibility of the SCSI hardware standard**.

Software drivers are required in a computer to "drive" the hardware. The SCSI software driver problem was first created when IBM defined BIOS (Basic Input/Output System) for the personal computer and Microsoft wrote the drivers supplied with MS-DOS. These drivers and the associated BIOS assumed a traditional approach to peripherals in which each device has its own adapter. There was no sharing of adapters by peripherals with differing device characteristics. The BIOS provided no support for separate software driver modules to "cooperate" through the usage of a common BIOS function and adapter. When daisy-chaining a diverse set of devices on a common SCSI adapter, this type of cooperation is necessary. As a result, whenever a new SCSI device is added to an existing SCSI chain, a new driver which combines the requirements for the new mixture of devices must be written and tested. The number of combinations can become very large.

The SCSI problem is easily described by relating our experience in using SCSI as an interface to our Bernoulli Box products. In 1980, we selected SCSI as the interface to connect the Bernoulli Box to the personal computer. In this environment, we provided a SCSI adapter which supported only our Bernoulli Box. There was no consideration of including devices other than a Bernoulli Box on the SCSI daisy-chain. A software driver was written and refined over a period of years to support the Bernoulli Box. Techniques were developed to create software drivers that allowed the removable high-capacity Bernoulli data cartridge to emulate a non-removable hard disk in such a manner that almost all software can use the Bernoulli Box with no changes to the application.

In 1985, we began to experience the SCSI driver problem. At that time, the Bernoulli Box Plus was developed which combined the Bernoulli Drives and an 80 megabyte hard file into a single subsystem. All devices had a SCSI interface and could share the common SCSI interface adapter card. This simple sharing of two similar but different devices required a rewrite and retesting of our software drivers at a price of over $200,000. The rewrite was caused by the need to implement a "traffic cop" function which allowed two device types to share a common adapter.

In 1987, we added CD-ROM support to the SCSI device driver. Microsoft's MS-DOS CD-ROM Extensions were used, but their use required a modification to the Iomega SCSI driver. Additional programming and testing were required. The problem of creating a new driver for every combination of attached devices was added a significant cost to product development. Product testing of new drivers has proven to be an even larger cost than programming. Clearly a SCSI driver software solution requires attention to both programming and testing expenses.

In 1987, we examined the wide proliferation of SCSI devices, the number of systems which could support SCSI and the trend in personal computers toward a low-cost, small footprint "single slot" system. A massive software driver problem was beginning to emerge. Due to the flexibility of the SCSI standard, wide variations of function were being provided by different manufacturers of the same class of systems. In addition, since the number of slots was decreasing, a slot would probably not exist on the new systems for our adapter. Thus, the luxury of having our own adapter and software driver support the Bernoulli Box would no longer exist after 1988.

A survey of available SCSI systems, peripherals and operating systems was conducted. At that time approximately 137 peripherals, 20 subsystems, and six operating systems were identified. Using the driver architectures prevalent in the industry and currently used by ourselves, over 9000 different peripheral, system and adapter combinations would have to be programmed and tested. A sizing of the resources required to provide complete driver attachability was between 150 and 200 person-years of system programming and testing. We found that new product development was rated not by the ability to develop a data storage peripheral, but by the ability to create the required software drivers. Clearly, a new solution was required.

The Open Architecture Drivers™ Solution

We defined a new software driver architecture to support SCSI and other peripherals. This new advanced approach to driver development resulted in the Open Architecture Drivers which support a wide variety of devices (see Figure 1). The Open Architecture Drivers provide a "building block" approach to SCSI drivers. This software "mix and match" building block capability complements the mix-and-match capability of SCSI.

Our analysis showed the need of the architecture to partition drivers into three functional areas. A series of driver kernels support a number of different operating systems including MS-DOS, OS/2, Unix, Novell, and Apple. These kernels are loaded as device drivers in the normal

Figure 1. Open Architecture Drivers — 1989 and Beyond

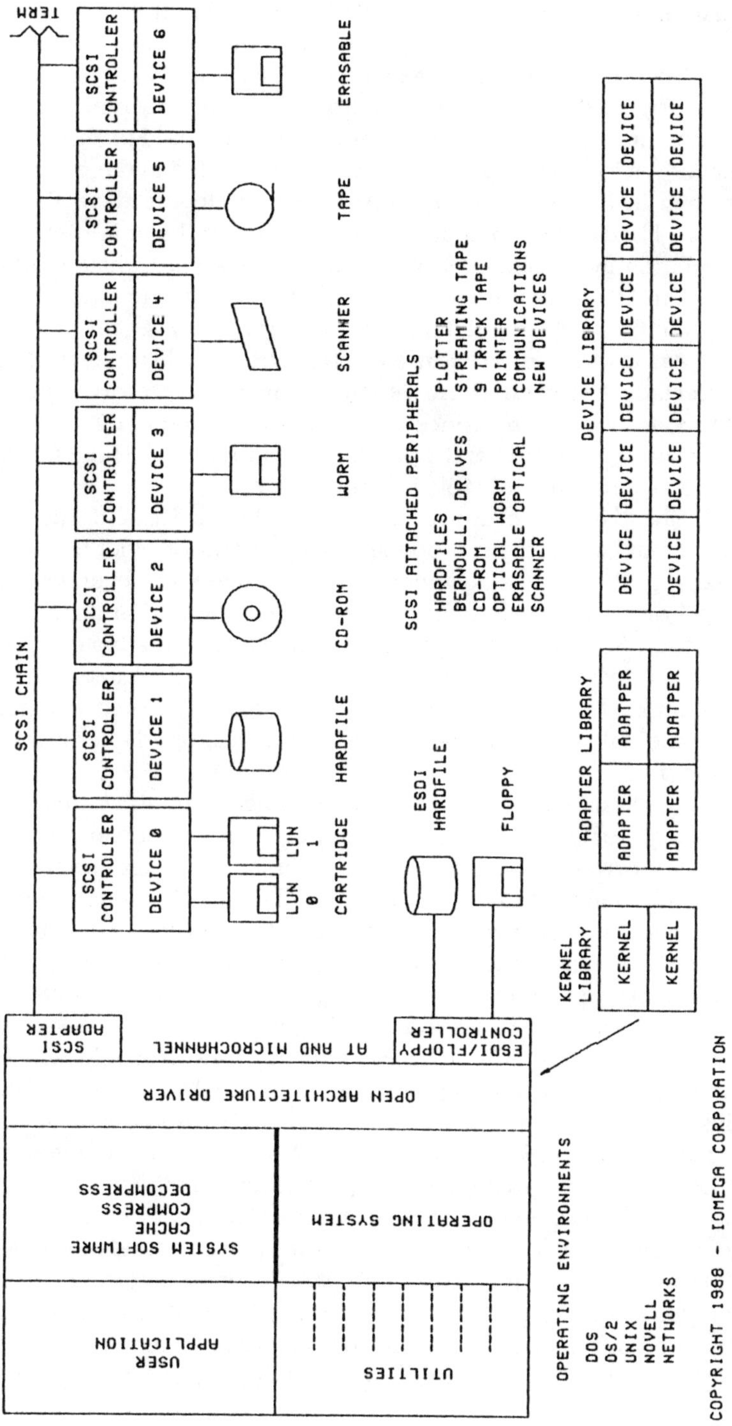

manner by providing a "DEVICE=" command in the CONFIG.SYS file for the system. Each operating system uses a different software driver kernel.

The other functional areas define device and adapter characteristics. The driver kernels are supported by device and adapter "tables". The tables contain all of the specific information required to support the adapters or devices. This information is not embedded in the driver kernels. As shown in Figure 1, the Open Architecture Drivers allow the user to access a library of adapter and device tables and driver kernels. A user configuration file is created which instructs the kernel which tables are to be used and how they are interconnected. The user can have several configuration files selecting different devices or functions.

An important attribute of the tables and the kernel is that the interface between them is the same for different operating systems. In other words, once a device or an adapter table is written, it can be shared across several operating environments. Thus, the creation of the adapter or device table is a one-time effort.

The partition of function between the device and adapter tables is such that each table can operate independent of other tables. For example, if a device table is written, it can operate with several adapters ranging from a simple low-function SCSI bus translation adapter to a high-function SCSI bus master adapter. Conversely, an adapter table will support all device tables. The kernel insures that the tables cannot and do not interact. Each table can thus be written and tested independently of all other tables. The addition of a new device or adapter is a simple one-time process.

No assembly language programming is required since the kernels and adapter tables can be written in C. Their creation and maintenance is straightforward. There is almost no limitation to the amount or type of function that the tables can provide. All tables are written following a fully specified state machine approach. The kernels use protected mode when operating on 286 and 386 class systems. The integrity of the system is thus maintained in a multi-tasking operating environment.

The kernels and associated adapter tables can support a wide range of adapter types. SCSI adapter chips are now available which will provide low-cost system implementation. A single chip is available costing less than $10 to interface the AT bus to SCSI. A two-chip set is available costing less than $15 to interface the Micro Channel Architecture to SCSI. These chips are low-function chips that serve as "bus translators".

Effective operation of SCSI requires drivers to be multi-tasking and multi-threaded. The Open Architecture Driver kernels provide this multi-tasking, multi-threaded capability. Where higher function and bus master adapters are used, the multi-tasking, multi-threading capability is invoked in the adapter, to free the operating system for other tasks. The Open Architecture kernels support both types of adapters. Adapters may operate in DMA or PIO modes, and as I/O or memory-mapped devices.

Pseudo Devices

An additional feature of the Open Architecture Driver is the creation of tables which define "Pseudo" devices. Pseudo devices are devices for which a physical device is not defined directly. The pseudo device notion provides for the creation of device tables that can support advanced device functions such as duplex or shadow writing of the same data to multiple peripherals. These notions can be expanded due to the complete flexibility in the creation of device tables. As an example, the following elements together would allow the automatic shadow writing of data to a network file server:

- adapter table for the network
- adapter table for a SCSI host adapter
- device table for the SCSI devices
- device table for the network server
- device table defining the pseudo device.

Other pseudo devices might combine a magnetic read-write device with a WORM device. This combination could allow a WORM drive to operate in a sequential character mode (variable length record) device, while the directory could be updated continually and maintained on the magnetic device. A removable cartridge could house both the magnetic (Bernoulli Cartridge) and WORM device to support this approach.

Device Support Utilities

Additional utilities can be attached to the Open Architecture Driver kernel. These utilities can implement functions such as cache, compression, decompression, encryption, and decryption. Attaching these functions to the driver kernel allows all attached devices and adapters to be supported. Thus, a single cache can support optical, magnetic or network devices.

Jukebox Support

The availability of small data cartridges introduces the capability of low-cost desktop jukeboxes. The jukebox is similar to ganged devices for which a pseudo device table is prepared to link multiple devices together as a single contiguous drive. The Open Architecture Driver pseudo device tables can support ganged devices. This ganging can be extended to jukebox support where the changing of the cartridge is handled as a device table transparent to the operating system.

SCSI device drivers which provide a mix-and-match selection of software modules complement the mix-and-match capability of the SCSI interface. With access to mix-and-match driver such as an Open Architecture Driver, the WORM user can share a single slot with other peripherals.

Operating Systems

New operating system functions are becoming available to support WORM drives. A WORM drive can support multiple hundred megabyte or gigabyte capacity files. Several hours of processing with high-performance 16- or 32-bit processors are typically required to process files of this size. A multi-tasking capability is most important to allow a background task to spend many hours performing these large processing jobs without requiring a dedicated personal computer. Access to multitasking on the high-performance system will allow the movement of data preparation from the mainframe and mini-computer systems to the personal computer.

The 8088 class desktop personal computer systems represents the major portion of the existing personal computers. These systems do not have sufficient performance to process large files but could be used with WORM drives for accessing pre-prepared data.

Optical drives provide storage capacities significantly greater than the 32MB limitations which exist in DOS 3.x and OS/2 1.0. DOS 4.x and OS/2 1.1+ break the 32MB barrier necessary to support the huge capacities of WORM media. These new operating systems are required for successful WORM applications.

File Managers

Closely associated with the new operating systems is the notion of more advanced file managers. MS-DOS and the early versions of OS/2 supported only the file structures that were associated with the magnetic read/write capabilities of the hard disk and the floppy diskette. These structures do not fit well with new peripherals such as the WORM drive. New file managers must be prepared which handle the write-once and archival nature of WORM applications. These new file systems must be installable on the operating system to support the WORM drive. Operating systems need to be extended where multiple file managers can attach to the operating system in order to support different peripheral devices. The user must be able to load the appropriate file system required for the format of the WORM disk being used. File systems must be capable of residing in any of the system memory including DOS extended memory.

An example of an early file manager is the Microsoft MS-DOS CD-ROM Extensions. These Extensions mapped the High Sierra logical format of the CD-ROM into the MS-DOS magnetic disk format to make the CD-ROM appear as another hard disk. The CD-ROM was assigned a drive letter and could then be accessed by any MS-DOS read-only application. Additional variations to the original High Sierra Format were also proposed including the CD-I (Compact Disc-Interactive) format. These variations require additional file managers to be defined. Multiple file structures and associated file managers are important requirements for systems working with optical data storage devices, especially WORM peripherals.

File managers and file format structures need to be extended to multiple file systems, particularly those that have been created to handle WORM's write-once nature. A number of such file systems have been created since WORM devices became available, and these often emulate the re-writability of magnetic media. WORM technology has an inherent archiving capability in which old or archived copies of the same file may exist on a cartridge. The WORM file manager must be capable of retrieving past versions of the same file. This capability does not exist for magnetic devices.

The WORM file structure has another requirement which differs from the normal magnetic hard file. The magnetic file structures provide for a directory and file allocation table (FAT) controlling the location of all file segments on the disk. Successful access to a hard disk file requires access to the directory. If the directory is compromised, the file can be unrecoverable since it may be scattered over the disk surface in individual data clusters. These clusters can be combined into a file only by way of the directory.

An additional requirement for file systems working with WORM devices is support of removability. The common usage of the non-removable hard disk has resulted in many applications and systems not considering the notion of removable media, but optical devices are removable. Removability must be supported in the operating system and its associated device drivers.

File System Standardization

Multiple standards are being discussed to support WORM devices. Although this is an excellent effort and should be pursued, standards work takes so much time that users and peripheral and system vendors will often create solutions before the standard has been accepted. Multiple WORM file systems will be used until the standards have been able to catch up with immediate needs. The installable file system capability can minimize the effect of the standards delay. With installable file systems, the user supporting multiple devices with different file formats can load a file manager for each file structure. As standards emerge, the number of file managers can be minimized as more and more systems implement the standard. However, the reading of archived WORM disks will require access to previously defined file systems.

Some of the file systems and structures which have been proposed for standardization include the following:

1. The generic file system for CD-ROM proposed by the High Sierra Group. With slight modifications this has become the ISO 9660 Standard. (The Microsoft MS-DOS CD-ROM Extensions map this format into the MS-DOS file system.)

2. A direct access structure for WORM which simulates the characteristics of a magnetic disk.

3. A sequential access structure for WORM which simulates the characteristics of a streaming tape.

4. A combination file structure supporting a WORM drive with a magnetic drive. The directory structure is maintained on the magnetic drive and user data is written to the WORM disk.

5. A file structure to support arrays of optical drives ganged together to span multiple gigabytes of storage. (Editor's note: See Chapter 13.)

6. A file structure to support digital data, audio and video on the same disk.

Most data is normally processed before it is ready for archiving. As such, file systems which support the manipulation of data on a rewritable magnetic or optical device will normally be used before data is stored on WORM media. A file management structure that can automate this process in an application transparent manner is required.

Conclusion

The SCSI architecture provides a powerful base for developing flexible device drivers. The greatest flexiblity can be realized by allowing a diverse set of peripherals to simultaneously use a common device driver and a common SCSI host adapter card. WORM technology will have its greatest impact only if standardized software providing operating system transparency becomes widely available. Without such software, WORM will not be able to achieve wide acceptance and will be relegated to specialized applications.

SECTION VI
OPTICAL STANDARDS

16
Current Status of Optical Media Standards

KEN HALLAM

The American National Standards Institute (ANSI), through its Accredited Standards Committee (ASC) X3B11, is attempting to establish formal standards for the interchange of optical disks.

The committee is composed of about 60 member companies with about 100 people who attend the meetings with some regularity. Members are mostly from the hardware side of the industry, but an increasing number of new members are from the software side. Meetings are held about once every two months with smaller working groups occasionally meeting more often. Activity is coordinated with another standards organization, the International Standards Organization (ISO), headquartered in Geneva, Switzerland.

The committee has several active projects for optical media broken out by disk diameter and media type, plus a separate project on file structures. Nearest to completion are the 5.25-inch projects.

The committee has four projects for 5.25-inch media — three for WORM and one for erasable optical media. There are two projects for 3.5-inch erasable optical media, one for 12-inch WORM media, and one for 14-inch WORM media.

5.25-inch WORM Media

Each of the three WORM projects describe a form of optical disk recording that cannot be interchanged with the other two. These types are known as Continuous Composite Servo (CCS), Sampled Servo with 4/15 modulation, and Sampled Servo with RZ modulation. Each type has its supporters.

A brief summary of the physical features of each type is given below:

Feature	CCS	Sampled 4/15	Sampled RZ
Servo	Continuous Groove	Sampled Pits	Sampled Pits
Modulation	RLL 2,7	4/15	RZ
ECC	LDC	Product Code	LDC
Clock	Modulation Code	Special Pits	Special Pits
Track Pitch	1.60 μm	1.50 μm	Variable
Capacity/side	300MB	320MB	450MB

All three methods have been described in draft documents, and voted on and approved by a majority of the committee members. The proposed standards will all undergo a period of review by X3, the parent committee, followed by a period of public review and comment before being published as official ANSI standards.

CCS supporters include Maxtor, Hewlett-Packard, Olympus, Hitachi, Fujitsu, Mitsubishi, Optotech and Matsushita. Sampled 4/15 supporters include LMSI, Pioneer, Hitachi, and Philips. Sampled RZ supporters include ISi and Honeywell.

5.25-inch Erasable Media

This project has only the CCS format proposed. It is based on the 5.25-inch WORM CCS but there are a few differences to account for the magneto-optic (M-O) nature of the read-write process. The goal of the committee was to allow a dual function drive that could handle both WORM and erasable CCS media. Such a drive would most likely be more expensive than one designed for only one or the other type of media; NTT (Nippon Telephone and Telegraph) demonstrated an early prototype of a multi-functional drive at an IEEE conference in 1988.

The optical erasable documents include a fairly extensive chapter on defect management which details how a scheme for defective sector retirement should be implemented. This project was near completion on the technical work at the beginning of 1989. It is likely that the erasable optical media draft document will be voted upon by the committee and approved to enter the review and comment phase by mid-1989.

As demonstrated at the Fall 1988 Comdex show in Las Vegas, a number of erasable optical drives are finally coming to market. These drives generally follow the proposed CCS erasable standard. However, the Canon M-O drive used in the NeXT Computer does not.

Pioneer 5.25-inch erasable optical disk and cartridge (Courtesy Pioneer Communications of America)

12-inch WORM Media

As there are already so many 12-inch optical media products on the market, it is unlikely that any manufacturer will change their product to conform to a new standard unless it offers some real advantages. For this reason, the 12-inch WORM project is not aimed at the present generation of products but instead is building on the concept of a new generation of 12-inch media that will not be compatible with any of the many existing formats. Work had only begun at the end of 1988 and project participants have estimated a completion date of 1990 or 1991.

14-inch WORM Media

This is a standard with little controversy since only the Eastman Kodak Company has built a 14-inch drive at this time. The draft standard is at the same position of the 5.25-inch erasable standard. It is about to go to a ballot by the technical committee, and then, if approved, forwarded to the review and comment phase.

ANSI X3B11 Committee Documents

5.25-inch WORM Media

Number	Name
X3B11/86-151R9	130mm WORM Media with Continuous Composite Servo (CCS)
X3B11/87-010	130mm WORM Media with Sampled Servo and 4/15 Modulation.
X3B11/88-192	130mm WORM Media with Sampled Servo and RZ Recording.

5.25-inch Erasable Media

X3B11/88-094R3	130mm Rewritable Media, Continuous Composite Servo (CCS).

File Structure and Labeling

X3B11/86-152	Optical Disk Logical Labels and File Structure (obsolete)
X3B11.1/89-XXX (number to be assigned in 1989)	Optical Media Volume and File Structure

17
File Structure Standards

KEITH GUNN

The components of an optical drive most completely described in reference manuals are:

- drive and cartridge dimensions
- format of data on disk (sector sizes, bit spacing, track format, reserved sectors, etc.)
- electronic interface (timing and other electronic details)
- software interface (commands, bus manipulation, and data transfer)

It has been viewed as desirable that all of these become standardized. Users frequently cite the "lack of standards" as a deterrent to buying products using optical disks. At the same time, users are unsure about what to ask for in this area. One senses that if Wang, FileNet, Plexus, and other integrators announced that Laser Magnetic Storage International (LMS) disks written on any of their systems could be read on any others, this would be a much more important announcement than that Maxell media would work in both Sony and Matsushita drives. On the whole, though, the standards effort is far from achieving any of the goals alluded to above.

Standardization is one field in which "Rome is not made in a day." So far, the ANSI (American National Standards Institute) X3B11 committee has produced a draft standard for cartridges for 5.25-inch media, and there may soon be a standard for labels. In all, there are 15 draft standards being worked on by ANSI X3B11.[1]

One of the most interesting areas for standardization is called "Logical Labels and File Structure for Digital File Exchange." "Label," in this context, means two different sorts of entities. One, the volume label (a volume is one side of an optical disk), holds information such as who wrote on the disk, when, on what system, and so forth. If the disk is logically divided into partitions, it will be necessary to create a standard for a

[1]Editor's note: See Chapter 16 for a list of ANSI X3B11 Committee Documents.

partition label to identify the locations of the partitioned regions.

ANSI also uses the term "file label" to refer to an on-disk structure that points to the locations of a file. Others have referred to the same thing through the concept of a "disk directory." In ANSI parlance, a directory entry is composed of a number of labels, one for the beginning and end of each extent of the file on the disk. File labels are stored in their own small region of the disk surface, away from the files. In the ANSI standard, they contain everything that is normally found in a Unix inode, i.e., owner and group identification, creation date and time, and more. But, like an inode, their primary function is to point to the file's logical addresses on disk.

The label structure is being standardized by ANSI through draft standard X3B11/86-152.[2] If two systems vendors agreed to support this standard, and if they both used the same model and make of drive, a large step would have been taken toward a situation in which a disk could be written by one system and read by [an]other.

The ANSI standard carefully distinguishes between a file system and a file structure. A file system is a portion of an operating system. It provides calls through which other operating system portions can be interfaced to it. A file structure is a method of arranging files on a disk's surface, within the constraints provided by the write-once disk, its sector lay-out, its limitations of writing a sector at a time, and so forth.

Another step, involving the writing of some interface code, would need to be taken before data would be fully interchangeable between the two systems. For this step, there are both operating system and file organization issues. One must consider how to translate between two systems the coded data which comprises the indexing information for each database. Standards committees could solve part of this problem through invoking a standard operating system like Unix. Then the data on the disk in the file labels could be captured into the Unix data structures (inodes and directory entries) when the file system is mounted, and/or written out when the disk is dismounted. However, this will not by itself address the application layer, which will differ from supplier to supplier, if only in the database which stores the index information.

Systems which incorporate jukeboxes require yet a higher level of software to catalog all the files stored in the disk collection.

Data Requirements and Optical Storage Data Structures

A complete optical storage solution needs to meet these requirements:

1. A disk must have self-contained data. That is, when the disk is

[2]Editors' note: This document is now obsolete.

brought to a compatible system that otherwise knows nothing about it, the disk must contain enough information about its own contents to allow the files to be cataloged and retrieved.

2. The system must store files reliably; that is, it must limit data damage when a system crash takes place during writing.

3. The file structure must allow for files that span more than one disk (called "continuation and striping.")

4. The operating system must support multiple copies of a given file (a file and its backups) on more than one optical disk or disk collection.

These are the firm requirements. There are many other desirable features, such as random access to a specified sector within a file, multiuser/multitasking capability, quasi-contiguous writing, transaction integrity, security, and accounting.

Conclusion

Different vendors' products manage information on optical disk differently because:

- no single product-oriented vendor dominated the early adoption of systems using optical disks.
- it is still early in the cycle of adoption of optical disks and jukeboxes.
- new ways of thinking are necessary to cope with a write-once storage device of enormous capacity.
- a file structure that exhibits high performance for one file size exhibits low performance for another.

There has been some speculation that IBM's entry into the systems market will cause offerings to center around IBM's supposed de facto standards. But there is little incentive for users with systems already installed to change to a new file format at this late date. Also, the use of optical disks for archival applications may never require data interchange standards.

However, there may be room to support an emerging standard for smaller disks (3.5-inch, perhaps), which are interchanged freely between users as a more robust, larger capacity "floppy disk."

18

Optotech Systems Architecture (OSA): A File System Architecture for Removable Optical Media

EDWARD BESHORE

Editors' Note: The OSA file system format is based on work and implementations performed by Optotech over a two-year period from 1986-1988. It was submitted to the ANSI File and Labels Committee as a working paper in August 1988 and to ECMA as ECMA document ECMA/TC15/88/12A in September 1988.

The OSA proposal was updated in late 1988 and formally presented to ANSI on January 23, 1989. The latest copy of the OSA proposal is available from Optotech at: Optotech, Inc., 740 Wooten Road, Colorado Springs, CO 80915 Attn: Edward Beshore (719.570.7500).

This is the first of a series of papers. Part II (not presented here) provides a detailed description of the OSA file system format. Subsequent papers will describe the operating system and low-level driver interface specifications and the details and conventions of logical file exchange.

Abstract

Optical media, both write-once and erasable, present numerous opportunities for capabilities that have not yet been fully attained. Optical media also presents unique challenges for the systems integrator who would exploit its benefits. This paper introduces [the] OSA, an architecture that implements a file system for both WORM and erasable optical drives. [The] OSA has been designed to provide full access to the potential of optical, and to relieve the difficulties associated with the technology.

Introduction

Today, most professionals in the computer industry are familiar with the promises of optical disk technology. Nevertheless, much confusion exists about what optical can and cannot do.

Write-once-read-many (WORM) technology was the first to come on the commercial scene a few years ago. Characterized by its ability to write data only once, WORM technology immediately found friends in those users who had a need to store data on an unalterable medium. Banks, government and insurance all have requirements for archival, permanent storage and the implicit version control WORM offers. At the same time, there were users who wished for the removability and storage density of optical, but could not economically or practically justify the tremendous consumption of optical media that WORM would force them to make.

Recent developments in erasable optical media now promise to provide a solution for users with more conventional data storage requirements. Retaining the removability and density of WORM, magneto-optic (M-O) disks can be written and erased an arbitrarily large number of times.[1]

It would seem that with this development that the path is clear for the optical drive industry. By supplying drives integrated with a popular peripheral interface, such as the Small Computer Systems Interface (SCSI), drop in replacements for existing magnetic drives would be possible. To a large extent this is true. Firmware for erasable drives can be configured to make them appear identical to conventional magnetic drives. M-O drives do, however, require that sectors be erased before they can be rewritten. This erase pass introduces a delay because media must spin twice under the optical head, once for the erase pass and once to write the data.

A *file system format* is a convention with which an operating system organizes sectors on a storage device. In this way the more complex structures of files, volume labels and directories are kept on a device like an optical drive. Likewise, *file system software* is the programming that resides inside of a computer operating system that implements the file system format.

File systems for WORM drives, because of their write-once nature, are not so easily constructed. Special software must be written that is aware of the fact that sectors can only be written once. Many WORM drive companies, and some third party firms, have written software that does just this, making WORM drives appear to be like any other erasable drive. This does involve the development of special disk formats, for which there are no commonly accepted standards.

Finally, some operating systems do not provide adequate mechanisms for properly managing removable media without some risk to the

[1]This should be contrasted with erasable disks that employ *phase change* media, which do have an upper limit to the number of write cycles they can sustain.

users data, UNIX being the most notable example. This further complicates the task of the systems integrator and value added reseller, and discourages those who would integrate optical into their products.

It seems that while the promise of optical is very real, that there are still some technical issues that remain in order for it to become an effective force in the mass storage industry. **It is the contention of this author that a simple file system format and interface standard can both mitigate some of the aforementioned difficulties with write-once and erasable while at the same time exploiting its promising characteristics.** [In this series of papers, the complete specification for such a file system, the Optotech Systems Architecture (OSA), will be introduced.]

WORM File Systems

One of the challenges with optical is the need to design a file system for WORM drives that provides an interface to both applications and users that appears updatable and erasable. (e.g., for an MS-DOS system, a drive should appear as "D:", for UNIX a drive should be a mountable file system, and for Macintosh a drive should appear as just another icon.)

One approach to providing such a solution involves tricking the existing file system by introducing a second level of indirection to the mechanisms which point to sectors or clusters of sectors on a disk. As sectors are referenced, the initial sector address is looked up in a table to find a physical location on disk. As sectors are updated, this table entry is modified to reflect the address of the newly written sector. The advantage of this approach is speed and relative ease of implementation, since such a mechanism can be employed at the physical interface level, which is where most operating systems allow user written device drivers. These techniques are also often capable of high performance. The disadvantage of this approach is that such implementations are specific to the native file system, discouraging transport to other machines. This technique can also be wasteful of disk space, especially in those systems that "cluster" sectors, like MS-DOS.

An alternative approach is to "capture" requests for file system accesses at the file open/close/read/write level. This allows the physical disk format to be independent of the host machine, promising interchange. Media conservation and highest throughput are also advantages of this method. On the other hand, file-level implementations require "hooks" into an operating system that are often not available. Fortunately, the trend in modern operating systems is to provide these hooks, primarily for the use of networks. Example[s] of such mechanisms are SUN's Network File System (NFS) and the UNIX 5.3 Remote File System (RFS).

Systems such as [MS-]DOS do not explicitly provide such access, although proven techniques do exist.[2]

Erase Latency

It seems clear today that magneto-optic (M-O) recording is the technology of choice in erasable drives. Able to undergo extremely large numbers of read/write cycles, M-O has demonstrated dramatic improvement in performance in the last 12 months. Nevertheless, inherent in M-O is the requirement to independently erase any written sectors before they can be rewritten. This means that a written sector must pass twice under the optical head to be rewritten, introducing a latency that halves M-O's performance relative to magnetic.

The solution to defeating this described latency is to decouple the erase of a sector from the rewriting of a sector. That is, if a file system kept two lists, a "garbage list" containing sectors to be erased and a "clean list" containing sectors that are erased, writing a sector simply would consist of using sectors off the second list, eliminating the need for an erase pass. Deleting or modifying a sector would consist of merely placing the sector address on the garbage list. When the operating system is not busy, or at times when the user does not demand the performance, erase passes could be performed on sectors in the garbage list and returned to the clean list. In a multi-tasking environment, erase passes could be performed by a low priority background task. Since it is an established responsibility of the file system to keep track of written and unwritten sectors, it is natural that such a mechanism could be part of an optical file system.

Removability

In many operating system environments, updating of disk file system structures is done on a periodic basis. This is often done in multi-tasking/multi-user systems for performance reasons. If a removable medium disk is installed on such a system, premature removal could result in considerable loss of data. It is important that controls be available to physically prevent removal when the file system has pending updates to perform. There are no standards for operating systems to signify to a drive that the medium must not be removed. Nevertheless, this responsibility is a natural chore for the file system. Since the file system software knows when updates are incomplete, it should issue prevent/allow medium removal requests to the drive (providing such functionality is supported) as required to insure the integrity of the medium.

[2]Such as trapping MS-DOS interrupt 21 (hexadecimal).

Logical File Interchange

The ability to remove a high capacity piece of media brings with it the potential for two important capabilities: 1) unlimited total storage capacity at a low cost, and 2) the freedom to move the media to other machines that have similar drives. This has been a feature of tape systems for some time. Indeed, tape is the sole way to routinely move high volumes of data between remote sites. If this same ability were within the domain of random access devices, an unprecedented exchange of data could occur.

The factor which limits the exchange of data between systems that are [not] alike is the format [in] which the data is written. It is standardized formats and programs to read those formats that have allowed the tape industry to exchange data between dissimilar systems. Tape systems remain relatively expensive considering their relatively limited usefulness to exchange and archive. The ability to extend such exchange to random access promises a single device that can be used for conventional data storage needs as well as the exchange and archive functions. With the proper format standards, removable optical media could be exchanged with no consideration for where it came from or where it was going.

Support for Dual-Mode Drives

Engineers suggest that one day drives will be available with the capability to read and write both M-O and WORM media by simply exchanging the cartridge as needs demand. Any file system implementation for optical needs to anticipate this need by providing the necessary functionality for both kinds of media. This will allow the user to pick and chose media according to the requirements of [the] application without requiring a re-initialization of the system or reinstallation of drivers and other devices. The file system must detect the media type and automatically adjust itself.

The Optotech Systems Architecture

Armed with the preceding discussion of the technical systems issues surrounding optical, it is possible to begin defining the characteristics for a file system to address those issues. The

Optotech Systems Architecture (OSA) is a Single File Format that allows:

Logical File Interchange. Extensibility is built into the format to allow for the varying requirements of diverse operating systems and machine architectures.

Random access and sequential. While primarily a highly efficient architecture for erasable and WORM media, [the] OSA will provide high performance in sequential file operations.

Multi-volume sets and striping. To accommodate datasets larger than the media, [the] OSA has hooks to allow for the simultaneous mounting of multiple volumes to form a single file system.

File version control. To accommodate the unique ability of WORM media to recover earlier versions of files, [the] OSA allows both WORM and erasable media to maintain an arbitrarily large number of file versions with each version being independently accessible.

Tagged structures for recovery. With the volumes of information committed to optical media, robust behavior and recoverability are critical to any optical file system. Internal data structures are uniquely tagged to allow recovery in the event of a catastrophic failure of hardware or software.

Efficient. [The] OSA is physical sector oriented, allowing updates to the resolution of the device sector size. Clustering of sectors is supported for those operating systems which require it.

Common to both M-O and WORM. [The] OSA's file structure for erasable is a simplification of the structure it maintains for WORM media. This means that differences between WORM and erasable are limited to a few locations in the file system software. [The] OSA can support automatic switching from WORM to erasable media. Additionally, erasable media can simulate WORM.

Decouple erase from write on M-O media. [The] OSA addresses the M-O erase latency by decoupling erases before writes. Erase passes can be handled at non-critical periods to improve drive throughput. A variety of mechanisms can be used to drive the separate erase pass. (Erase at end of command, erase at media insert/eject, background erase on multi-tasking systems.)

An Interface Specification which defines:

Communication with the operating system. [The] OSA defines a standardized, orthogonal interface which allows easy interface with a variety [of] operating systems.

Communication with the drive interface. [The] OSA also defines a standard interface for drive communication. While device communication is the responsibility of the implementor, [the] OSA defines and limits the required functionality of such low-level drivers.

Portable and small. Written entirely in ANSI "C", OSA's source code size is 3-5 thousand lines, keeping generated code to reasonable limits.

Conclusion

It is the conclusion of this author that much of the promise of optical lies not in the media, but in the file system that uses that media. Many of the popular objections can be eliminated with the same approach. [The] OSA is an architecture that allows practical implementation of these concepts.

Acknowledgments

It is necessary to acknowledge the contributions of those Optotech group members that will make [the] OSA a practical reality. Jeff Dulude started the process of discovery several years ago with the first optical file system here at Optotech. Jim Harper and Todd Putnam applied the lessons and experiences of the early generations of file systems to advance and demonstrate a "second generation" approach to the problem. Useful discussions with Stephen Moraco and Dan Matekja helped to solve several sticky problems. Finally, thanks must go to Margaret Sandor for making the whole thing actually work.

19
The SCSI Connectivity Crisis

THOMAS TEWELL

As the Small Computer Systems Interface (SCSI) becomes more popular, other I/O interfaces are losing market share. However, is the PC market ready for SCSI? Although SCSI is an ANSI standard, a serious problem arises due to the lack of standards for writing SCSI host adapter software to operate SCSI devices. As a result, since most optical devices have a SCSI interface, the integrated optical-based products sold today are usable only with a particular vendor's SCSI host adapter. This chapter investigates this problem and describes how the industry is responding to solve it.

The Winchester Disk Standard

By the mid-1980s, production of Winchester disk drives ("hard drives") became a multi-billion dollar industry. As many PC owners began to use hard drives, the need for cartridge tape drives for backup and data interchange arose. Realizing why it is so easy to integrate a hard drive into the PC environment allows for insight why it is not as easy to integrate SCSI devices.

Integrating a hard drive into the PC environment is easy because of the existence of a well defined hardware register set at the hard drive controller level. When IBM introduced the PC/AT with a hard drive controller, its hardware interface became the industry standard. Anyone who wanted to write an operating system or hard disk interface software could use the same protocol. Every operating system available for the AT (including MS-DOS, Unix, Xenix and OS/2) either uses the disk interrupt interface (software interrupt INT 13H[1]) or communicates with the device at the hardware level. Thus, the standard was born.

The SCSI Interface Problem

The situation with SCSI is quite different. IBM has not yet formally introduced a SCSI host adapter into the PC environment, but a lot of other

[1]The "H" suffix indicates a hexadecimal number.

companies have. The demand for SCSI software has grown as SCSI becomes the predominant interface for optical devices. As this market continues to evolve, developers of operating systems and integrated products are plagued with the problem of writing software that contains an ever-increasing amount of hardware-specific code. Since there is no standard SCSI support in most operating systems, optical product developers have no standard access method. As a result, their software must bypass the operating system and communicate directly with the hardware.

Multitasking operating systems such an Unix usually prohibit application programs from directly accessing the hardware. When this is the case, product developers must write device drivers that follow rules dependent upon the operating system. This creates a problem in that writing device drivers is often beyond the expertise of system integrators.

Once a developer does choose a particular vendor's SCSI host adapter, the software which uses it is married to that board. Hence, device drivers must be developed for various boards in order to have a versatile product. Even different models of boards from a single vendor may not be software compatible. In addition, since some SCSI device features have not yet been standardized, the software may also only work with peripherals from certain vendors. A prime example of the latter is the audio interface of CD-ROM drives. While this is being standardized in SCSI-2, CD-ROM drives today are inter-compatible for data but not for audio.

The problem can be represented as a three-dimensional matrix with SCSI host adapters on the first axis, SCSI devices on the second axis and operating systems on the third. In order to support a number of SCSI host adapters, operating systems and devices, the optical developer is forced to write what could literally be hundreds or thousands of hardware specific pieces of code (or device drivers) for use with an application program.

The Common Access Method (CAM)

The solution to this tremendous problem is obvious: operating systems must have a standard, well defined SCSI entry point that developers can use to send SCSI commands to the host adapter. This is shown in Figure 1 (the HBA boxes represent the host adapters from a number of vendors). If this standard SCSI entry point existed in the most popular operating systems, integrated optical products could be standardized.

Another problem exists regarding who writes the hardware-specific code that is integrated with the operating system. The answer is again obvious: it is the responsibility of the SCSI host adapter manufacturer to provide such a module for integration by the optical product developer or operating system vendor. Many host adapter manufacturers are now doing just that.

Figure 1. An Architecture Providing a Standard SCSI Entry Point (Courtesy Columbia Data Products)

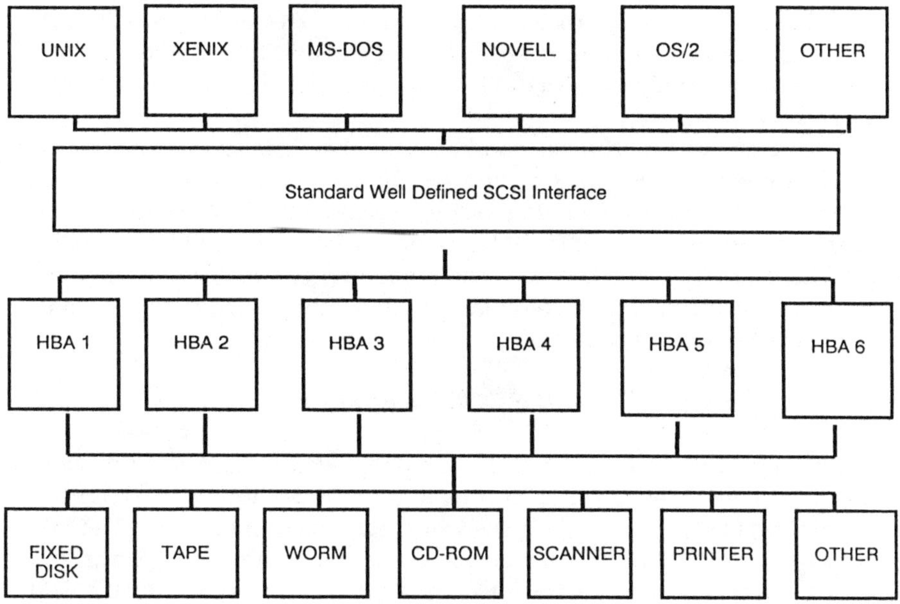

Because this access method problem is not isolated to any one company, the responsibility to create a standard SCSI entry point falls upon the entire PC industry. It affects peripheral, host adapter and operating system vendors, along with computer manufacturers and application developers. The industry has responded by forming an ad hoc committee known as the SCSI-2 Common Access Method (CAM) Committee.

It is the goal of the CAM Committee to define a set of calls and I/O requests to assist developers in writing code to support SCSI in the PC environment. Referring again to Figure 1, the "Standard Well Defined SCSI Interface" is what the CAM Committee refers to as the SCSI Interface Module (SIM). The CAM Committee is defining the details of this SIM.

SIM is defined as a piece of software that is linked with the operating system and executes the SCSI Command Descriptor Block (CDB) passed to it. The caller (a device driver or application program) will set up a request packet structure and pass it to the SIM. As of January, 1989, this request packet structure is not yet completely defined by the CAM Committee.

Although it is logical to try to define a SIM layer that can be common to all operating system environments, it is not practical due to their dissimilarities. For example, address pointer problems arise since some operating systems operate in real mode and others operate in protected mode. To overcome this, both kernel level and user level access to the SIM entry point must be provided. Some operating systems virtualize their memory, creating problems for first-party DMA SCSI host adapters, i.e., host adapters with an on-board DMA capability. In addition, some require multi-threaded operation while others only require a single-threaded mode.

As a result, the general consensus of the CAM committee is that while portions of the SIM structure will be common among the various operating systems, an operating system dependent (OSD) portion will be attached somewhere in the SIM structure. The entry point to the SIM module cannot be standardized. The remainder of this chapter describes some of the problems encountered in integrating SCSI with the most popular PC operating systems.

MS-DOS SCSI Integration

Integrating SCSI into the MS-DOS operating system does not pose any major problems. Since MS-DOS runs in real mode, addresses passed to the SIM will be physical addresses which stay fixed in memory. The SIM is free to use ROM BIOS functions, and it is single-threaded. Hence, it is logical to choose a software interrupt as the entry point into the SIM module. This is the standard access method for device classes, e.g., video functions use INT 10H, disk functions use INT 13H and keyboard functions use INT 16H.

The kernel processes (such as device drivers) are free to use software interrupts. An application program such as a tape backup utility is also free to use software interrupts. The SIM module can be loaded either by a ROM BIOS or by loading a device driver at boot time by way of the CONFIG.SYS file.

The only problem encountered in integrating SCSI with MS-DOS occurs when running an operating environment such as Windows/386 or DESQview/386 on top of MS-DOS. These operating environments place the 80386 processor into virtual mode, changing the addresses from physical to virtual. There is no problem for SCSI host adapters that use programmed I/O or even first-party DMA as long as virtual addresses are used. However, there is a problem for those adapters that use first-party DMA with physical addresses. It is fortunate that most SCSI host adapters do not have this problem because there is no easy solution.

Novell Netware SCSI Integration

Netware is an operating system that allows networked computers to share a common set of resources, e.g., hard drives, laser printers and/or optical devices. The computer running Netware is the "server". Since application programs do not run on the server in dedicated mode, no user level entry point is needed in the SIM module. The SIM module will only run in kernel level mode, i.e., only device drivers will communicate with it.

Contrary to popular belief, Netware operates in a single-threaded mode at the device driver level. Disk channel requests are queued and issued to the channel in a FIFO manner. Since a device driver typically acts as a single disk channel, it does not need to be multi-threaded. However, some vendors have written device drivers that operate multiple disk channels. Since such a driver can receive multiple requests (one for each channel it operates), it must be multi-threaded. As a result, creating a multi-threaded SIM is up to the developer. It is not a manditory feature.

SIM developers will find that integrating a module into the Netware operating system that can be used and shared by various device drivers is a difficult task. The Netware operating system has no facilities for dynamically linking drivers into Netware at boot time. All driver are linked into the Netware kernel when it is created at configuration time. A SIM module would have to be either part of a hard disk device driver that is linked into the Netware kernel, or part of a ROM BIOS that is capable of operating in protected mode. Unfortunately, most host adapters do not have enough on-board ROM space to support both a protected mode BIOS and a real mode BIOS, along with boot code.

Unix/Xenix SCSI Integration

The Unix operating system is a complex environment for SCSI integration. It operates in protected mode, and it is a multi-user, multi-tasking operating system. Device drivers must queue requests for the device(s) they support. The SIM module will be required to accept requests from device drivers (kernel mode) or application programs (user mode).

In addition, the Unix operating system itself can issue a request to the device driver (and consequently to the SIM) to perform an I/O operation. The associated data buffer may have a virtual address, and may consist of portions of memory that are not physically contiguous. If a SIM module operating a DMA-capable host adapter must use such a non-contiguous buffer, it is the responsibility of either the device driver calling the SIM module or the SIM module itself to break the operation into multiple requests. However, if the host adapter supports a "scatter/gather" capability to automatically access these non-contiguous portions of memory, this feature should be enabled instead.

Unix device drivers are almost exclusively interrupt driven. This means that the SCSI host adapter interrupts the computer when it has completed an operation. The computer then jumps to the SIM module's interrupt routine to handle completion of the request. If multiple device drivers are using the SIM module, it must be able to call the interrupt routine of the device driver that started the SIM operation. This is necessary to signal completion of the operation and to start the next request in its queue. Failure to do so results in deadlock for the device.

Integration of the SIM module into the Unix operating system requires its being linking with the kernel routines at configuration time. Unix has no facilities for dynamic configuration similar to the MS-DOS CONFIG.SYS file. Hence, the integrator of the SIM module must have a link kit for the Unix operating system being used. The SIM module must be written as a device driver and must support **ioctl( )** requests to perform user level (application program) SCSI operations.

OS/2 SCSI Integration

OS/2 is unique in that although it operates in both protected and real mode, its device drivers receive requests in a single format independent of the microprocessor's mode at the time a request is issued. This is known as bi-modal operation, and request packets sent to the SIM must be bi-modal. This fact poses a problem for the SIM because although bi-modal memory is reserved for device driver use, it is a very limited resource under OS/2.

The SIM module can be loaded into memory as a character device driver by way of the CONFIG.SYS file. It can also be loaded as a portion of one of the start-up device drivers such as DISK01.SYS, or it may be part of a protected mode ROM BIOS (ABIOS).

If the SIM module is loaded as a device driver, the calling driver that wishes to use the SIM module must attach itself to the SIM via the Device Helper Service routine **AttachDD( )** (available as of OS/2 version 1.1). This routine returns the real mode segment and offset along with a protected mode selector and offset to the caller in the SIM device driver. These pointers are the address of the SIM entry point in the SIM device driver. Application programs are free to operate devices via SIM by communicating with the SIM device driver via **ioctl( )** requests, or by communicating with a device driver that is "attached" to the SIM device driver (see Figure 2).

Since OS/2 is a multi-threaded operating system, the SIM interrupt routine must call the interrupt routine of the calling device driver to finish the current operation and start the next request. Since the microprocessor can be in either real mode or protected mode at interrupt time, it is the SIM's responsibility to determine the current mode and call the interrupt routine with the calling device driver's data segment set up properly. In addition, the CS (code segment/code selector) register must be set up as appropriate for the current mode.

Figure 2. Device Driver "Attached" to an OS/2 SIM Device Driver (Courtesy Columbia Data Products)

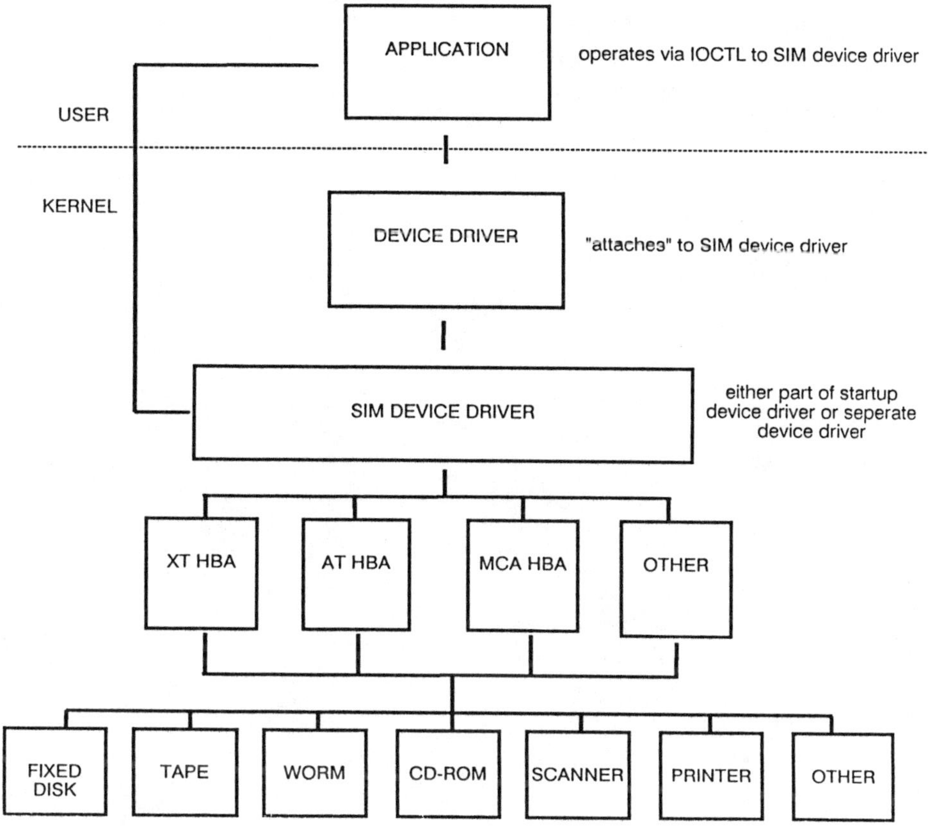

Conclusion

SCSI is an important part of the optical industry. Although SCSI itself is a standard, a standardized access method for SCSI host adapters is essential to create integrated products that are as vendor- and operating system-independent as possible. Although work remains to be done, the industry is committed to the task by way of the SCSI-2 Common Access Method (CAM) Committee.

CAM Committee Information

For those interested in joining the CAM Committee, the membership fee is $2000. For those interested in receiving the documentation generated by the CAM Committee, the fee is $200. All inquiries should be directed to the following address:

CAM Committee
14426 Black Walnut Court
Saratoga, CA 95070
ATTN: I. Dal Allen
408.867.6630

Appendix 1 Overview of WORM and Erasable Drives

This section consists of four tables that compare the basic characteristics of major WORM and erasable optical drives:

Table 1. Overview of 12-inch WORM Drives
Table 2. Overview of 5.25-inch WORM Drives
Table 3. Overview of WORM Jukeboxes
Table 4. Overview of 3.5-inch and 5.25-inch Erasable Drives

Information on the following characteristics is provided:

Interfaces	Onboard Memory buffer size
Seek Times	Data Transfer Rates
Double or single sided media	Capacity per side
Media RPM	Format (CAV/CLV/MCAV)
ISO Standard Conformance	Media diameter

Drives and jukeboxes listed in these tables are currently available for purchase in the U.S. today (January 1989). We have attempted to include the drives and jukeboxes which are available in the U.S. for purchase and which were introduced at the 1988 Fall COMDEX Exposition. These tables are based on published specifications and personal communications with hardware manufacturers. We have attempted to make these charts as current and accurate as possible. However, we suggest that readers obtain manufacturer product specifications and additional descriptive information since specifications are subject to change.

Eastman Kodak and Pioneer Communications of America

There are two drives which did not fit into any of the aforementioned tables: the 14-inch WORM drive manufactured by Eastman Kodak Company, and Pioneer Communications' 8-inch WORM drive. Specifications for these two drives are listed on the next page.

Model	**Kodak 6800 8001/8002**	**Pioneer**
Media Diameter	14-inch	8-inch
Interfaces	SCSI, IPI-3	SCSI
Controller Memory	64KB	256 KB
Data Transfer Rates:		
Burst	4-10 MB/sec	660 KB/sec
Sustained	1.0 MB/sec	308 KB/sec
Seek Times:		
Maximum	700 ms	—
Average	450 ms	250 ms
Track-to-Track	9 ms	—
Capacity per side	3.4GB	750 MB
Double-sided media	Yes	Yes
Rotational Rate (rpm)	786-1632	450
Vector Format	QLV[1]	CAV
ISO Standard Format	Yes[2]	No

[1]QLV (Quantized Linear Velocity) is Eastman Kodak's term for MCAV.

[2]Eastman Kodak has developed a standard format for its 14-inch WORM media. This format uses sampled servo technology.

Table 1. Overview of 12-inch WORM Drives*

Vendor Model	ATG 1001	Hitachi 301A-1	LMSI 1200E	Optimem 1000	Optimem 2400	Sony WDD-3000	Toshiba WMS 500A
Embedded SCSI Controller	No	No	Yes	Yes	Yes	No	Yes
Interfaces	SCSI PC-bus	SCSI IEEE-488(GPIB)	SCSI ISI	SCSI proprietary	SCSI proprietary	SCSI parallel	SCSI
Controller Memory	2KB	64KB	44KB	4KB	64KB	64KB	64KB
Data Transfer Rates/sec: Burst, Sustained	1.25MB 479KB	1.5MB 440KB	1.33MB 262KB	1.25MB 479KB	1.25MB 625KB	1.1MB 300KB	1.26MB 0.5-1MB
Seek Times: Max. Average Track-to-Track (ms)	190-400 150 5	— 200 —	330 150 —	250 150 3	250 150 3	190-500 250 1.2	— 160 —
Capacity per Side)	1GB	1.31GB	1GB	1GB	1.2GB	1.6GB (CLV) 1.05GB (CAV)	2.5GB
Double-sided media	Yes	Yes	Yes	No	Yes	Yes	Yes
Sector Format	CAV	CAV	CAV	CAV	CAV	CLV/CAV	MCAV
Rotational Rate (rpm)	1122	600	480	1122	1122	360-720	617

* None of these drives meet the ISO standard.

Table 2. Overview of 5.25-inch WORM Drives

Vendor Model	Embedded SCSI Controller	Interfaces	Controller Memory	Data Transfer rates/sec: Burst, Sustained	Seek Times: Max/Avg/Track-to-Track (ms)	Double-sided/ Capacity per Side (MB)	Rota-tional Rate (rpm)	Sector Format	ISO Standard Format
Cherokee Tracker	No	SCSI, ESDI	64KB	1.5MB| 625KB	--/135/1	Yes/260MB	1613	CAV	No
Fujitsu MS2505B	No	SCSI, ESDI	64KB	1.5MB, 480KB	200/100/1	Yes/360MB	1800	CAV	No
Hitachi OD101-1	No	SCSI	--	1.5MB, 690KB	--/93/--	Yes/300MB	1800	CAV	No
IBM 3363*	No	SCSI	--	2.5MB, ---	---/275/3.5	No/200MB	1800	CAV	No
ISi 525WC	No	SCSI, PC Bus	8KB	---, 312KB	200/135/1	Yes/115MB	1800	CAV	No
ISi 525GB	No	SCSI, PC Bus	64KB	---, 812KB	--/90/1	Yes/600MB	1800	CAV	No
LaserDrive 810,820,840,850	No	SCSI	64KB	---, 272.5KB	--/175/--	Yes|405MB	557-1155	CLV	No
LMSI LD-510	Yes	SCSI	64KB	1.25MB, 600KB	--/60/1.5	Yes/327 MB	2160	CAV	Sampled
Maximum Storage APX 3000	No	ESDI	8KB	312KB, 240KB	200/135/1	Yes/122MB	1800	CAV	No
Maximum Storage APX 4000	No	ESDI	16KB	5.0MB, ---	**	Yes/400MB	1800	CAV	No
Maxtor RXT-800S	Yes	SCSI	--	1.25 MB, ---	324/168/4	Yes/400MB	334-668	CLV	No
Mitsubishi MW 5D1, 5U1	Yes	SCSI, ESDI	--	1.5MB, 400KB (write)400KB (read)	--/80/--	Yes/300MB	1800	CAV	Continuous
Mountain Optech SEL-2	No	---	---	---, 275KB	475/195/1.5	Yes/100MB	1200	CAV	No
Panasonic LF-5000	No	SCSI	--	1.3MB, 312KB	-/230/-	No/200MB	882	CAV	No
Pentax LW-S501	Yes	SCSI	64KB	2.5MB, 530KB	---|40|---	Yes/326MB	1800	CAV	Continuous
Pioneer S-5001	No	SCSI, proprietary	256KB	1.5MB, 742.5KB	-/60/-	Yes/327MB	1800	CAV	Sampled
					324/168/4	Yes/400MB	(Variable)	CLV	No
Ricoh 5040-WL	Yes	SCSI	256KB	1MB, 312KB	475/195/1.5	Yes/200MB	1200	CAV	No
Shugart 5984***	No	SCSI, PC Bus	--	1.25MB, 210KB					
Toshiba WM-D070	No	SCSI	64KB	1.5MB, 692KB (CAV) 325-650KB (MCAV)	-/90/-	Yes/300(CAV), 450MB(MCAV)	1800(CAV) 900(MCAV)	CAV, MCAV	No

* The IBM 3363 is based on the Panasonic LF-5000.
** Maximum Storage refers to "an effective 28ms access time from a systems level perspective."
*** The Shugart 5984 is the former Optotech 5984.

Table 3. Overview of WORM Jukeboxes

Vendor Model	Maximum Disks	Disk-to disk avg. (sec)	Capacity	Drives per jukebox	Media size	Interface	WORM Drives Usable
Access* ODSR	20	6-12	40GB	1-2	12"	RS-232	LMSI
Cygnet 1800 Series	141	11	369GB	1-5	12"	RS-232	LMSI, Optimem, Hitachi
Cygnet 5000 Series	25	4	30GB	1-2	5.25"	RS-232/SCSI	(numerous)
Eastman Kodak 6800 Library	150	6.5-7	1.02TB	1-3	14"	RS-232	Kodak
FileNet OSAR 64	64	7-8	168GB	1-4	12"	RS-232	LMSI, Hitachi
FileNet OSAR 204	204	7.5-9	534GB	1-4	12"	RS-232	LMSI, Hitachi
Hitachi OL 301S-11/12	16	7-8	42GB	1-2	12"	SCSI	Hitachi
Hitachi OL 301S-12/22	32	7.5-9	84GB	1-2	12"	SCSI	Hitachi
Hitachi OL101-11/21	24	6.5	14.4GB	1-2	5.25"	SCSI	Hitachi
Hitachi OL101-12/22	48	7	28.8GB	1-4	5.25"	SCSI	Hitachi
Mitsubishi MW-5G1-A	56	4-6	34GB	1-2	5.25"	SCSI	Mitsubishi
Mitsubishi MW-5G1-B	152	4-7	90GB	1-4	5.25"	SCSI	Mitsubishi
Optotech Optofile**	66	10	26GB	1-4	5.25"	RS-232	Shugart
Pioneer DJ-1/DJ-2	20	14	30GB	1-2	8"	SCSI/ proprietary	Pioneer
Ricoh RJ-5160	20	6-7	16GB	1-2	5.25"	SCSI	Ricoh
Sony WDA 3000-10	50	6	160GB	1-2	12"	SCSI	Sony

* The Access Corporation manufactured ODSR is also sold by LMSI.

** This product has not been formally released; it would probably be released with a Shugart nameplate.

Table 4. Overview of 3.5- and 5.25-inch Erasable Drives(1)

Vendor Model	Media Diameter (inches)	Interfaces	Controller Memory	Data Transfer Rates/sec: Burst, Sustained	Seek Times (max/avg/ track-to-track) (ms)	Capacity per Side	Double-sided Media	Sector Format	Rotational Rate (rpm)
Sony SMO D-501	5.25	SCSI modified EDSI	64KB	1.2MB, 680KB	180/90/20	297/325MB	Yes	CAV	2400
Canon OM 500D	5.25	SCSI modified EDSI	64KB	1.5MB, 260KB	92/130/10	256MB	No	CAV	3000
Matsushita JU-9500	5.25	SCSI, EDSI	---	--, 925KB	--/75/--	300MB	Yes	CAV	2400
Maxtor* Tahiti I	5.25	SCSI	---	4MB, 1.25MB	70/35/1	466/512MB 298/326MB	Yes	MCAV** CAV	1800-2200
Ricoh RO-5030E	5.25	SCSI	256KB	1.2MB, 300KB	-/44/-	297/326MB	Yes	CAV	1800
Sharp JY-500	5.25	SCSI	---	2.4MB, 150KB	200/67/--	325MB	Yes	CAV	900
Verbatim TMO 35/60	3.5	SCSI	64KB	1.5MB, 262KB	65/30/3	60MB	No	CAV	2400

(1) Except for Canon, Matsushita and Verbatim, all CAV media conform to the ISO continuous composite servo format. Olympus Corp. offers the ME-D501 drive. However, no information was available at the time of publication.
(2) If two figures are quoted, these are for 512 and 1024 byte sector options.
* This drive will be sold by Maxoptix Corp., a Maxtor subsidiary. Maxtor abandoned its 3.5-inch Fiji I drive.
** Maxtor calls this ZCAV or Zoned Constant Angular Velocity.

Appendix 2 Glossary of Terms and Acronyms

Whether they consist of one word or several words, the terms listed below are in alphabetical order, letter by letter, up to the comma in the case of inversion. In the case of multiple definitions of terms, these are consecutively numbered.

A

acceleration - The rate of change of speed with time. In optical storage, one measure of the severity of the job to be accomplished by the focus and tracking servos in correcting flatness.

access time - The time to get to a specified location in or on a memory device. For disk drives, quoted access times usually refer only to the positioning time for the radial actuator, neglecting servo settling and rotational latency; average access times for disk drives usually describe a radial motion of one-third of a full stroke. See Latency.

access time - controller (read) - The time measured from the drive's receipt of a SEEK command (if necessary) from the controller to the time the first byte of data is received by the controller. Therefore, it includes seek time and latency, as well as the time to read and transfer the first byte of data.

access time - controller (write) - The time measured from the drive's receipt of a SEEK command (if necessary) from the controller to the time the first byte of data is written to the disk. Therefore, it may include seek time, head settling, latency, and writing the first byte.

access time - host (read) - The time measured from the controller's receipt of the last byte of a READ command block from the host to the time the first byte of data is available to the host.

For controllers that perform a simple read-ahead or some sophisticated caching algorithm, the READ command may not require any disk access since the necessary data is already available in the controller buffer. For these controllers, host read access time would only include command validation and DMA (or other data transfer) set-up time to send the first byte of data to the host. For controllers that always require a disk access, host read access time consists of command validation, seek time, latency, reading, error detection and correction, and DMA (or other data transfer) set-up time to send the first byte of data to the host.

ANSI (American National Standards Institute) - An organization which approves standards used by numerous industries in the U.S.

ASC (Accredited Standards Committee) - A committee which works on projects intended to become ANSI standards.

B

B - Abbreviation for bytes. Used as a suffix, e.g., MB.

b - Abbreviation for bits. Used as a suffix, e.g., Kb.

backwards compatible - Sometimes "downward compatible"; said of a new product which can be used with equipment or media originally designed for use with an older product. An example is an erasable medium which can be written and read by a drive that was originally produced to read and write WORM media.

bad sector - An unusable portion of a disk caused by a media defect. A bad sector table retains these locations and prevents their access.

BIOS (Basic Input/Output System) - A set of ROM-resident device drivers for an IBM PC or compatible computer. Drivers are included for the keyboard, console, printer, floppy disk and hard disk.

block - An amount of data moved or addressed as a single unit; the least amount of data to be read or written at a time. Deciding what size a block should be involves trade-offs. Error correction will use the least additional storage space when blocks are long, but storage space is wasted if a data file is smaller than a block. Typical block sizes in WORM drives are 512, 1024, 2048 bytes.

burst error - In error correction for a storage device, the loss of many consecutive bits of information because of some flaw in the medium such as a scratch or dirt. The distinction is with continuous noise which corrupts data in a different way, requiring a different kind of error correction. In optical memory, most data loss is due to burst errors. The design of an error correction code (ECC) depends on how often error bursts are likely to occur and how long the longest burst is likely to be.

burst mode - A method of transferring data that does not permit an interrupt to occur.

C

cache - Generally, temporary storage for data to which access must be very quick.

cartridge - An enclosure (generally of plastic) in which an optical medium (disk) is kept for protection. Some vendors captivate their media in the cartridge (this mode is called "spin in"), providing a window for the laser beam; others remove the medium from the cartridge inside the drive. Also called a cassette.

CAV (Constant Angular Velocity) - Describes the characteristic of a disk which always spins at the same rotational rate, so that the time taken to scan a track is the same at all radii.

CD-ROM (Compact Disc, Read-Only Memory) - A version of the standard compact disc intended to store general purpose digital data, although CD audio data can also be included. Its data capacity is upwards of 600MB.

CCS (Common Command Set) - A set of standard SCSI commands and data structures defined in a document produced by a task group of the SCSI ASC (X3T9.2). Revision 4.B (23 June 1986) is the definition by which a device is termed "CCS-compliant", but it will be part of the SCSI-2 standard. The CCS allows a driver to dynamically determine the characteristics of devices attached to a SCSI port.

CCS (Continuous Composite Servo) - A physical format for optical media in which servo information is continuously encoded on the disk. It is one of three competing formats for standardizing 5.25" WORM media, and the only proposed 5.25" erasable optical format.

CIRC (Cross-Interleaved Reed-Solomon Code) - Using a sophisticated method of error detection and correction (a layered error correction code) that involves techniques of data delay and data rearrangement techniques, corrected data can be one bit error in a trillion bits. CIRC detects and corrects up to two errors in one code word and interpolates for long error bursts. The maximum complete correctable error burst length is 4,000 data bits, and the maximum worst case interpolatable burst is 12,300 data bits assuming that no random errors occur at the same time.

CLV (Constant Linear Velocity) - Describes the characteristic of a disk which rotates more slowly when outer radii are being scanned so that the relative velocity between a writable "cell" and the track is maintained at a constant value. This keeps the linear density of data constant over the whole disk, but creates practical problems due to the non-constant time taken to scan one track and the need to speed up and slow down the disk as various radii are scanned.

compression - An encoding technique that saves storage space by eliminating gaps, empty fields, redundancy, or unnecessary data, to shorten the length of records or blocks. Provides for the use of fewer data bits than originally required without information loss. A decoding technique implements the reverse operation to convert it to the original data.

CRC (Cyclic Redundancy Check) - A simple form of algebraic error correcting code.

D

defect - Some irregularity in a medium which disturbs its ability to store recorded data. Defects in an optical disk include bumps, depressions, dirt, missing sensitive material, etc. Because of the high density of optical recording, even micrometer sized defects are of consequence.

defect density - The fraction of the total active area of a medium obscured by defects.

Digital Paper™ - A relatively new optical storage flexible media that has a storage capacity of one gigabyte on a single-sided 5.25-inch optical disk. BOSCO (Bernoulli Optical Systems Company), an offshoot of Iomega Corporation, is developing a 5.25-inch WORM drive that uses "floppy" WORM disks.

Developed by ICI Imagedata, part of ICI Films which is a business unit of ICI Americas, Inc., this "floppy" opticalmedia is produced by sputtering a reflective layer onto a polyester film substrate and then coating the material with a dye polymer layer. The dye can be tuned to suit the infra-red wavelength of the writing laser. Data is encoded by the difference in reflectivity between the unburned material and the micropits formed by laser action. The data densities achievable are a function of the wavelength of the laser. Current technology can produce and resolve pits of one micrometer in diameter using solid state lasers with a wavelength of 780 to 830 nanometers. A data density of greater than 10MB per square inch is attainable.

DRAW (Direct-Read-After-Write) - Describes the method of error checking in which data written to an optical disk during one disk rotation is read for accuracy on the subsequent rotation. Recorded data on an optical disk may be read immediately after writing (recording); no processing is required.

DRDW (Direct-Read-During-Write) - Describes a method of error checking data on an optical disk in which data is written and verified during the same disk rotation. Refers to the ability to read the information during the writing process.

E

ECC (Error Correction Code) - A method of data recovery that allows the full recovery of a single physical block of user data. An encoding scheme turns a bitstream into a longer bitstream whose length comes from carefully designed redundancy. This is intended to enable the encoded bitstream to survive corruption by random noise and burst noise and still be decodable to the original bitstream without missing or incorrect data. Examples are CIRC and convolutional code.

EDC (Error Detection Code) - Used in conjunction with ECC to allow the detection of errors for correction.

ECMA (European Computer Manufacturers Association) - Standards body headquartered in Geneva, Switzerland whose functions in Europe are similar to those of ANSI in the U.S.

erasable - Rewritable. See also magneto-optic.

F

Faraday effect - Certain substances, when exposed to a magnetic field, will change the polarity of light passing through them. This polarity change is called the Faraday effect. Optical disks using the Faraday effect must be transmissive, rather than reflective.

FAT (Fat Allocation Table) - A table maintained by MS-DOS and OS/2 for the chain of sectors which comprise a disk file. Each logical disk typically contains a redundant pair of FATs.

FIFO (First-In, First-Out) - A queue for storage of commands or data.

firmware - Software stored in read-only memory (ROM).

focus servo - Used in an optical disk drive to keep the reading and/or writing light spot focused on the information bearing surface, despite imperfections in the medium and drive mechanisms or externally imposed shock and vibration.

form factor - The size and shape of a product. For example, most 5.25-inch Winchester drives have the same dimensions so that they can fit interchangeably into computer cabinets. For the same reason, 5.25-inch optical drives have the same form factor as Winchesters.

G

GB - Gigabyte; 2^{30} bytes. The prefix "giga" means one billion.

H

handling zone - The part of a disk or cartridge that may be touched by a handling mechanism, e.g., in a jukebox.

heap - An array representation of a binary tree of data entities. Some WORM software products use a data heap to store a hierarchical file system in order to allow random file modifications in a manner which efficiently uses disk space on the write-once medium.

I

import/export slot - The slot used to add disks to or remove disks from a jukebox; also referred to as an exchange slot or mailbox.

inode - A data structure containing administrative information for a Unix disk file, e.g., name, type, size and location of contents.

interleaving - The process of breaking up and reordering blocks of data to cause a long error burst to be turned, after de-interleaving, into many short bursts, each of which can be corrected by the error correcting code (ECC) in use.

inventory - To compile a mapping table indicating the storage slot of each volume in a jukebox. This is done by reading a volume label from each disk surface in a jukebox.

IPC (Inter-Process Communication) - An operating system level scheme for message passing between programs.

IPI (Intelligent Peripheral Interface) - A standard for an interface between a CPU and a storage peripheral device. The IPI interface handles data rates up to 10 Mb/sec and is gaining support from several large companies including Eastman Kodak and IBM.

ISO (International Organization for Standardization) - Standards body formed after World War II to precipitate international standardization. Its functions are similar to ANSI and ECMA.

J

jukebox - An automatic media handler for optical disks and drives; also called a library. A jukebox may support multiple disks online with offline disks quickly accessed mechanically using a robotic arm. Jukeboxes are also used for magnetic tape drives.

K

KB - Kilobytes; 1024, or 2^{10} bytes.

Kb - Kilobits; 1024, or 2^{10} bits.

kB - 1000 bytes.

kb - 1000 bits.

Kerr effect - Certain substances, when exposed to a magnetic field, will rotate the plane of polarization of light reflected from them. This phase change is called the Kerr effect.

L

latency - The component of the delay in access to data which comes from waiting for a disk to rotate to the desired azimuth. Average latency for a disk drive is usually calculated as one-half the rotational period.

LBA (Logical Block Address) - The number used to locate a particular block of data on a disk surface.

LDA (Laminated Disk Assembly) - An optical disk structure developed by Eastman Kodak for their 14-inch WORM media.

M

magneto-optic (M-O) - An optical storage technology which combines laser and magnetic methods to read and write from a platter. Information is written by local magnetization of a magnetic medium, using a focused light beam to produce local heating and consequent reduction of coercivity so that a moderately strong, poorly localized magnetic field can flip the state of a small region of high coercivity material. Reading is done either magnetically with inductive heads in close proximity to the medium, or optically through rotation of the plane of polarization of probing light via the Faraday effect or Kerr effect.

mapping - In a jukebox environment, the process of translating a volume name to a disk's slot number.

MB - Megabyte; 2^{20} bytes. The prefix "mega" means one million.

MCAV (Modified Constant Angular Velocity) - MCAV is a media format. In MCAV, the tracks are divided into bands or zones. Within any one band, the disk spins at a constant angular velocity and there is a fixed number of sectors per track. The relation between velocity and band location is similar to the velocity versus radius curve for CAV operation. MCAV allows greater data density than CAV, but without the performance compromise of CLV.

mount - **(1)** An operation which makes the contents of a volume available to a file system. (2) The act of determining the location of a volume in a jukebox and insuring it is spun up in a drive.

ms - millisecond; 2^{-3} seconds. The prefix "milli" means one thousandth.

O

OCR (Optical Character Recognition) - A process of recognizing characters or numbers in printed form through the use of photoelectric technology. Also called optical scanning.

optical head - An assembly within an optical drive containing the components that reflect laser light on the data surface of the disk and convert the reflected light into electrical signals that can be interpreted as data. Components in the optical head are the laser, lenses, prisms, a focusing mechanism and a photodetector.

o.s. - Abbreviation for operating system.

OSI (Open Systems Interconnect) - A mass storage interface standard promulgated by the ISO.

Q

QLV (Quantized Linear Velocity) - See MCAV (Modified Constant Angular Velocity).

R

rewritable - erasable. See also magneto-optic.

RFPI (Remote Front Panel Interface) - The remote electrical connection to the front panel controls of a disk drive. Used by a jukebox to spin up or down a disk in a drive.

S

SCSI (Small Computer System Interface) - A standard 8-bit parallel interface frequently used to connect computer peripherals to a computer. SCSI provides a logical rather than a physical command set in order to allow common commands to be used with a multitude of device types. Approved in 1986 as ANSI standard X3.131-1986 (also known as "SCSI-1"). SCSI-2 is currently in the standard review process.

sector - A triangular section of a disk surface within a track. A block of data is addressed by its track and sector numbers.

seek error - The drive's laser is unable to accurately locate user requested data as a result of physical and/or mechanical problems such as vibration, disk surface irregularities, and poor laser focusing.

seek time - The time required to make a storage unit ready to access a specific location by selection or physical positioning. In optical disk technology, the time required to position the optical read/write head to the desired track.

It should be measured from the moment the drive receives a seek command from the controller to the time the controller is informed (and validates if necessary) that the desired track has been reached. For other than controller designers, seek time may be a mildly interesting piece of information but not a particularly useful one. Traditionally, disk drive manufacturers supply three average seek times: track-to-track, full-stroke, and one-third stroke.

servomechanism - A combination of detector and actuator which continuously follows some variable quantity; examples are the focus and tracking servos of optical disk drives.

slot number - Numeric indicator of a location within a jukebox; could be a storage slot, optical drive or the mailbox (import/export slot).

spin up - The time during which a drive accelerates a stationary disk to its operational speed.

superblock - A block on a Unix disk which describes the state of a file system, e.g., size and maximum number of possible files. It normally follows the boot block and precedes the inode list.

T

TB - Terabyte; 2^{40} bytes. The prefix "tera" means one trillion.

track - A circular path on which information may be stored on a disk surface. A track encompasses one rotation of the disk, and is divided into sectors.

tracking servo - The servo used in an optical drive to keep the reading and/or writing light spot centered on the information track, despite imperfections in the medium and drive mechanisms or externally imposed shock and vibration.

transfer rate - The rate at which data is transferred to or from a device, especially the reading or writing rate of a storage peripheral. Usually expressed in bits or bytes second.

transfer rate - controller (burst) - The number of bytes transferred per second on the system bus between the host (or host adapter) and the controller buffer. The difference between the controller burst transfer rate and the drive user data transfer rate is one of the main factors used in determining how a group of controllers can concurrently transfer data on the system bus without any of their respective drives "hiccupping" (losing a rotation). As long as the controller buffer is getting rid of data faster than it is receiving it, a drive need not lose revolutions except for certain error handling situations.

transfer rate - drive (absolute) - This is the average number of bytes transferred between the drive and the controller buffer per second. Note that the rate includes all bytes transferred including ECC and CRC bytes. For controller designers this drive transfer rate is of interest; for end-users this is usually of little or no interest.

transfer rate - drive (user data) - The number of bytes of user data transferred between the drive and the controller buffer per second. It will be affected by the same characteristics given in the definition of the absolute drive transfer rate.

transfer rate - subsystem (read) - The number of bytes transferred to the host during execution of a READ command divided by the elapsed time in seconds from the controller's receipt of the last byte of the READ command until the (SCSI) command complete message is sent.

The variations in times due to the different controller algorithms enable controller vendors to legitimately be proud of the effective read transfer rate of subsystems which include their controller. A slower drive transfer rate can be masked by a caching algorithm so that the subsystem has an apparent instantaneous access time and its transfer rate approaches the controller burst transfer rate.

transfer rate - subsystem (write) - The number of bytes transferred from the host during execution of a write command divided by the elapsed time in seconds from the controller's receipt of the last byte of the WRITE command block to the time that a completion status is available to the host.

The events required to execute a write command differ among magnetic, WORM, and erasable optical drives. For erasable optical drives it may include SEEK time, latency, erasing all sectors to be written, reseeking to the first sector, and writing the data. Since WORM media cannot be certified by using a write operation, some drives require extra disk rotations to verify the data after it is written. Magnetic disks do not need the erasing or reseeking steps.

Some controllers provide completion status after the last data byte is received, but before the data is written to the media. This is sometimes advantageous time-wise, but can be a problem if anything prevents successful writing subsequently.

U

unmount - (1) An operation which makes the contents of a volume unavailable to a file system. (2) The act of spinning down a drive, removing its disk, and placing it in a storage slot within a jukebox.

V

volume - (1) One unit of removable storage; the contents of one optical disk surface. (2) A "named" optical disk surface in a jukebox; its "name" (label) is usually stored in a prescribed location on its surface.

volume verification - The process of reading a volume label from a prescribed disk surface location and verifying it against what was expected.

W

WORM (Write-Once, Read-Many) - An optical technology which allows data to be written once and to be read back indefinitely.

Z

ZCAV (Zoned Constant Angular Velocity) - See MCAV (Modified Constant Angular Velocity).

References

Bach, Maurice J., *The Design of the Unix Operating System.*Englewood Cliffs, NJ: Prentice-Hall, 1986.

Kernighan, Brian W., Rob Pike, *The Unix Programming Environment.* Englewood Cliffs, NJ: Prentice-Hall, 1984.

Parker, Sybil P. (Ed.), *McGraw Hill Dictionary of Computers.* NewYork, NY: McGraw-Hill, 1984.

Ralston, Anthony (Ed.), *Encyclopedia of Computer Science* (first edition). New York: Van Nostrand Reinhold Co., 1976.

Rothchild, Edward, *Glossary of Optical Memory Terms.* San Francisco,CA: Rothchild Consultants, 1985.

Walsh, Myles E., *Understanding Computers: What Managers and Users Need to Know.* New York: John Wiley & Sons, Inc., 1981.

Appendix 3
Recommended Readings

Altman, W. P., Claffie, G. M., and Levene, M. L. "Optical Storage for High Performance Applications in the Late 1980's and Beyond." *RCA Engineer* 31 (1986): 46-55.

Bainbridge, R. C. "The Role of Standards in the Emerging Optical Digital Data Disk Storage Systems Market." In *Proceedings of the Society of Photo-Optical Instrumentation Engineers*, 27-28. Bellingham, WA: SPIE, 1984.

Berg, B. A. "Critical Considerations for WORM Software Development." *Optical Information Systems* 7, no. 4 (1987): 329-33.

Berra, P.B., and Troullinos, N.B. "Optical Techniques and Data/Knowledge Base Machines." *IEEE Computer* 20, no. 10 (October 1987): 59-70.

Bican, F. "Mass Storage Devices: The WORM Turns." *PC Magazine* 7 (1988): 199-226.

Boggs, R. L. "Road to Optical Digital Disk Systems: The Cautious But Optimistic User Will Lead the Way." *Journal of Information and Image Management* 19 (1986): 10-13.

Bonnebat, C. "Information Storage Technologies — Some Recent Trends and Current Prospects Analyzed From the Media Manufacturers Standpoint." *IEEE Transactions on Magnetics*, MAG-23 (1987): 9-15.

Bouwhuis, G., J. Braat, A. Huijse, J. Pasman, G. Van Rosmalen, and K. Schouhamer-Immink. *Principles of Optical Disc Systems.* Accord, MA: Adam Hilger, Ltd., 1985.

Bracker, W. E. "Optical Data Storage: Theory, Hardware, Software and Applications." In *Proceedings of the National Computer Graphics Association Graphics 87*, 75-90. Fairfax, VA: National Computer Graphics Association, 1987.

Burgess, J.G., and N. C. Ramsay. "FileTek Storage Machine Applications." *Digest of Papers for the IEEE Symposium on Mass Storage Systems.* October 31 - November 3, 1988. Monterey, CA, 1988.

Campbell, D.K. "Drive Issues for High Performance Magneto-optic Recording." In *Topical Meeting on Optical Data Storage — Summaries of Papers*, 2-5. New York, NY: IEEE, 1987.

Carringer, M.W. "Real World Jukebox Implementation for Digital's VAX/VMS." *Computer Technology Review*, Summer 1988.

Christodoulakis, A., and C. Faloutsos. "Design and Performance Considerations for an Optical Disk-Based, Multimedia Object Server." *Computer.* 19, no. 12 (December 1986): 45-56.

Cinnamon, B. *Optical Disk Document Storage and Retrieval Systems.* Silver Spring, MD: Association for Information and Image Management, 1988.

Courtot, M. "The Impact of Standards for Optical Information Systems on Current Micrographic Products and Systems." In *Conference Proceedings of Optical Information Systems '86*, Judith Paris Roth, 96-101. Westport, CT: Meckler Publishing Corporation, 1986.

DeHaan, M. "Optical Technology: What's Mature and What's on the Horizon." *ESD: The Electronic System Design Magazine.* 17, no.9 (1987): 41-49.

Dulude, J. R. "Software Transparency and Write-Once Optical Disk Drives." In *Optical Meeting on Optical Data Storage — Summaries of Papers*, 172-173. New York, NY: IEEE, 1987.

Erickson, R. and Bovee, D. "Innovative Software Design Utilizing WORM Technology." In *Proceedings of Optical Information Systems '87 Conference.* Judith Paris Roth, 120-125. Westport, CT: Meckler Publishing Corporation, 1987.

Francis, B. "PC Back-up's Optical Understudy." *Datamation* (December 15, 1988): 57,60.

Freedman, J. B. "The Institute for Computer Science and Technology at the National Bureau of Standards (NBS/ICST) Optical Digital Data Disk Standardization Activities." In *Proceedings of the Society of*

Photo-Optical Instrumentation Engineers, 77-79. Bellingham, WA: SPIE, 1987.

Freese, R. P. "Optical Disks Become Erasable." *IEEE Spectrum* 25, no. 2 (1988): 41-45.

Freese, R. P., M. DeHaan, and A. A. Jamberdino, eds. *Optical Mass Data Storage: Proceedings of the SPIE (The International Society for Optical Engineering) Meeting.* Bellingham, WA: SPIE, 1986.

Gait, Jason. "The Optical File Cabinet: A Random-Access File System for Write-Once Optical Disks." *IEEE Computer* (June 1988): 11–22.

Gardner, R. H, V. W. Halling, T. A. Rinehart, A. W. Funkenbusch, M. A. Khan, D. W. Siitari, and R. P. Freese. "Status of M/O Erasable Media Production." In *Proceedings of the Topical Meeting on Optical Data Storage*, 120-122. New York, NY: IEEE, 1987.

Gardner, R. N., S. Webster, S, M. A. Khan, T. A., Rinehart, and A. W. Funkenbusch. "M/O: Its Emergence as the Dominant Erasable Technology." In Optical Mass Data Storage: *Proceedings of the SPIE (The International Society for Optical Engineering) Meeting*, edited by R. P. Freese, etal., 48-55. Bellingham,WA: SPIE, 1986.

Gunn, Keith. "File Structure Standards." *Optical Memory News* 63, (1988): 6-7.

Heinemann, D. D. "Optical Controller Adds WORM to DEC." *Computer Technology Review* (1988).

Hoaglund, A. S. "Information Storage Technology: A Look at the Future." *Computer* (July, 1985).

Isailovic, J. *Videodisc and Optical Memory Systems.* Englewood Cliffs, NJ: Prentice-Hall, Inc., 1985.

Ito, S. and Takakashi, N. "HITFILE 650 Optical Disk Filing System." *Hitachi Review* 36, no 4 (1987): 231-220.

Jipson, V. B. "Erasable Optical Recording Technologies." In *Topical Meeting on Optical Data Storage — Summaries of Papers*, 146. New York, NY: IEEE, 1987.

Kalstrom, D. *Compatibility is the Key to Success for New Computer Technologies.* Plasmon Data Systems, Inc., 1988.

Knight, G. "The Optimem 1000 Optical Disk Drive." In *Topical Meeting on Optical Data Storage — Summaries of Papers*, WC-A4/1-3. New York, NY: IEEE, 1984.

Kuttner, P. "Optics for Data Storage: Optical Disk Technology." In *Laser Beam Scanning: Opto-Mechanical Decisions, Systems*, edited by G. F. Marshall, 303-409. New York, NY: Marcel Dekker, Inc., 1985.

Lange, G. R. "Practical Specifications for Characterizing Write/Read Performance of Optical Disk Media." In *Topical Meeting on Optical Data Storage — Summaries of Papers*, 54-57. New York, NY: IEEE, 1987.

Lee, T., Chen D. "Optotech 5984 Drive Overview." In *Optical Mass Data Storage: Proceedings of the SPIE (The International Society for Optical Engineering)*, edited by R. P. Freese, et al., 116-127. Bellingham, WA: SPIE, 1986.

"LMSI-Hitachi Ad Hoc 5.25-inch Standard." *Optical Memory News*, 61/62 (July-August, 1988): 1, 8.

Lowe, J. B., C. A. Lynch, and E. B. Brownrigg. "Publishing Bibliographic Data on Optical Disks: A Prototypical Application and Its Implication." In *Proceedings of the Society of Photo-Optical Instrumentation Engineers (SPIE), Third International Conference on Optical Mass Data Storage*, 227-236. Bellingham, WA: SPIE, 1985.

Lou, D. Y. "Data Integrity in the LD 1200 System." In *Topical Meeting on Optical Data Storage — Summaries of Papers*, 174-176. New York, NY: IEEE, 1987.

Lynch, C. A. "Optical Storage Media, Standards, and Technology Life Cycle Management." *Records Management Quarterly* 20, no. 1 (1986): 44-54.

Magel, M. "Write-Once and Erasable Alternatives." *AV Video*, (November 1988): 36-38,4 7.

Maker, J. "Rigid Optical Disk Assembly by Eastman Kodak Company." In *Topical Meeting on Optical Data Storage — Summaries of Papers*, 82-85. New York, NY: IEEE, 1987.

Mallery, D. "Optical Allusions." *DEC Professional* (1987).

Malloy, R. "The ISI WC525 Optical Disk Drive." *Byte* 12, no. 8 (1987): 231-33.

Manns, B. and Wilder, D. "Interfacing a Mainframe Database Retrieval System with an Optical Disk Image Storage System." In *Digest on Papers — Eighth Annual IEEE Symposium on Mass Storage Systems*, 7-11. New York, NY: IEEE, 1987.

Meng, B. "Systems Architecture: Optical Disks Slip in Compatibility." *Digital Design* 16, no. 1 (1986): 28-37.

Mitsuhashi, Y. "Standardization Activities for Optical Data Disk in Japan." In *Proceedings of the Society of Photo-Optical Instrumentation Engineers*, 71-73. Bellingham, WA: SPIE, 1984.

Nugent, W. R. "Error Detection and Correction Systems for Optical Disks: Issues of Media Defect Distribution, Defect Growth, Error Management and Disk Longevity." In *Optical Mass Data Storage: Proceedings of the SPIE (The International Society for Optical Engineering)*, edited by R. P. Freese, etal., 10-15. Bellingham, WA: SPIE, 1986.

Office Productivity Using Image Storage and Retrieval Systems. Saratoga, CA: Electronic Trend Publications, 1988. $295.

Ooi, B.C., A. D. Narasimhalu, I.F. Chang. "Integration of Write-Once Optical Disk with Multimedia DBMS." In *User-Oriented Content-Based Text and Image Handling - Proceedings of RIAO '88.* Cambridge, MA: Massachusetts Institute of Technology, 1988.

Optical Technology's Impact on Paper, Microform, Magnetic and Tape Storage: A Technology Impact Report Describing the Growth Opportunities and Applications for CD-ROM, CD Interface Disks, WORM, and Erasable Optical Drives. Saratoga, CA: Electronic Trend Publications, 1988. $1,250.

Rash, W. "A Quintet of WORMs." *Byte* 13, no. 2 (1987): 146-152.

Rosch, W. L. "WORMs for Mass Storage." *PC Magazine* 6, no. 12(June 23, 1987): 101-110.

Rosch, W. L. "Backup Choices from Tapes and Disks to WORMs." *PC Magazine* 6, no. 12 (June 23, 1987): 135-168.

Rothchild, E. *Rewritable Optical Media and Technology Markets.* San Francisco, CA: Rothchild Consultants, 1988.

Rothchild, E. "An Eye on Optical Disks." *Datamation* (March 1, 1986).

Saffady, W. *Optical Disks for Data and Document Storage.* Westport, CT: Meckler Publishing Corporation, 1988.

Saffady, W. *Optical Storage Technology 1987: A State-of-the-Art Review.* Westport, CT: Meckler Publishing Corporation, 1987.

Saffady, W. *Optical Storage Technology 1988: A State-of-the-Art Review.* Westport, CT: Meckler Publishing Corporation, 1988.

Sander, I., and S. Slovenkai. "Magneto-Optical Recording with a Compact Optical Head." In *Proceedings of the Society of Photo-Optical Instrumentation Engineers (SPIE): Third International Conference on Optical Mass Data Storage,* 182-185. Bellingham, WA: SPIE, 1985.

Schroeder, C. "Information Standards and Optical Disk Systems." *Inform* 1, no.2 (1987): 12-13.

Schwerin, Julie B., Parke Lightbown, Connie Bailey, and Howard Kaikow. *CD-ROM Standards: The Book.* Oxford, England and Pittsfield, VT: Learned Information (Europe) Ltd. and InfoTech, 1986.

Shifman, J. "Error Correction and Detection for 5.25-Inch Optical Disks." In *Optical Mass Data Storage: Proceedings of the SPIE (The International Society for Optical Engineering,* 278-297. Bellingham, WA: SPIE, 1986.

Simpson, D. "Erasable Optical Disks: When, What, Why?" *Mini-Micro Systems* 20, no. 12 (December 1987): 15-18.

Simpson, D. "Write-Once, Read-Many, Why Wait?" *Mini-Micro Systems* 21, no. 12 (December 1988): 76-83.

Tanaka, K., Watanbe, I., Sugahara, H. "The Technology Trends in Optical Disk Storage." *Information Proceedings of the Society of Japan* 28, no. 8 (1987): 1075-83.

Thoma, George, J. Cookson, F. Walker, and S. Hauser. "Interfacing Optical Disks to a Document Image Storage and Retrieval System." *Journal of Imaging Technology.* 12, no. 5 (October, 1986).

Thompson, T. and Nick Baran. "The NeXT Computer." *Byte* 13, no. 12 (November 1988): 158-175.

Understanding Computers: Memory and Storage. Alexandria, VA: Time-Life Books, Inc., 1987.

Verhueven, J. A. "Standardization Activities of Optical Digital Data Technology in European Computer Manufacturers Association (ECMA)." In *Proceedings of the Society of Photo-Optical Instrumentation Engineers*, 74-76. Bellingham, WA: SPIE,1984.

Vitter, J.S. "An Efficient I/O Interface for Optical Disks." *ACM Transactions on Database Systems* 10, no. 2 (June 1985): 129-162.

Warren, C. "Software Tools, Utilities Drive Optical Disks." *Mini-Micro Systems* 19, no. 15 (December 1986): 33-44.

Welch, B. J. "Big Eight Firm Backs Write-Once Optical Storage." *Info-World.* (March 24, 1986).

Zajaczkowski, J. "Future Standardization Development Projects Within the ANSI." In *Proceedings of the Society of Photo-Optical Instrumentation Engineers*, 68-70. Bellingham, WA: SPIE, 1984.

Zelinger, S. "The Optical Disk Jukebox." *Inform* (December 1987): 34-38.

Appendix 4
Directory of Companies

Access Corporation
1811 Losantiville Drive
Cincinnati, OH 55441
513.396.9600
The Engineering Document Image Control System uses either a 5.25- or 12-inch drive with the ODSR, an optional 16- or 20-platter jukebox. The ODSR is also sold by LSMI. This System is used for the creation, storage, distribution, and control of engineering/manufacturing documents, including drawings.

Adaptec, Inc.
691 South Milpitas Blvd.
Milpitas, CA 95035
408.945.8600
SCSI chip and host adapter vendor.

Advanced Graphic Applications, Inc. (AGA)
90 Fifth Avenue
New York, NY 10011-7696
212.337.4200
DISCUS is an IBM-PC-based WORM system using MS-DOS. A version of DISCUS uses erasable optical storage

Alphatronix
4900 Prospectus Drive, Suite 1000
POB 13687
Research Triangle Park, NC 27709-3687
919.544.0001
Developed an erasable subsystem for DEC, Sun, and IBM-compatible computers based on the Sony erasable drive.

American National Standards Institute, Inc. (ANSI)
1430 Broadway
New York, NY 10018
212.642.4900
Organization associated with standards for all industries. Publishes the official SCSI standard specification.

Aquidneck Systems International, Inc.
650 Ten Rod Road
North Kingstown, RI 02852
401.295.2691
WORM drive systems integrator. Developer of Optical Archiving System (OAS), a WORM controller that offers universal compatibility.

Arix Corporation
821 Fox Lane
San Jose, CA 95131
408.432.1200
Formerly Arete Systems Corporation. Multiprocessor-based superminicomputer manufacturer offering a WORM subsystem with software to support an updatable Unix file system.

Art Tech Gigadisc (ATG)
Avenue du General Eisenhower
BP 1270
31047 Toulouse
Cedex, France
Formerly Alcatel Thomson. 12-inch WORM drive manufacturer.

Berg Software Design
POB 3488
Saratoga, CA 95070
408.741.5704
408.741.5010
Consulting firm specializing in device driver software for SCSI, WORM and CD-ROM devices. Owned by Brian A. Berg, co-editor.

Canon America, Inc.
One Canon Plaza
Lake Success, New York 10042-1113
516.488.6700
5.25-inch erasable drive and media manufacturer.

Capital Software, Ltd.
845 Third Avenue
New York, NY
212.755.6870
Developer of WORM-based subsystems for the PICK operating system.

CBEMA (Computer and Business Equipment Manufacturers Association)
311 First Street, N.W., Suite 500
Washington, D.C. 20001-2178
202.737.8888
An industry trade group that administers the Approved Standards Committees (ASCs). ASCs work on projects intended to become standards of the American National Standards Institute (ANSI).

Cherokee Data Systems, Inc.
1880 South Flatiron Court, Complex H
Boulder, CO 80301
303.449.8850
Rugged 5.25-inch WORM drive manufacturer.

Columbia Data Products, Inc.
1070B Rainer Drive
Altamonte Springs, FL 32714
407.869.6700
SCSI firmware and device driver vendor for various environments including MS-DOS, Unix, Xenix, and OS/2.

Computer Structures, Inc.
580 College Avenue
Palo Alto, CA 94306
415.856.2021
Software consulting and development firm owned by John Levy, a book chapter author.

Cygnet Systems, Inc.
601 West California Avenue
Sunnyvale, CA 94086-4831
408.773.0770
5.25-inch and 12-inch jukebox and software manufacturer.

Document Automation Consulting
266 Alvarado Road
Berkeley, CA 94705
415.486.1024
Consulting firm owned by Keith Gunn which focuses on standards issues, including the implication of emerging standards for document content such as ISO 8613, ODIF, and DCA. Publisher of *New Standards for Document Image Compression*, a report on IBM's current attempt to promulgate its own standard to replace Group 3 and Group 4 compression as the worldwide standard.

Dorotech France
81 rue Corot
92410 Ville d'Avray
France
(1) 47.09.38.38
Developer of DoroFile™, a Unix-based WORM product. Distributed in the United States by Zetaco Corporation.

Eastman Kodak
343 State Street
Rochester, New York 14650
716.724.5130
Offers Optical Disk System 6800, a 14-inch WORM/jukebox-based system.

ENDL Associates
29112 Country Hills Road
San Juan Capistrano, CA 92675
714.364.9626
Consulting organization owned by Ken Hallam (Chair of X3B11, the ANSI Technical Committee on Optical Media standardization) and I. Dal Allan (Vice Chair of X3T9.2, the ANSI Technical Committee working to standardize SCSI and ESDI). Publishes the *ENDL Letter.*

FileNet Corporation
3565 Harbor Blvd.
Costa Mesa, CA 92626
714.966.3400
Offers integrated WorkFlo™, a WORM-based document and image storage and retrieval system using single drives or jukebox devices.

FileTek, Inc.
6100 Executive Blvd.
Rockville, MD 20852
301.984.1542
Offers the Storage Machine/1™, an integrated WORM-based system using a jukebox device. SM/1 uses off-the-shelf and customized software in an integrated storage and retrieval system.

Fujitsu America, Inc.
Computer Products Group
3055 Orchard Drive
San Jose, CA 95134-2017
800.626.4686
408.432.1300
5.25-inch WORM drive manufacturer.

Global Engineering Documents
2805 McGaw
Irvine, CA 92714
800.854.7179
714.261.1455
Printer and supplier of technical documents, including the SCSI-2 working draft.

Hitachi America, Ltd.
Computer Division
950 Elm Avenue
San Bruno, CA 94066-3904
415.872.1902
5.25-inch and 12-inch WORM drive and jukebox manufacturer.

IBM Corporation
Low-End Optical Products
General Products Division
Tucson, AZ 85744
602.799.1000
Offers Model 3363, a 5.25-inch WORM drive based on the Panasonic L-F5000 WORM drive.

Information Storage, Inc. (ISi)
2768 Janitell Road
Colorado Springs, CO 80906
719.579.0460
800.333.WORM
5.25-inch WORM drive manufacturer.

Integrated Automation (IA)
1301 Harbor Bay Parkway
Alameda, CA 94501
415.769.5400
Optical disk drive and jukebox integrator. Offers WORM-based integrated systems for engineering information management.

Iomega Corporation
1821 West 4000 South
Roy, Utah 84067
801.778.1000
Bernoulli Optical, a subsidiary of IOMEGA, will introduce in 1989 a flexible WORM ("floppy WORM") drive using Digital Paper, a new optical storage media that has a storage capacity of one gigabyte on a single-sided 5.25-inch disk.

KOM, Inc.
145 Spruce Street
Ottawa, Ontario
Canada K1R 6P1
613.238.7766
WORM and jukebox integrator. OPTIFILE™ is a WORM drive magnetic disk emulation product for DEC and other operating systems.

Laser Magnetic Storage International, Inc. (LMSI)
4425 ArrowsWest Drive
Colorado Springs, CO 80907-3489
719.593.7900
5.25- and 12-inch WORM drive and jukebox manufacturer.

LaserDrive
1101 Space Park Drive
Santa Clara, CA 95054
408.970.3600
5.25-inch WORM drive manufacturer.

Maximum Storage, Inc.
5025 Centennial Blvd.
Colorado Springs, CO 80919
719.531.6888
5.25-inch WORM drive manufacturer.

Maxtor Corporation
211 River Oaks Parkway
San Jose, CA 95134
408.432.1700
5.25-inch WORM and erasable optical drive manufacturer.

Micro Design International, Inc.
1235-D Commerce Road
Morrow, GA 30260
404.968.6658
Offers a variety of software products including the Xenix mountable and the LaserBank™ transparent WORM systems. The firm offers OPAL™, an online file system for Unix, Xenix and MS-DOS that allows the transfer of files between these operating systems.

Micro Dynamics, Inc.
8555 Sixteenth Street, Suite 802
Silver Spring, MD 20910
301.589.6300
Offers MD-MARS™, the Multi-user Archival and Retrieval System, a Macintosh-based 5.25-inch WORM drive and jukebox subsystem.

Mitsubishi Electronics America, Inc.
Computer Peripherals Division
991 Knox Street
Torrance, CA 90502
213.515.3993
5.25-inch WORM, erasable optical and jukebox manufacturer.

Mountain Optech
2830 Wilderness Place, Suite F
Boulder, CO 80301
303.444.2851
Rugged 5.25-inch WORM drive manufacturer.

NeXT, Inc.
3475 Deer Creek Road
Palo Alto, CA 94304
415.424.8500
Manufacturer of the NeXT Computer which uses the Canon erasable optical drive as its primary storage device.

Optical Storage Solutions
1001 Galaxy Way, Suite 310
Concord, CA 94520
415.825.3441
Offers the OS-DOS™ family of operating system- and WORM drive-independent magnetic file system emulation products.

Optimem
A Cipher Data Products Company
297 North Bernardo Avenue
Mountain View, CA 94043
415.961.1800
12-inch WORM drive manufacturer.

Optisys
8620 North 22nd Avenue, Suite 109
Phoenix, Arizona 85021
602.997.9699
Offers the OptiDriver™ WORM software product for magnetic file system emulation under MS-DOS.

Optotech, Inc.
740-770 Wooten Road
Colorado Springs, CO 80915-3518
719.570.7500
Developing an ISO-standard 5.25-inch erasable M-O drive. Shugart purchased manufacturing rights to its WORM drive.

Panasonic Industrial Company
Computer Products Division
2 Panasonic Way
Secaucus, NJ 07094
201.392.4603
5.25-inch WORM drive manufacturer.

Pegasus
55 Crest Avenue
Walnut Creek, CA 94595
415.938.3345
415.439.7845
WORM and erasable optical drive and jukebox integration company.

Perceptics Corporation
Pellissippi Center
POB 22991
Knoxville, TN 37933-0991
615.966.9200
Systems integrator of optical disk subsystems using 12-inch WORM drives and Cygnet jukeboxes in applications for image and data storage and retrieval in CAD/CAM, medicine, satellite, banking, and oceanographic applications.

Pioneer Communications of America
Optical Memory Products Division
1058 East 230th Street
Carson, CA 90745
213.513.1016
5.25-inch and 8-inch WORM drive and jukebox manufacturer.

Plexus Computers, Inc.
3833 North First Street
San Jose, CA 95134
408.943.9433
Manufacturer of a WORM-based mixed mode (data and images) database system called XDP™.

Ricoh Corporation
3001 Orchard Parkway
San Jose, CA 95134
408.432.8800
5.25-inch drive and jukebox manufacturer.

Rothchild Consultants
256 Laguna Honda Blvd.
San Francisco, CA 94116-1496
415.681.3700
Offers optical memory marketing and technical consulting services worldwide. Publications include *Optical Memory News* and the *Optical Memory Report.* Offers a continuing information service, Optical Systems Information Service, and sponsors the Technology Opportunity Conferences.

ST Systems Corporation
4400 Forbes Blvd.
Lanham, MD 20706-9008
301.794.5000
Optical disk systems integrator.

Sharp Electronics Corporation
Sharp Plaza
Mahway, NJ 07430-2135
201.529.8200
5.25-inch WORM and erasable optical drive manufacturer.

Shugart Corporation
9292 Jeronimo Road
Irvine, CA 92718
714.770.1100
5.25-inch WORM drive manufacturer. Purchased manufacturing rights to the Optotech 5984 WORM drive.

Sony Corporation of America
Optical Storage Technology
Sony Drive
Park Ridge, NJ 07656
201.930.6025
5.25-inch and 12-inch WORM and erasable optical drive, jukebox and media manufacturer.

Space Telescope Science Institute (STScI)
3700 San Martin Drive
Baltimore, MD 21218
301.338.4700
Institute operated for NASA by the Association of Universities for Research in Astronomy (AURA). Responsible for conducting the scientific operations of the Hubble Space Telescope (HST) to be launched aboard the Space Shuttle in 1989.

Storage Dimensions
A Maxtor Company
2145 Hamilton Avenue
San Jose, CA 95125
408.879.0300
Integrator of Maxtor WORM and erasable drives. Offers the LaserStor™ family of WORM-based subsystems for the IBM-PC/XT/AT and PS/2 computer systems with LaserCache™ software, a package that uses the magnetic hard disk to cache data moving to and from the WORM disk.

Toshiba America, Inc.
Disk Products Division
9740 Irvine Blvd
Irvine, CA 92718
714.583.3000
5.25-inch and 12-inch drive and jukebox manufacturer.

TRW Financial Systems, Inc.
2001 Center St.
Berkeley, CA 94704
415.548.8572
WORM and jukebox systems integrator.

U.S. Design Corporation
A Maxtor Company
4311 Forbes Blvd.
Lanham, MD 20706
301.577.2880
Integrator of Maxtor 5.25", LMSI 12" and Sony 12" WORM drives for DEC and Sun computers. Software products include JukeVOS for the Sony jukebox.

Verbatim Corporation
An Eastman Kodak Company
435 Indio Way
Sunnyvale, CA 94086
408.773.5777
3.5-inch erasable optical drive and media manufacturer.

Wang Laboratories, Inc.
One Industrial Avenue
Lowell, MA 01851
508.459.5000
The Wang Integrated Image System (WIIS) is a 12-inch WORM-based integrated image document and office information system based on the Wang VS that captures information in image form including text, handwritten forms, annotated printed documents, line drawings, and photographs.

Zetaco Corporation
6850 Shady Oak Road
Eden Prairie, MN 55344
612.941.9480
Distributor of DoroFile™, a Unix WORM product developed by Dorotech of France.

Index

Contributors

Brian A. Berg, president of Berg Software Design, has been in the software industry for fifteen years, including the last ten years as a consultant. He has implemented device drivers and real-time software under Unix, MS-DOS, MTOS, VMS and AOS. Since 1985, he has implemented a number of systems which use WORM and CD-ROM optical storage. His consulting activities have been with firms including Arix (Arete Systems) Corp., Plexus Computers, Inc., Tab Products Co., Raytel Systems Corp., E-mu Systems, Inc., TRW (Teknekron) Financial Systems, Optical Media International, Acctex Information Systems and Sequent Computer Systems. He has spoken and moderated at a number of conferences including Optical Information Systems '87 and '88. He participates in and helps organize the IEEE Asilomar Microcomputer Workshop held annually near Monterey, California. He has published in *Mini-Micro Systems* as well as *Optical Information Systems*, of which he is a contributing editor. He has a B.S. in mathematics from Pacific Lutheran University and attended computer science graduate classes at Stanford University.

Edward Beshore, manager of the Software Engineering Group at Optotech, Inc., oversees the development of peripheral firmware and subsystem software products. Prior to joining Optotech, he was lead programmer at the University of Arizona for their imaging experiment on the Pioneer 11 spacecraft mission to Saturn. His primary responsibilities were the development of image processing and data communications software. He has also held a senior engineering position with Boeing Computer Services Company where he developed programming tools for avionics software development. He served as engineer at the Multiple Mirror Telescope Observatory at the University of Arizona where he developed telescope and instrument controls systems software. He has a B.S. in astronomy and physics from the University of Arizona.

Keith Gunn, founder of Document Automation Consulting, is involved with assisting end-users in the establishment of requirements for document imaging independent of the recommendations made by system integrators and product suppliers. He was manager of System Engineering of the Document Management Division at Litton Integration Automation where he managed the emergence of new architectural standard and analyzed a broad case of applications in such market areas as package delivery, banking and brokerage and aerospace. He has also served as vice president of Bartlett Systems, a system analysis firm in the field of Space defense specializing in imaging sensors for ballistic missile early warning and tracking and space-borne sensing of gaseous pollutants. He served as chief engineer at Block Engineering, a firm whose specialty is Fourier Spectroscopy. He has an A.B. in astronomy from Harvard University and has done graduate work in physics at Georgetown University in Washington, DC.

Ken Hallam, president of ENDL Associates, has over 25 years experience in the computer industry. His marketing experience at IBM, Ampex, Memorex and Western Digital, plus 10 years as an active member of several Accredited Standard Committees, give him a unique perspective on the technical and marketing decisions facing the industry today and in the future. He has held management positions in design engineering, test engineering, field service, marketing and planning. He is currently chairman of the ANSI Technical Committee on Optical Media standardization, X3B11. He is a U.S. delegate to ISO (International Standards Organization) TC97/SC23 and was selected as a technical editor of the ISO standard for WORM media.

Larry W. Holmstrom, director of business development for Iomega Corporation, works in the areas of optical and high-capacity removable magnetic products and system software development. He was vice president of development for Bonneville Telecommunications where he was responsible for the development of nationwide FM-subcarrier data broadcasting and an associated satellite network. During 19 years with IBM, he gained experience with product development, electronic testing, factory automation, real-time machine control, integrated circuit manufacturing, product management and planning. While at IBM (Boca Raton, FL) he managed IBM's highly successful "Writing to Read" program. He is listed in *Who's Who in American Education* and has received IBM's Invention Achievement and Outstanding Contribution Awards. Also, he has been awarded numerous patents and was nominated as Outstanding Young Electrical Engineer. He has a B.S.E.E. from Utah State University and a M.S. in computer science from Syracuse University.

Choi T. Kwok has been technical director at Advanced Graphics Applications, Inc. since 1986. He has developed AGA's magneto-optic device driver as well as scanner software for OS/2. He has also developed graphics (WYSIWYG) applications, and a full-text retrieval (word search) engine. Among his responsibilities are product documentation and software quality assurance control. He has a B.S. in physics from Rensselaer Polytechnic Institute.

James G. Lanford, president of Micro Dynamics, Ltd., has over 15 years of experience in designing, implementing and managing computer software and hardware projects. He has worked at such firms as Memorex and EDS. He designed MacLabeler Plus, a programmer's disk utility with an advanced object-oriented graphical interface, and PostHaste, an integrated PostScript programming environment. He is the chief architect for Micro Dynamics' Multi-user Archival and Retrieval System (MARS). In addition, he has designed the Browser program, a system which enables analysts to extract intelligence from large free-text databases and navigate large data structures with linear and non-linear display of data utilizing WORM storage. He has a B.A. in electronics from California State University at Chico, and has done graduate work at The George Washington University in Washington, DC.

John V. Levy, president of Computer Structures, Inc., has been a consultant since 1982. He specializes in hardware and software project management and product development issues, and has been active in the computer field since 1966. While at Digital Equipment Corporation in the 1970s, he supervised hardware and software development and received seven U.S. patents for his work on the Massbus I/O channel and the SBI backplane bus of the VAX-11/780. He was later employed at Tandem Computers and Apple Computers before starting his consulting firm. He received a B.E.P. in engineering physics from Cornell University, an M.S.E.E. from Cal Tech, and a Ph.D. in computer science from Stanford University.

Eva C. Marsh joined Cygnet Systems, Inc. in 1984 as finance industry marketing manager and currently holds the position of marketing communications manager. Prior to joining Cygnet, she spent 11 years with Wells Fargo Bank in various management positions. She left the bank as vice president and manager of the real estate division. Prior to this position, she was responsible for the bank's check processing division, and was head of the Data Processing Center. She has a B.S. in economics from the University of San Francisco and has attended programs for senior executives at Harvard University and the Massachusetts Institute of Technology.

Ian MacRae, manager of research and development, KOM, Inc., is responsible for the development of OPTIFILE-based systems. A software manager for eight years, he has been involved in the design and programming of a variety of systems since 1972. As co-founder and software designer for Quadrex Information Systems of Montreal (1981-1984), he created a word processor. He has a B.A. in mathematics from Carleton University in Ottawa, Canada.

Al McDowell is currently responsible for managing the Laser Magnetic Storage International (LMSI) product line of 5.25-inch WORM and CD-ROM optical drives. He is a principal member of the X3B11 Optical Media Standards Committee. His optical storage experience began in 1978 with founding and managing of the Star Systems Division of Exxon Enterprises, which he sold to StorageTek in 1981. Prior to joining LMSI in 1988, he was responsible for marketing optical storage and tape products with Fujitsu America. He has a B.E.E. from Syracuse University and a Ph.D. in business economics from Cornell University.

Sanjay Ranade, senior computer scientist with ST Systems Corporation, has over 12 years of experience in computer system development and integration, including image processing, new computer architectures and microprogramming. With other ST Systems Corporation scientists, he has designed a VAX-driven archive and distribution system using optical disks, T-120 cassette tapes and conventional magnetic disks. His publications have appeared in *IEEE Journal of Systems, Man and Cybernetics, Pattern Recognition,* as well as *Optical Information Systems* of which he is a contributing editor. He has a Ph.D. in computer science from the University of Southampton, England.

Judith Paris Roth, president of Advanced Information Management Technology, Inc. (AIMT), has been involved with optical storage technology since 1979. She is editor-in-chief of *Optical Information Systems* magazine, interactive videodisc editor of *Optical Information Systems Update* and chairperson of the annual OIS Conference and Exposition sponsored by Meckler Corporation. Author of *The Essential Guide to CD-ROM* and *CD-ROM Applications and Markets,* she has written extensively about optical storage technology in *Popular Computing, Journal of the American Society of Information Science, High Technology,* and *Educational and Instructional Television.* She has an M.L.S. from Syracuse University and attended the Information Systems Seminar at the Sloan School of Management at the Massachusetts Institute of Technology in 1981.

Peter M. B. Shames is chief of information systems development at the Space Telescope Science Institute. He is responsible for the development of advanced systems projects and for the data system architecture and long-range planning. He is a member of the National Research Council Space Science Board Committee on Data Management and Computation (CODMAC). His activities include the development of the NASA Science Internet, chairing of the Data Management Task Force of the NASA Science Applications and Information System (SAIS) Working Group. He is also chairman of the NASA Earth Science Applications Data System (ESADS) panel on networking. He has a B.A. from the University of New

Hampshire and has done graduate work in computer science at Cornell University.

Roy J. Slicker has been in the computer industry for 15 years developing both hardware and software for systems and applications. For the past seven years he has been involved with rotating optical media. He was a founder, president and chief operating officer of Optical Storage Solutions, Inc., a software company developing systems level software for the WORM optical storage. While at OSS he spearheaded the sales and market development efforts of the firm. Mr. Slicker is a member of the ANSI X3B11 committee created to develop hardware and software standards for WORM disks. In late 1988, he left OSS to form Pegasus, a firm which develops both system and applications level software for CD-ROM, erasable and WORM optical storage. Pegasus has received a contract to develop a Sony jukebox interface for the Novell network for installation in the Federal Executive Branch.

Thomas Tewell is director of engineering at Columbia Data Products, Inc. He has been actively involved in SCSI software design and development since 1985. He has written SCSI device drivers for numerous operating systems including MS-DOS, Unix, Xenix, Novell Netware, and OS/2. He has been involved with developing SCSI products for Western Digital, NCR, AT&T, and other major OEMs, and is actively involved in the SCSI-2 Common Access Method (CAM) Committee.

Fonald Yee is technical coordinator for the Systems Engineering and Testing Department of ST Systems Corporation's air traffic control software development. He is primarily responsible for providing the technical direction and support for the Oceanic Display and Planning System (ODAPS) being developed for air traffic control over the North Atlantic. He has over 14 years experience in the design, development, and implementation of large applications systems. He has worked in diverse application areas including education research, finance and administration, air traffic control, and space science utilizing a variety of state-of-the-art hardware and software systems including optical disks, LANs, DBMS, and data communications software. He has both a B.S. in physics and an M.S. in computer systems from American University, and an M.S. in computer science from the University of California.

Rob G. Zwick is manager of the Optical Products Division of Optisys, Inc. He has been active in the microcomputer industry since 1980. He has worked for startup organizations such as Western Information Systems, a computer distributor, and Tecex, an optical disk integrator. He is experienced with manufacturing, new product introduction, advertising and national sales promotion as well as new product development, engineering, and design. He has a B.S. in computer science from Arizona State University.